LOOK FOR THE LIVING

'Why do you look for the living
among the dead?'

Peter Selby

LOOK FOR THE LIVING

*The Corporate Nature of
Resurrection Faith*

FORTRESS PRESS
PHILADELPHIA

First American Edition by
Fortress Press 1976

© 1976 by SCM Press Limited, London
and Fortress Press, Philadelphia

Library of Congress Catalog Card Number 76-15884
ISBN 0-8006-1245-0

Printed in Great Britain   1-1245

Contents

Preface

The period during which this book has been in the making seems in retrospect very like a three-legged race. My desire has been that my theological understanding might move together with the challenges and excitements of the work of lay training in which I have been engaged. It has not proved an easy partnership, and indeed cannot be in a situation where change is all that is guaranteed.

What has happened is that from time to time one or other of the partners has clamoured for concentrated attention. This book, based on a doctoral thesis presented in the University of London in 1974, represents the fruit of those periods when I have attempted to see that my ideas of biblical interpretation should correspond with the practice as I was witnessing it in my work, and also should raise questions and offer new directions. As a result, I am aware that it is less directly and explicitly related to the fundamental issues of discipleship as I find them arising in lay training than I might have wished; that seemed to be what was necessary at the time, and I hope that the extent to which my thinking is a response and a contribution to dealing with those issues is nevertheless apparent.

I have been constantly aware of the debt which I owe to my teachers at the Episcopal Theological School in Cambridge, Massachusetts, and in particular to Dr Harvey Guthrie and Dr Lloyd Patterson, whose course on 'Biblical Eschatology and the Church' has continued to offer me a framework of theological thinking which can move critically with change. Those who have worked with me in the Southwark Diocese over the past seven years, whether as colleagues or as participants in training ventures of various kinds, have contributed enormously to my thinking, and have frequently responded with patient criticism when I have assailed them with my untried thoughts. This has been especially true of Mr John Nicholson who has been my immediate colleague throughout the period; it has long since ceased to be possible for me to estimate the amount which I owe to our shared experience and conversation.

Professor Christopher Evans of London University was my supervisor while I was writing the thesis, and gave me not only of his knowledge on the subject of the resurrection traditions, but also his generous interest in the questions raised by my work in the field of training; the weekend in which he shared in some of that work was a particularly memorable contribution to the experience of those who participated and to the development of my ideas. I have been grateful also to those who have been prepared to read some of the material and make comments, particularly to Professor Maurice Wiles and Dr Cecilia Goodenough.

As the mental three-legged race has gone on, Jan, my wife, has found herself sometimes spectator, sometimes navigator, and sometimes finding imaginative ways to tie the two partners in my mind together again. This book represents a great deal of our journeying together.

PETER SELBY

1

WHAT ARE WE LOOKING FOR?

The centre of Christian faith is the raising of Jesus from the dead. There
has not been much disagreement about that. From Paul onwards
Christians have held this to be so. If the resurrection falls we fall with it
and our words, our discipleship and our worship fall too. The centre of
the Christian year is the celebration of Easter and the unique claim of
Jesus upon his followers is sealed by the fact that he was raised from
the dead.

But if Christians have been unanimous that the resurrection of Jesus
is at the centre of their faith, they have not been unanimous about
much else. To ask what the resurrection was, or is, is immediately to
become aware of a vast range of viewpoints, not only about what
happened in the days immediately following the death of Jesus, but
also about what the implications of those vital few days might be. In
some ways it is easy to imagine that this is a new situation, but a look
at the immense amount that has been written in the centuries between
the writing of the New Testament and our day shows just how constant
and how vast has been the controversy about what belief in the resurrection involves.[1]

Much of the argument now is about the question 'What happened?'
There is no Christianity without that question, without some concern
with the details of that part of the past which lies at the heart of the
faith. A vast amount has been written, not just about what the Easter
event was (as we shall see later), but about the connection between
faith and history.[2] Historical research and faith are uneasy partners;
critical methods, particularly about so distant a time, do not usually lead
either to certainty or to conviction but more often to scepticism and
doubt. Even those who claim that their historical researches show the
resurrection to be something highly probable admit, and even rejoice,
that in the end a decision about it has an irreducible element of faith.[3]

However the idea that resurrection faith consists of an element of historical inquiry and an element of faith takes us very little further. How much historical inquiry? What are we inquiring about? And what is this faith that can make up the difference between historical uncertainty and religious conviction? These questions all remain to be answered, and this book is concerned with where to look for these answers. There has been a vast amount of looking, and much of it in some very unfruitful places. To survey the attempts to apply the mind of the historian – in some cases it would be truer to say the detective – to the days immediately following the death of Jesus is to enter an area of much ingenuity and little success, a place where some fascinating information emerges but where the living one is not to be found.

On the other hand there have been those who have despaired of history as a way of access to the risen Christ and have entered instead upon the question 'What does the resurrection mean for me?' as being the only possible question which can be asked about it; their efforts have produced some inspiring and poetic images of new life being born in the midst of personal experience, and some bizarre speculation about how the old life might continue beyond the grave.

These ways of looking for the resurrection of Jesus depend on separating things which the New Testament writers hold firmly together: event is separated from meaning, past from present and future, course of events from destiny of mankind, the life of the individual from the health of the community. To look for the resurrection is to look for something which held together all these elements which much contemporary looking pulls apart. Concern about the nature of the raising of Jesus is also a concern for the nature of faith itself, and that concern requires neither mere historical inquiry nor mere personal reflection. To look for the resurrection is to look for that which the New Testament community found at the heart of its life, and requires therefore that we look at the life of that community and particularly at those aspects of its life which it held to flow from the raising of Jesus.

The contention that the events of the days immediately following the death of Jesus can only be considered in relation to the faith and experience of the New Testament community is not some sleight of hand by which the hard historical issues can be avoided, and it certainly does not represent a crude identification of the raising of Jesus with the rise of faith in his followers. We do not, however, live at a time when it is possible simply to accept Westcott's view that 'nothing but the antecedent assumption that it (the resurrection) must be false could have suggested the idea of deficiency in the proof of it'.[4] Historical criticism, as well as the positivist demand that we say what we mean, requires us to enter into the historical quest with rigorous honesty. It also brings us again and again to the recognition that what we have in the New Testament is a record of the experience and beliefs of a community, and it is those about which we are asked to decide when we look for the risen Christ. We must go further than Gore, who said that the dis- crepancies among the various accounts of the resurrection do not give rise to doubt;[5] those discrepancies provide access to the different ways in which members of the early Christian community understood the resurrection and the experiences which they associated with it, and so provide us with a way of looking for faith.

On the other hand, to say that concern with the present experience of the individual and with our fate beyond death are not adequate ways of looking for the resurrection is not to rule those concerns out in favour of a concern with community alone; rather it is to say that the discovery of significant patterns of living and dying which can speak to us as individuals depends upon looking for the meaning of risen life within our community, as the first Christians found it in theirs. We shall take issue very strongly with the view that a concentration on an experience of resurrection which belongs primarily to the interior life of the individual is the best way to seek the risen Christ; however much such a concentration may avoid the boredom and remoteness which may often seem to belong to the historical, and the conflict and risk which belong to any attempt to engage with the issues of life in com- munity, it remains true that the resurrection of Jesus was known in and by a community. It was the shared life of a community that made it possible to believe that Jesus had been raised from the dead as well as to find the way to new life. Just as the historical question about what happened after the death of Jesus can only be considered alongside the experience of the New Testament church which made the Easter stories credible, so all that we know about the early Christians' quest for personal meaning and for hope beyond death is closely connected with the fact that they were part of a community which had been entrusted with a mission and with a message which had to be proclaimed to all mankind.

So to look for the resurrection of Jesus is not to look for the answer to a question about a small piece of the past on its own or to questions of the meaning of personal existence on their own; it is to seek what happened to the earliest Christians and the nature of the task to which they believed themselves to be committed. To look in this way is to encounter the fact that belief in the resurrection of Jesus is not, and cannot be reduced to, either acceptance of information about the past or a sense of purely personal fulfilment or a hope that there is life beyond death; the resurrection of Jesus relates to the way in which a community staked its whole life on something that was new and totally demanding of its zeal and its allegiance.

This is because resurrection, as we shall see, belongs to the language of ultimate right and ultimate wrong, of eschatology, of the final purpose of all things. To look for the resurrection of Jesus is therefore also to look for a way of speaking of those realities in living which command total obedience and which express the destiny of the universe. It is to face the fact that the earliest Christians declared that in Jesus God had brought about the final scene in the drama of his activity, and that their whole corporate hope was directed towards the fulfilment of the purpose which God had inaugurated in Jesus.

The entertaining of such a hope does not merely expose a person to the possibility of disappointment. Hope for the survival of death might be disappointed if it turned out that the belief in survival was false; but that would be a disappointment of which we should, by definition, know nothing. Any hope that something will happen will be disappointed if nothing happens; but the kind of hope of which the resurrection speaks could turn out to be wrong in a much more radical sense.

The two disciples on the way to Emmaus said that they had hoped that Jesus was the one to redeem Israel (Luke 24.21) and the disappointment they there express is to be understood as more than an awareness that a hoped-for event had not taken place; what had been disappointed was their hope for something that was more than an event which might or might not take place; it was hope for that which had determined the shape of their life and which, they had believed, would determine the whole future of the world. What, as the story is there told, had been shattered was the expectation that Jesus was the one who carried the divine commission to usher in the fulfilment of God's purpose for the world. The account which we are offered suggests that the position from which the disciples started was of people looking for one who was to complete all that God had promised, and their bewilderment arises because the death of Jesus seems to mean that he was not that one.

The story is the prelude to a declaration that the Christ must suffer all these things 'and so enter into his glory' (Luke 24.26) and to the realization that their hopes for Jesus were not after all disappointed; but the prelude makes it plain that the hope was founded within the context of certain expectations about the world and not merely about a particular event that might happen. The issue which needed to be settled was whether Jesus was indeed God's agent for the fulfilment of his purpose for the world and therefore whether he was the one in whom all men should believe or not. It was an issue on which depended not merely how individuals should order their life but also to whose cause they should commit themselves. To believe in his resurrection was to stake their life upon the hope that what God had in store for the world was what he had shown in Jesus. It was therefore a hope involving the risk of disappointment not only in the sense that what had been hoped for might not take place, but also in that men might turn out to have placed themselves in opposition to God in the critical struggle between him and his opponents. The resurrection of Jesus meant that, contrary to all Good Friday appearances, and indeed because of what had then taken place, it was Jesus whom God had made his agent and whom he called all men to follow. To deny the resurrection was not merely to be mistaken, it was to take the wrong side.

> . . . this Jesus, delivered up according to the definite plan and fore-knowledge of God, you crucified and killed by the hands of lawless men. But God raised him up . . . (Acts 20.23 f.).

The contrast here expressed is not limited to that between the guilty and the innocent. It is between those who were engaged in frustrating God's purpose for the world and the one in whom that purpose was carried out. The resurrection gospel proclaimed that he is the one in whose hands lies the ultimate judgment of man.

> God . . . has fixed a day on which he will judge the world in righteousness by a man whom he has appointed, and of this he has given assurance to all men by raising him from the dead (Acts 17.31).

Faith in the resurrection of Jesus was therefore a decision that it was Jesus who was to be judge, and that it was in following him that one would be found righteous at the judgment.

Thus the resurrection of Jesus was perceived within the framework of expectation which the history of the Jews had brought into being. This expectation was linked to their belief in a righteous and all-power-

ful God who would bring his will to pass in the world. The resurrection
of Jesus did not fit easily into that framework, as can be seen from the
immense amount of argumentation in the New Testament on the
subject of the unexpected, suffering Messiah; it can indeed be said
that inasmuch as it thrust the Christian community outwards in mission
it contributed to the destruction of the framework within which it was
perceived. To this it will be necessary to return later. What is certain is
that the resurrection was understood within a context which allowed it
to be something which had happened in the world and held out promise
for the world. That context allowed the resurrection of Jesus,
apparently, to be misunderstood in various ways, as will be seen later;
but it did not allow the resurrection of Jesus to become either wholly
past or wholly private. It required those who were invited to believe it
to expect a certain future and to commit their lives to the pursuit of it.

The problem which poses itself as soon as any contemporary expression of the resurrection faith is examined is that the framework of
Jewish eschatology within which it was originally understood is no
longer the way in which we generally look at the world. It is not widely
supposed that the world is moving towards its final judgment by Jesus.
This is not to say that such language is no longer used by Christians;
only that when it is used as the language of their faith it has no obvious
reference points within the world-view of their contemporaries. The
vigorous arguments of Paul and Mark that the Messiah whom all were
expecting was Jesus carry little weight when a Messiah is not being
looked for. Thus the resurrection of Jesus has now to be received
within the context of quite different expectations, if that can be done
without being false to the original proclamation. That will mean striving
after an interpretation which offers criteria by which the truth or
falsity of the resurrection faith can be established, and the truth must
be of the kind that requires that element of moral risk which the New
Testament hope displays.

This is particularly necessary in view of the immense evocative
power of the resurrection image. Life out of death is in some sense and
at some point what everybody seeks, and the image can therefore be
harnessed in relation to a great variety of hopes. Some of these hopes
will be like the resurrection of Jesus only in their power; they may even
be fulfilled, but at the cost of a surrender to ideals very far from the
ministry of Jesus, for when life is to be achieved out of death a whole
range of questions immediately present themselves. Whose life from
whose death? What kind of life from what kind of death? Inasmuch as

resurrection faith is to be held now, there is then a need for moral criteria; there are ethical indications to be looked for if the image of life through death is to be validly used.

Such criteria can begin to emerge if one can be certain that it is the resurrection of *Jesus* of which one is speaking. Yet such certainty does not depend on our hopes for the future but upon our view of the past. The moral risk of hoping for a certain kind of future is therefore tied to the intellectual risk of making certain affirmations about the past. There can be no possibility of undertaking the preaching of a resurrection faith without the resolution of those issues which have now become pressing as a result of the historical debate about the nature of the New Testament evidence and the direction in which it points.

So this book represents an attempt to restore the connections which the original resurrection faith shows between faith and history, between past, present and future, between the fate of the person and his life in community. In the next chapter we shall clearly see what happens when these connections are not taken with the seriousness they deserve, so that resurrection faith becomes remote or bizarre or simply private. The vital question is what we are looking for and where we are to look; our very separate questions about what happened and what it means to me will appear in a new light when they are seen in the context that the original Easter proclamation provides. What we are looking for is a way of declaring and pursuing the dimension of a purposeful common life, which was the basis on which Jesus was known as the one whom God had raised from the dead.

2

WHERE ARE PEOPLE LOOKING?

Resurrection faith does not die easily. However much the wind of scepticism blows, and however difficult it may seem to argue for the resurrection of Jesus on purely historical grounds, there remain still fairly large numbers of people who regard the language of Easter as in some sense their language, and the hope of the resurrection as their hope. While it may be true that the majority of these present-day believers hold to their convictions without any great awareness of the historical questions surrounding the records which we have of the days following the death of Jesus, they have nevertheless maintained their belief even while being inescapably part of a world in which beliefs of that kind would be subject to a prevailing scepticism of which they could hardly be unaware. Beliefs do not, of course become rational or true just because a number of people hold them, however large that number may be; nevertheless there must be a presupposition that people have reasons for believing what they do, and that such reasons are the proper subject of theological examination. Such an examination may only lead to the conclusion that the reasons are inadequate and the beliefs themselves confused, but without such an examination no attempt to describe resurrection faith or its rationality would be adequate.

We shall consider here two main types of resurrection faith; that which connects it chiefly with our quest to survive death, and that which relates it to our quest to give meaning to our personal lives. The former kind finds its support for belief mainly in such evidence as there is that human beings survive death, while the second does so on the basis of certain patterns of death and resurrection which can be discerned in a person's life. In looking at these two types of resurrection faith and the way they are felt to be supported we shall be asking how far these ways of understanding the resurrection are faithful to the New

Testament witness to the raising of Jesus and how far they fall short of it. In so far as they do fall short of it they raise the question, to which we turn in the third section, how far it is possible for present experience and present human questioning to give access to our past in general and to the origins of resurrection faith in particular.

Resurrection and Survival

Belief in the resurrection of Jesus is connected for many with their desire to postulate man's survival of death, and support for it is therefore found in the evidence that is claimed to exist for the life after death. For many believers this is the point at which Easter relates to their deepest needs and affirmations. This is hardly surprising when the association both of the resurrection of Jesus and of the Pauline argument found in I Corinthians 15 with life after death has been strengthened by its use at funerals for generations, in some cases a fixed liturgical use, and since the mystery of death is a constant pre-occupation it is natural that an image which appears to speak to the quest for survival should be felt to be supported by such evidence of it as there is. Furthermore, it is a fact that believers have always felt that the resurrection of Jesus gave some assurance about the future of man beyond death. It appears to speak to the question implied by mortality, and however difficult it may be to understand its precise implications for a future life, it nevertheless affirms unequivocally that death is not the last word about life.

Even among those who regard the resurrection proclamation as having primarily to do with survival, the evidence from psychical research is variously evaluated. One who is prepared to make use of it for apologetic purposes is M. C. Perry. In *The Easter Enigma*, he attempts to show that the appearances to the disciples had many of the characteristics of those 'veridical hallucinations' experienced by those who purport to have had contact with people who have died. He attempts to analyse resurrection faith as a 'fourfold cord', based on our information about apparitions of the dead, the New Testament data, our speculations about survival and the views which we derive from Christian theology. He marshalls some of the cases which have become known to those engaged in parapsychological research, and very carefully considers what the criterion would be for separating veridical appearances from those which are not.

The criterion is that 'the apparition should be significantly correlated with some verifiable event occurring to the ostensible communicator',[1] and if the apparition was said to be that of a dead person it had to 'convey verifiable information which could not have been obtained by any normal means on the behalf of the percipient'.[2] Since it is not suggested by the New Testament material that Jesus 'conveyed information' to his disciples after his resurrection, other than the information which is itself in question, namely that he was alive, this can have no relevance to the discussion of the resurrection appearances. The comparison of the accounts of appearances in the New Testament can do no more than establish what kind of a happening the appearances were. All that can be shown by such a study is that

> if we accept as possible and meaningful the notion that Jesus survived death and communicated with his disciples, then we can show that the resurrection appearances and their consequences are consonant with this interpretation, and that other interpretations are unlikely.[3]

What this leads into is a measure of speculation about the nature of the 'resurrection body'. In view of the fact that the disciples would have held a Jewish view of survival, involving resurrection of the body rather than immortality of the soul, Jesus

> caused their minds to project an apparition of his body as they had known it. This would demonstrate to them, in the only way in which they could understand, that it really was he who was teaching them and that he had truly conquered the power of Death.[4]

Estimates of the results of parapsychological research vary, and so therefore will estimates of Perry's argument. He elaborates it to the point where a distinction is made between the kind of appearance which Paul experienced on the Damascus road and the kind experienced by the earliest apostles, and is thereby able to form a conclusion about the origin of the belief in the ascension; at the end of the forty-day period there was a decisive shift from the 'physical body' type of appearance to the 'heavenly glory' kind as seen by Stephen before his death and Paul at his conversion.[5] Despite the elaboration of the argument, however, Perry at the end makes no great claim for it. His argument does not, he considers, embrace more than a thousandth part of the full Christian belief in the resurrection. An understanding of survival could do no more than give a clue to the way in which the appearances took place.[6]

Perry's account is a very interesting attempt, in some detail, to relate a fairly uncharted area of knowledge, psychical research, to some of the data of the Christian tradition. As a historical reconstruction, however, it suffers from being based on a handling of the New Testament which takes no account of the theological concerns of the writers, as his treatment of the forty days and the ascension, just described, bears out. Because he makes no allowance for the influence of theological considerations on the way the stories are told, he is quite prepared to believe that a harmonization of the differing accounts is possible. The conclusion to which he comes is such as to strike all but the most conservative scholars as fanciful.

> So far, then, our attempt at harmonization has gone admirably. We have used up all the material in the Gospel accounts up to this stage and have come across no discrepancy more serious than a doubt as to the precise number of angels seen by the women at the tomb or the precise moment at which they first saw them.[7]

This manner of dealing with the material is based on the presupposition that the accounts of the resurrection appearances had no other purpose than to establish that Jesus was alive. It is not surprising that even when Perry concludes his book with the observation that his analysis of the resurrection of Jesus covers no more than the thousandth part of the Easter faith, the remaining part which he says he has not covered has to do with the quality of the eternal life which is offered to the believer. An examination of the New Testament accounts of resurrection faith will show that Perry's account has completely upset the balance. Even the motif of eternal life itself contains far more than the assurance of something beyond death for the believer. This thousandth part which Perry offers would, on its own, only lead to a very distorted view of what the resurrection faith really was.

The idea that religious belief might find support in some of the data revealed by research into the paranormal has also been advanced, from a more philosophical point of view, by H. H. Price. His Sarum Lectures of 1971 are devoted entirely to this theme,[8] and although he says that he accepts that there is a distinction between the paranormal and the spiritual,[9] the lectures in fact link the two together very closely. His interest in the paranormal ranges more widely than Perry's, to include the relationship of intercessory prayer to telepathy and of spiritual capacities to extra-sensory perception. The last two chapters, however, are concerned with life after death, and it is here that his view of the resurrection appearances, described in an appendix, assumes importance.

It is noticeable that views of the life after death which Price attacks most strongly are those which are associated with rewards and punishments, heaven, hell and purgatory.[10] It is no part of our purpose here to defend these doctrines; but it is extremely doubtful whether the total elimination of the ethical dimension from traditional language about the next world is possible without losing the primary purpose of such doctrines, which was to express the eternal significance of the choices which human beings make. To say this is not to condone the exploitation of fear which was often so prominent a feature of the church's proclamation of the last things; it is simply to make the point that belief in that kind of life after death was very much a part of belief in a God who made strong ethical demands and whose rule was absolute.

Price's concern with the after-life is, however, quite unrelated to ethical considerations. His concern is only to elucidate from the evidence what kind of next world there might be, whether it is an 'embodied' or a 'disembodied' one. This is reflected in the way in which he treats, in an appendix, the New Testament accounts of the resurrection appearances and the empty tomb. There is no suggestion that the New Testament accounts had any other motive than to describe a paranormal phenomenon. The following two passages, the first about a resurrection appearance and the second about the empty tomb, convey Price's main concern:

> Of all the post-Resurrection appearances, the one which is most easily credible, at least to a psychical researcher, is the Emmaus narrative in Luke 24.13 – 35. That is because the phenomena reported are purely visual and auditory. Nothing at all is said about tangibility. The only puzzling episode is the breaking of the bread. Was the bread physically broken? Or was this too a purely apparitional event? I suspect that it was.[11]

> What became of the body which died on the Cross? Shall we say that in the tomb it was 'de-materialized' and then 're-materialized' during those two and half days, and that the resurrected body was *visibly* similar to the one which had been laid in the tomb but in other ways was very different (for instance, 'alive for ever more')?[12]

From such a resurrection faith the notes of eschatological fulfilment, mission and newness of life which characterize the New Testament witnesses' proclamation that Christ was risen are all missing. It is hard to see what light is shed on the gospel of the resurrection by Price's tentative conclusion (at the end of the appendix just quoted) that Christ's resurrection body probably had 'four-dimensional mobility', or in what way such an argument could lend support to faith as the New Testament understands the term. Man's deep longing to transcend death is hardly answered by the offer of four-dimensional mobility.

Yet the relationship between the resurrection of Jesus and man's desire to transcend death cannot be ignored in any account of the way in which that faith has been handed on. This is not only so because of the place that desire has in the way the faith is held today, but because from a very early point in the church's history it had become one of the primary concerns involved in belief in the resurrection. Quite apart from the more extreme speculations, there is ample evidence of the attempt by the early fathers to relate their belief about Jesus to the question about what happens to a person when he dies. At the most extreme, these speculations would strike the present-day reader as ludicrous. Thus, Athenagoras' question about what would happen if a particle of one body had, after burial in the earth and decomposition, been eaten by another human being, and his assertion that God would be able to reassemble the particles of the bodies of the dead even if they were decomposed or burnt,[13] appear as flights of fancy even wilder than the Sadducees' question (Matt. 22.23-28) about what would happen to a resurrected woman who, in her lifetime, had been married to seven brothers in succession. The manner in which the resurrection would take place, and the conviction that it would take the form of the 'resurrection of the flesh' are also matters of great concern to Tertullian and Irenaeus.[14]

Yet it would be a mistake to assume that the fathers' concern with the resurrection of the dead was merely a concern with personal survival. The terms in which they discuss the subject make it clear that they are also concerned with God's relation to the world he has created, and so with resisting the devaluation of the creation which is implicit in the Hellenistic doctrine of the immortality of the soul. Under the guise of a concern with the survival of those who had died, a strong attack on the dualistic world-view of the time is being made, and God is declared to be concerned with the future of the world of matter as well as with the soul. As Norris writes, the doctrine of the resurrection of the body confirmed the doctrine of creation, for

> as every Christian writer of the patristic period was, to one degree or another, aware, the doctrine that the world is God's creation 'out of nothing' contradicts [Hellenistic] ideas at several points. For one thing, it must refuse to admit that matter, now regarded perforce as the creature of God, can be by nature alien from its Creator; and this

refusal was lent further support by the doctrine of the bodily resurrection.[15]

This anti-dualistic aspect to the church's understanding of the resurrection, even when it is concerned with the question of survival after death, is one of the cardinal points which form the basis of H.A. Williams' interpretation of the resurrection, to which more detailed reference will be made later.

The possibility of the body's resurrection now in the present is thus of no mere theoretical interest. It is a matter of urgent concern to us all.

What does it mean?

It means my body being raised up to its own life. It means mind and body no longer making war on each other in a bid for domination, but recognizing that they are both equally me. When I can feel that I am my body, and that this does not in any way contradict the fact that I am my mind, then I shall have had experience of resurrection. For it is death that separates and life which unites. To be raised to life, therefore, is to discover that I am one person. In the experience of resurrection body and mind are no longer felt to be distinct.[16]

As the examination of the arguments of Perry and Price has shown, there is a real risk that an attempt to argue for the resurrection of Jesus on the basis of the evidence for survival might lack this anti-dualistic emphasis. Such an argument seems in fact to relate to quite a different issue from that which preoccupied the fathers of the church. Their affirmation was that through Jesus the whole person, and in particular the flesh, can take part in what God has in store for man beyond death, an affirmation which takes a life beyond death for granted. Modern believers ask for assurance that there is a life after death at all, and try to find that assurance in the resurrection of Jesus. This change in the nature of the affirmation is of the greatest importance. The survival that is being sought, and of which confirmation is being found in the raising of Jesus, is no longer one which is able to make a comment on this present life − 'that matter cannot of its nature be alien from its Creator'. What is now sought is an assurance of continued life which has no comment to make on present life except that it is to continue.

This change in the character of belief in the resurrection becomes even more apparent when those passages in the New Testament which appear to make a comment on life beyond death are compared with the way in which they are heard now. The problem of death certainly con-

cerned the early church almost from the beginning, but it was a problem caused not so much by the fact of grief and bereavement or by a
concern for the future of the self, but rather by the implications which
the deaths of some believers were seen to have for the church's faith in
the imminent end of all things and for the coming of God's kingdom.

> We want you to be quite certain, brothers, about those who have
> died, to make sure that you do not grieve about them, like the
> other people who have no hope. We believe that Jesus died and rose
> again, and that it will be the same for those who have died in Jesus:
> God will bring them with him. We can tell you this from the Lord's
> own teaching, that any of us who are left alive until the Lord's
> coming will not have any advantage over those who have died. At
> the trumpet of God, the voice of the archangel will call out the
> command and the Lord himself will come down from heaven; those
> who have died in Christ will be the first to rise, and then those of us
> who are still alive will be taken up in the clouds, together with them,
> to meet the Lord in the air. So we shall stay with the Lord for ever.
> With such thoughts as these you should comfort one another
> (I Thess. 4.13-18, JB).[17]

Such a passage reflects a world-view far removed from our own, and
such thoughts are not, at any rate in an unexpurgated form, likely to be
of much use in comforting either the dying or the bereaved. Those who
hear the funeral collect which asserts that we have been taught 'not to
be sorry as men without hope for them that sleep in him' would be
unlikely to assent to the apocalyptic hope which clearly lies behind a
passage such as this. It is evidently written in answer to the question
posed by the death of Thessalonian Christians prior to the advent of
the Lord, and offers the assurance that they will not thereby have lost
their share in the kingdom of Christ when it comes. As it stands it
offers an answer in terms that could not be accepted now to a question
that is not being asked. The same has to be said about the other passage
most frequently understood as offering, through the resurrection of
Jesus, hope of life beyond death, the fifteenth chapter of I Corinthians.

> But in fact Christ has been raised from the dead, the first fruits of
> those who have fallen asleep. For as by a man came death, by a man
> has come also the resurrection of the dead. For as in Adam all die,
> so also in Christ shall all be made alive. But each in his own order:
> Christ the first fruits, then at his coming those who belong to Christ.
> Then comes the end, when he delivers the kingdom to God the
> Father after destroying every rule and every authority and power
> (I Cor. 15.20-24).

What is here being described is not the survival of death but the Christian apocalyptic scheme, and if this does offer an account of life beyond the grave it certainly offers much more besides. This is confirmed by the discussion which follows, about the nature of the risen body.

> Some one will ask, 'How are the dead raised? With what kind of body do they come?' You foolish man! What you sow does not come to life unless it dies. And what you sow is not the body which is to be, but a bare kernel, perhaps of wheat or of some other grain. But God gives it a body as he has chosen, and to each kind of seed its own body. For not all flesh is alike, but there is one kind for men, another for animals, another for birds, and another for fish. . . . So it is with the resurrection of the dead. What is sown is perishable, what is raised is imperishable. It is sown in dishonour, it is raised in glory. It is sown in weakness, it is raised in power. It is sown a physical body, it is raised a spiritual body (I Cor. 15.35 – 39, 42 – 44).[18]

If this passage states anything about the Christian understanding of death, it is that death is necessary. The life beyond death is apparently assumed; what is emphatically asserted is that it cannot be attained without the occurrence of death.

The same difficulties apply in the case of those passages from the gospels which appear to offer hope beyond death. In the dialogue with the Sadducees about the resurrection (Matt. 22.23 – 33), two things become clear in what appears in any case to be more in the nature of a rabbinical contest than an attempt to offer a coherent doctrine of the life beyond death. In response to the Sadducees' story about the woman who had been married to seven brothers and their question to whom she would be married at the resurrection, Jesus says,

> You are wrong, because you know neither the scriptures nor the power of God. For in the resurrection they neither marry nor are given in marriage, but are like angels in heaven. And as for the resurrection of the dead, have you not read what was said to you by God, 'I am the God of Abraham, and the God of Isaac, and the God of Jacob'? He is not God of the dead, but of the living (Matt. 22.29 – 32).

Apart from an unwillingness to answer the question in the terms in which it has been put, it is first clear that Jesus is not prepared to talk about the resurrection as some kind of continuation of the life we now know, with its assumptions and limitations. And, secondly, in so far as he is willing at all to offer some grounds for belief in a future life, it is on the basis of an argument about the nature of God and not about the nature of man.

Another text which is frequently assumed to offer some assurance on this subject is the conversation between Jesus and Martha before the raising of Lazarus.

> Martha said to Jesus, 'Lord, if you had been here, my brother would not have died. And even now I know that whatever you ask from God, God will give you.' Jesus said to her, 'Your brother will rise again.' Martha said to him, 'I know that he will rise again in the resurrection at the last day.' Jesus said to her, 'I am the resurrection and the life; he who believes in me, though he die, yet shall he live, and whoever lives and believes in me shall never die' (John 11.21 – 26).

In their context, Jesus' words are clearly intended to transform the traditional Jewish expectation of the resurrection by claiming for himself that total significance which the Jews maintained could only belong to the end of all things. It is hard to overestimate the change which is effected in their meaning when they are spoken to a group of bereaved people nowadays: they are likely to hear the words not in the sense that their greatest longings and expectations for the world have been fulfilled in the life of Christ on earth, but that Christ offers hope for individual life beyond the grave.

Thus while the hope for survival of death may offer a path by which people can enter into resurrection faith, it is still a path strewn with obstacles. For the resurrection of Jesus was not in the first instance proclaimed as a response to the quest for a means of transcending death, and the language in which it was proclaimed, even when the fate of individuals who have died is being discussed, does not seem likely to commend itself. As a result, the resurrection faith is likely to be appropriated in response to the desire for immortality only in a severely censored form. In the process, the understanding of a God with a purpose for the world, the commitment to a proclamation of the truth about all mankind implicit in the Christian mission, and the sense of the new criteria of judgment offered in Jesus are likely to vanish, and the language of the New Testament resurrection faith will have been tamed in the service of the vague and attenuated belief that the person who appears to have died is not really dead.

That does not mean, however, that the hope for life beyond death cannot be available as the point at which the resurrection faith meets the contemporary hearer. The resurrection proclamation has been handed on in the church precisely because of its capacity to embrace idioms and vocabularies, hopes and expectations, very different from those which were current when it was first believed. The risk is that the language and the current expectations predominate to the extent that the resurrection faith is appropriated to confirm what people believe, or wish to believe, anyway. The creative possibility in a situation where the resurrection proclamation is addressed to a different complex of expectations is that it will illuminate and transform them as well as be able to be expressed through them.

If the language of resurrection faith has little appropriateness where grief at personal loss is the predominant factor, as at most funerals, then it will be even less appropriate to those occasions where, as after the death of a person who has had to endure a long illness, the predominant sense is that death has come as a relief. The idea of death as an enemy, which is presupposed in so much of the New Testament's thinking about it, and the Christian proclamation of Christ as victorious over it, will have little to say. Yet the language is not always inappropriate. There are occasions when death comes as the unsought interruption of a life which had embodied those convictions about the world which New Testament resurrection faith presumes. On such occasions, although the cultural gap remains, the language of the New Testament reverberates because death has raised a question not just about the life of that individual but also about the cause, the mission, the quality of life, which the dead person embodied. It then becomes possible to cross the gap which separates us from those whose life was staked on the imminent second advent of the Lord because the life of the person who has died has offered a coherence and a faithfulness which, while not the same as that which was available to the New Testament Christians, nevertheless bears its unmistakable marks.

An example of the way in which the language of resurrection can be given relevance to the quest for the survival of death by means of its coherence with other factors is offered by the reflection of William Stringfellow. After working as a lay member of a Christian team in East Harlem, he found at a certain point that he was critically ill, and had not much longer to live. Sometime later, when he had unexpectedly recovered, he reflected thus on his coming to terms with the likelihood of his own imminent death.

> The decade locates me, at its outset, deeply in the midst of work as a white lawyer in Harlem, but it closes in fragile survival of prolonged, obstinate, desperate illness. It begins in social crisis, it ends

in personal crisis. For me, these two crises are equally profound, because the aggression of death is the moral reality pervasive in both and, moreover, the grace to confront and transcend death is the same in each. Indeed, I do not think the two episodes, which roughly mark my personal boundaries of the past decade, are essentially distinguishable. I doubt, in other words, that I could have had the capability to lately survive radical disease, unremitting pain and the shadow of death, had I not spent those earlier years in the Harlem ghetto, discerned there something of the moral power of death, and learned, from neighbors, clients and Harlem inhabitants at large, something of the triumph of life which human beings can enter and celebrate despite death's ubiquity and strength. Harlem is the scene in which I first comprehended the veracity of the resurrection — and that prepared me, more than any other single thing, for devastating illness and ruthless pain. Had I known only what I had heard about the resurrection in Sunday school or from pulpits or from within the American white Anglo-Saxon Protestant ethos, I believe I would surely have died — most likely toward the end of 1968.[19]

What has been said so far might seem to lead to the conclusion that resurrection language can only be used appropriately with reference to the deaths of martyrs and saints. This would be to assume that the coherence of belief which supplies meaning to the resurrection language can only be offered by the dying or dead person, when in fact that coherence of belief was primarily, in the New Testament, the property of the community which had the resurrection to proclaim. It may well be that the sense of appropriateness which the language of resurrection has when it is used about outstanding lives arises because those lives have exhibited what it is properly the function of the believing community to exhibit; but the New Testament church found the death of a member a problem not simply because of natural grief but chiefly because it appeared that one person would not be there to share the fruits of the mission in which they were together engaged. It is to that problem that any New Testament hope of transcending death is addressed, and inasmuch as that language continues to be used when people die it directs those who use it to the consideration of how the structure of belief and action which both caused death to be the theological problem which it was and supplied the answer to that problem can be reflected by a different church in a different world. It is not that resurrection faith cannot be appropriated on the basis of man's quest for the power to transcend death, or indeed on the basis of whatever evidence there may be to suggest that he does; it is rather that that quest and that evidence have to be re-evaluated in the light of the other elements which belong to the full picture of resurrection faith.

The Resurrection in Personal Experience

One of the boldest attempts to give an account of how resurrection can be experienced in life is made by H. A. Williams in *True Resurrection*. His criticism of most treatments of the subject is that they focus entirely on the past or the future.

> Resurrection, at least in Western Christendom, has invariably been described as belonging to another time and place. The typical emphasis has been upon the past and future — a past and future with which our connection can only be theoretical, however correct the theory is held to be. So, for example, a book about the resurrection is naturally assumed to be a discussion either about what can be held to have happened in the environs of Jerusalem and Galilee on the third day after Jesus was crucified or about what can be held to be in store for us after our own death.[20]

This can certainly not be said about Williams' own book. He devotes no place to historical discussion, and as the paragraph just quoted makes clear, his attitude to inquiry about the past and to speculation about the future is that neither can be more than a cerebral pursuit. They have no power to excite or to give life. If the past were to be used by a politician as a focus of national unity or aspiration, 'it would be the contemporary issues which excited and inspired, of which the past event would be no more than a convenient representation.'[21] The future similarly has no power to cause us to choose differently. 'Like all theory, the future has no teeth.'[22] Whether this estimate of the past and the future are acceptable remains to be examined; suffice it here that it leads him into a wide-ranging survey of the ways in which resurrection can be and is a present fact, with an impressive range of examples. The artist who at first experiences only emptiness but then finds his imagination stirred into life, the married couple whose relationship has been slowly drying up but suddenly blossoms forth with new depths; these and others whom he instances are, in his view, undergoing resurrection.[23]

One of the factors in the way of such experience of resurrection has been the dualism latent in much of the Christian church's teaching. The Platonic exaltation of mind over body has led either to the body being killed off and its desires quelled, or else to its being indulged in an act of conscious rebellion against the old master, man's reason. Resurrection has then to be experienced as the recovery of the essential unity of the self and of the integrity of mind and body. This brings to life not merely the body but the mind also, and not only the person having the experience but also the world in which he lives.

> Yet the experience of resurrection returns and I know myself again as one person for whom to be body is to be mind and to be mind is to be body. And this experience of oneness within myself invariably brings with it the experience of oneness with the external world. I no longer feel separated from the people and things I live among. While remaining fully themselves and preserving their own inalienable identity, they also become part of what I am. The separation between me and them is overcome so that I share an identity with them. My own resurrection is also the resurrection of the world.[24]

One of his stories is of a widow and her lover, who are an instance of the way in which liberation was discovered in the unity of mind and body, so that the physical, from being the opponent of the mental and spiritual, became the means of their expression.

> They too, like St Paul, heard the voice of the Eternal Word. St Paul heard the Word through the medium of the religious interests which were his chief concern. The characters in our stories heard the Word through the medium of their respective preoccupations. But whatever the media, fear was cast out. Dualism was transcended. And those concerned were raised in their bodies to newness of life.[25]

The dualism which is death-dealing to the body is also, in Williams' view, death-dealing to the mind. In the place of mystical knowledge offering communion with others and with the environment has been substituted mere scientific knowledge which appears to bring possession but in reality brings death. Resurrection for the mind reinstates a sense of communion with what is known in place of the domination over it which is the quest of the scientific and technological mind. It was as 'a detached theoretician', Williams says by way of example, that Job was unable to make sense of his misfortune, and he was only saved by his ultimate refusal to abandon his experience of what he was in favour of the theory of rewards and punishments with which his friends sought to explain what had happened to him.

> Then the Lord spoke to Job out of the whirlwind. Reality was revealed to Job at first hand in all its terrifying power and ruthlessness. It was seen in its giant strength to belong to an order which smashed to pieces the theoretical cage in which Job and his friends had sought to keep it captive. In his experience of reality as it truly was in itself, and in the consequent break-up of the projection upon

it of his own fantasies, Job died and was raised from the dead. There was no more querulous insistence upon the injustice of life. All was now awe and wonder at the terrifying mystery through which he had lived.[26]

What the resurrected mind possesses is not intellectual certainty, but something more like the knowledge that is mediated by works of art. This was also the kind of knowledge mediated by Jesus, whose concern was with the present moment and not with speculation, with parable and not with doctrine, for his knowledge was of the sort which brings man into communion with man and with God.

Death-resurrection is a pattern discernible also in attitudes towards the good. In the realm of the ethical, men are also imprisoned in a death-dealing past, whereby society identifies what is good with what most conveniently conforms to its own mould. When the two communities in Northern Ireland identify what is good with the prejudices of their particular group, they are the prisoners of history, and of a past which has distorted their perception of the good.[27] Jesus' ethical demands, on the other hand, were not grounded in either rules or social conformity, but in the conviction that the power of the resurrection could be brought to bear on situations no matter how intractable they seemed.[28] The person who is emancipated from his own dead past is able to emancipate others, and in this way even to change the way the past is perceived. 'Do not Christians in the light of resurrection call that Friday good?'[29]

> In social as in individual matters, ethical behaviour or goodness is not conformity to an existing value or the attempt to articulate an existing value. Ethical behaviour or goodness is resurrection. It is bringing creative insight to bear upon a social situation so that whatever in that situation is deadening to human development may be changed into something life-giving. Goodness is the fruit of imagination, the product of life coming to consciousness, and this can happen only in the now and with regard to contemporary situations.[30]

Death and not resurrection is also the effect of some traditional Christian attitudes to suffering. Suffering is not punishment for sin; it is undesirable and is to be prevented wherever possible. Yet it is part of human experience, and when viewed in the light of resurrection can be the vehicle of new insight. Williams instances representations of suffering in some works of art, where despite the deep acknowledgment of pain there is nevertheless a note of triumph. Or it can be seen in Beethoven's triumph over his deafness,[31] or within the experience of more ordinary people who after being confronted by a level of suffering far greater than they are able to bear discover within themselves capabilities which had previously lain dormant. By such a miracle suffering becomes a source of resurrection.

> Yet when, by miracle, we accept the suffering, receive it, take it on board, then we find that this limited self is an illusion, that we are infinitely more than we ever imagined, so that we can after all take the suffering and in taking it become fuller, deeper, richer people, because a dormant potential within us has been roused to activity and life, and we know ourselves to be more than previously we had even a hint of. Thus does the destructive power of suffering become creative and what is death-dealing become life-giving.[32]

Williams is willing to admit, however, that even if resurrection is to be discerned when the body becomes an instrument of life rather than something to be controlled and killed, when knowledge becomes communion instead of possession, when goodness becomes the action of liberation and not conformity to a dead past, and when suffering is taken into the self to become the raw material of new perception and life, nevertheless the matter of physical death cannot be left unconsidered. 'For it is precisely in physical death that life's destructive forces reach their climax and appear to win their final victory.'[33] The response to this issue must not however be one which does not take as its starting-point the kinds of experience of resurrection which he has previously been considering. Resurrection within life begins from the sense of powerlessness and proceeds through an experience of miracle. This is so already in life, and in death it will be no greater miracle. What is given by way of new life is something beyond what is expected or even conceived, and likewise the Christian anticipation of death is that of one who expects to receive far more than has so far entered his mind. This expectation Williams calls 'hope' in contrast to the mere hope for the continuance of what is already known and appears to be taken away, which he calls 'desire'. The sense of powerlessness followed by miracle, as it is repeated in life, prepares us for dying.

> Such undefined hope and its fulfilment we have already experienced here now. The experience involved a break with ourselves as belonging hopelessly to the past and our being raised up to the creative call of our own future. Physical death is the last and final break with our past. We cannot prove that the miracle of resurrection will automatically follow. But we can take to heart the fact that it has invariably done so hitherto. 'Old things are passed away; behold, all things are

become new.' We could say that God's turning to us is new and strange every morning. Those aware of that fact can hardly fail to hope.[34]

Resurrection faith such as Williams outlines it is both profound in its content and beautiful in its expression. He has been quoted here fairly extensively[35] because he represents the bold imagination that is needed if resurrection faith is not merely to be shouted to men from the housetops but actively related to their lives. His impatience with versions of that faith which depend primarily on historical research or speculation about the future arises not from any unwillingness on his own part to consider in depth what the tradition in which he stands signifies, but upon the conviction that the reality to which the tradition draws attention is still the reality of human experience at its most profound. The attitudes expressed in the book on a variety of topics are intended to be 'resurrection attitudes', and so they are.

This suggests that the kind of historical question in which Williams professes to have no interest is rather taken for granted than omitted. In his earlier book, *Jesus and the Resurrection*, he anchored his discussion to the events of Holy Week and Easter, but even so he moved straight to their implications for the faith of the reader, and one may suspect that both his reluctance to involve himself with historical questions and his declaration that they are beside the point rest on a willingness to take the New Testament as it stands and not to be concerned with any difficulties which it may be possible to discern in it. His assumption may in fact be that the New Testament writers were performing a task not at all dissimilar to the one which he has set himself, namely, to draw attention to certain features in the experience of their readers which fitted with the language of resurrection, and that undoubtedly was a part of what those writers intended.

It is equally clear, however, that this was not all they intended, and it may therefore be asked at what points Williams' procedure omits to take account of significant elements in the resurrection faith. It would not be accurate to say that there is no counterpart in Williams' thinking to the New Testament writers' concern to say that something had happened in the world; he too is concerned very much with what happens there. Yet there is a sense in which his resurrection is very much 'in the eye of the beholder' and it is upon the beholder, or rather the believer, that resurrection comes. The resurrection has become a way of looking at all events rather than being itself an event. The New Testament writers seem to wish it to be both. The words quoted above,

'Do not Christians in the light of resurrection call that Friday good?', are particularly important in this respect. If the omission of the definite article with 'resurrection' is intended in some sense to change it from something that happened to a way in which Christians came to understand the cross, then Williams' position is open to two criticisms: historically it leaves questions completely unanswered about how that new understanding was reached, and theologically it involves God with human responses but not with events. The response to such criticisms would undoubtedly be that events are meaningless without human responses and interpretations; that is correct so far as it goes, but events are not merely human responses.

These criticisms also illustrate the risks involved in basing resurrection only upon the present. When we are told, for example, that the painter's sudden inspiration is an experience of resurrection, it is necessary to ask what criteria are operating in this choice of language. At what point would such experiences become too trivial to merit that description, so that it would become not a new way of looking at events which makes them life-giving rather than death-dealing, but rather a way in which theological concepts become so restricted that their full import for the believer is simply concealed? If all difficulties in life are crosses and all renewals are called resurrections, what has happened to that dimension of the New Testament proclamation which made the resurrection the anticipation of the final destiny of all men?

It is significant that in *True Resurrection* Williams' use of the scriptures is confined to those areas where individuals are brought to a new understanding: Job, Jacob's wrestling, the new life-style proposed for a person by Jesus, Paul, but in his personal experience rather than in his theological proclamation. The book both in its attitudes and in its style may leave the reader temporarily unconcerned with the awkward issues of whether resurrection is something that happened and is happening, and of how we are to know. That the book is based on some very clear personal answers to those questions cannot be allowed to obscure the fact that these are real questions, and that it is the task of theology to give articulate rather than implicit answers.

It is not simply churlishness on the part of the theologian that he is forced by his material to draw attention to the historical fact that religious language and the religious sphere of meaning have frequently been pressed into the service of questionable objectives, and that this has become apparent when resurrection experiences which begin by producing in individuals and groups genuine signs of a new beginning and a fresh start in righteousness end by confirming the individual's or the group's return to the situation they had thought to leave behind. In such a case resurrection is not merely appropriated in a trivial sense, but is used to justify values very far indeed from those which Williams for example clearly holds.

Like other theological issues, this may be illustrated by the situation which confronted the German churches during the rise of Nazism. The speeches of Nazi leaders were full of references to religion in general and to the resurrection in particular. Germany, it was freely said, was undergoing resurrection. The shackles of Versailles were being thrown off and a new life of freedom emerging. The millions who had been ground into poverty by the combination of world-wide depression and the load of reparations required from Germany were now building, among other things, the most advanced motorway system in the world. A nation was recovering its independence and self-respect. So the language of resurrection came very naturally to the lips of the politicians in the first instance, and was then ideally suited to the maintenance of a sustained propaganda campaign in which the churches were enlisted as allies.

The benefit of hindsight makes it easy to forget the plausibility with which this must have struck the ears of even the most idealistic — indeed, especially the most idealistic — of Christians in Germany. It also belongs to the complexity of things that those who thought to resist Hitler, and above all to resist his assumption of the Christian vocabulary in the service of National Socialism, found themselves forced to do so by way of the condemnation, in an almost inarticulate fashion, of any theology which took human experience as its starting-point. Barth's affirmation of the uniqueness of God and of his accessibility solely by means of his revelation in Jesus Christ were far less easy to understand, let alone believe, than were the utterances of the German Christian movement on behalf of a Nazi-Christian synthesis. Nevertheless, this resistance was made, and some of its issues may be seen focussed in a letter written by friends of Bonhoeffer to the Council of Brethren of the Old Prussian Union after a 'resurrection festival', held on 9 November 1935, for those who had fallen in the Nazi rising at Munich in 1923.

On 9th November, the German people witnessed a 'resurrection festival' for those who fell in Munich in the year 1923.

We note that this was a state celebration with explicitly cultic forms and deliberately using biblical terminology. By an express decree of the Minister of the Interior, the Christian churches have been asked to take part in this celebration by the use of banners. Here the Evangelical Church has been led astray into a manifest violation of its confession. There should have been a clear statement on the subject of this day, making a firm distinction between the Christian resurrection hope and this popular-idealistic idea of resurrection. The least that might have been done would have been to give visible expression to the church's position by refraining from displaying any flags. The state seems to have sensed this: on the radio broadcast, those who could not accept this 'devotion' (*sic!*) were several times asked to refrain from it.

We know that many pastors have been distressed at not having been given any guidance on this serious occasion. They have been left alone in their difficult decision. They must now be under the impression that they will also remain unprotected if penal consequences ensue from their decision to stand by the confession. We know that investigations into the matter have already been begun by the police in Pomerania. And the parishes are in severe danger of having their faith damaged because they have not been shown clearly that this 'positive Christianity' of the state has nothing to do with the message of Jesus Christ.

1. We would ask the church government most urgently to be mindful of its office of guardian in view of the pseudo-Christian state cults which are increasing and to make a clear pronouncement on the subject without delay, in pursuit of the Dahlen Declaration of March of this year.

2. We would ask the church government to make a regulation about the use of flags, so that the occasions on which flags are to be flown on churches are carefully considered. We would ask the church government to take up a position *post eventum* concerning 9th November of this year for the sake of pastors and their parishes.[36]

The event which lies behind this letter is an example, albeit an extreme one, of the risks involved in the attempt to discern resurrection within the experience of the believer. The image of death and resurrection is a powerful and evocative one, but precisely for that reason it can be used to serve causes very far from those which were believed to be implied by the resurrection of Jesus. In such an apparently trivial matter as the showing of flags on church buildings, the problem of identifying any particular event with the pattern of the resurrection becomes apparent. The lesson of the German church struggle for the Christian theologian is at least the need to be able to speak of the resurrection of Jesus in a way that leaves it independent of, and therefore capable of exercising a critical role in, the affairs of men, even if at certain points those affairs appear to illustrate it or to conform to the model offered by it. The apparently very theologically conservative and very church-centred claim about Jesus' resurrection, as it is made in this letter, in effect amounted to a demand that the church preserve the integrity of that past which brought it into being, while using it to evaluate the events through which it was passing. The consequences of a total identification of the values of Christianity with the political system against which Bonhoeffer and others struggled are now a matter of history. Those particular consequences were, it is true, very extreme, and it may be argued that the manner of the resurrection proclamation should not be decided by a unique manifestation of its subversion through an evil ideology. But the need to preserve a resurrection pro- clamation which is to some degree able to function independently of the experiences with which it is identified is not only illustrated by such an extreme example. The capacity of any experience, once it has been designated a resurrection experience, to become the model of what a resurrection experience must be like, limits the openness of those who have had that experience to recognize resurrection experiences of very different kinds.

It was pointed out in the first chapter that the language of resurrec- tion is the language of eschatology, and refers to the decisive and final act of God in restoring his kingdom; it is language about the end of all things. It remained so even when used to describe what had happened to Jesus. What in Jewish eschatology had been a single divine act became for the church two acts, which were nevertheless still one, a first- fruits and a harvest, the resurrection of Jesus and the resurrection of all, the anticipation of the end and the end itself. This pattern was repeated for the individual believer also; he entered into the resurrection of Christ at his baptism, and then lived in anticipation of his own resurrec- tion at the end of the age. There were many aspects of the life of the community which were pointers to that unique divine act of the raising of the dead, but they were pointers or implications only, and not the event itself. There was therefore about any experience available within the life of the Christian community, however significant it was felt to be, a provisional and incomplete character. The early Christians, and this is a dominant theme in I Corinthians, misunderstood themselves if they imagined that by the Spirit they were in full possession of the kingdom of God, of eternal life and of the consummation which belon- ged to it. They were to be prevented from such misunderstanding by the knowledge that what they were experiencing was both the result of the resurrection which had happened to Jesus and also the pointer towards the resurrection which awaited them and all mankind.

A political party which has attained some objective or a small group which has worked painfully through difficult relationships to a level of understanding previously undreamt of will, if such language comes naturally to them, feel inclined to call what they have undergone a 'resurrection'. In doing so, they will be in danger of making an identification rather than establishing a relationship. Human experience can point to and be felt to flow from, can confirm faith in and increase understanding of, that final act of God which is claimed to have happened to Jesus and to be going to happen to the whole world; but however closely the two are connected, they are not the same. The march of oppressed peoples to freedom may seem to those engaged in it to be resurrection, as Paul was able to compare the conception of a child in Sarah's 'dead' womb to resurrection; but both these are images of something which can never be fully contained within them, the resurrection of the dead of which the resurrection of Jesus was the anticipation. If that resurrection is to provide a way of understanding these other events, it has to do so on its terms and not on theirs; otherwise resurrection faith in this generation will not resemble that of the earliest Christians in any but the most superficial way. For what the early church wished to offer was not a useful vocabulary nor even a profound symbolism, but the truth about the world that had been declared by the raising of Jesus from the dead.

If this analysis is correct, the examples of which Williams writes provide an important means of illuminating resurrection faith, but at the same time raise a crucial question. The resurrection of Jesus has never been understood or proclaimed without reference to the experiences of believers, and to that extent the theologian is required to indicate, as Williams does, the kind of experiences which can be understood as a pointer to the resurrection of Jesus; but he is also committed to inquiring whether that which is pointed to has any existence apart from those experiences which do the pointing. We shall see that the raising of Jesus from the dead was not proclaimed in the beginning without some reference to theological realities which were implied by it and which it was possible for believers to experience for themselves; for that reason, it is difficult to discover what kind of event lay behind the resurrection faith. But historical research has shown that the resurrection proclamation bore witness to something which had brought those experiences into being and without which they could not be understood. What saved those experiences from becoming the private possessions of those who had had them and gave them universal significance was the conviction that they were but confirmations of the purpose of God for the world as revealed in the raising of Jesus.

Resurrection faith did, then, concentrate, as Williams would wish a contemporary exposition of it to do, on the present; but it did so because the present had the power to give access both to a past and to a future. That past and that future were not, as Williams suggests, merely theoretical, because the past to which the present was giving access was something that had actually taken place, and the future to which it promised access was the only future which there was for the world, and to which, therefore, mankind had to adjust itself. The theological question is not how present experience can be a *substitute* for the discovery of that past which concerns what happened to Jesus or of that future which is held out to the world, but rather how present experience, and what kind of present experience, can *mediate* to believers in the present day knowledge about that past and that future.

This theological question is brought to a head by the resurrection since it proves singularly difficult to apprehend in terms of a separation between objectivity about the past and commitment in the present. Gaining access to a part of the past by means of the present commitment of the believer appears, by modern historical standards, a strange procedure; yet it seems to be the only possible one. On the other hand, that part of the past, the resurrection of Jesus, once discovered, must retain an integrity of its own so as to be capable in its turn of being used as a criterion for distinguishing between those present experiences and attitudes which can be seen as signs of the resurrection and those which cannot. Unlike modern historians, Christians claim as evidence for something which has happened in the past their experience of and commitment to the risen Lord whom they discern in the pattern of their present life; again unlike modern historians, Christians also claim that that past event for which their present experience is evidence, is the event which determines the true meaning and pattern of all events. If such claims are so out of keeping with historical ways of thinking, it remains to be asked whether there are other means of access to and relationship with their past which men employ in circumstances where history fails to offer that means. What connection do people make between their past and their present?

Past and Present in Human Understanding

The quest for aspects of present experience which might be part of a contemporary expression of the resurrection faith led to a consideration first of the human desire to transcend death and secondly of aspects of life which might be thought to furnish examples of resurrection experiences. Both avenues of exploration, it was concluded, must form part of that contemporary expression of the resurrection faith, but both can in important respects fall short of faithfulness to what the New Testament is concerned to offer. In particular, further thought needs to be given to how these two avenues of exploration can give a way of knowing about the resurrection as both something that has happened and as something which determines the destiny of man. Whether present realities can give access to the past in this way needs now to be considered, and for this it will be necessary to examine some situations which can serve as examples of the interplay between present commitment and knowledge of the past; not all of these examples will appear to have equal status, but together they may provide some insight into the complexity of that combination of argument, experience and reflection which appears to belong to belief in the resurrection of Jesus Christ.

The first such example illustrates the way in which the sense of a shared past can unite, while its absence divides. Two men are out walking. Their conversation is animated, full of gesticulation, mirth and excitement. Names occur again and again. As we draw nearer to them we hear that their talk is of the past; they are reminiscing. They have not met for a long time, but for two years during the second world war they were constant companions. They tell of mutual friends, of the idiocies of commanding officers, of exploits with tanks, with the enemy and with women. They are reliving the most significant years of their life, and as they do so, for a brief time, their present experience becomes more significant.

Meanwhile their wives are at their respective homes. They chose not to come out that evening on that particular walk. Reminiscences of the war hold no interest for them. They had not, after all, been with their husbands at that time. They had been at home, trying as best they could to look after young and growing children. It had been a difficult time, and in a sense it still is. They are not separated physically from their husbands now, but they are separated by a past they do not share.

It was the same past, and neither disagrees with the other's version; the wife, in each case, understands that her husband did have the experience he claims, and the husband understands that his wife had to put up with all that she says. They both suspect each other of a little exaggeration; the war was not so exciting as the husbands suggest, nor perhaps quite as difficult a time as the wives say. But by and large it is not the truth about events that is at issue. What is very much in dispute is which version is to count as a true picture of that particular part of the past, and what is to count as *our* past. The past is the deep bond which unites the two men on their walk; it reintroduces them to the realm of significance and value. But the past is also what divides husband from wife, and the knowledge of the excited conversation on the husbands' walk breeds envy and resentment in their wives. For it is a past that does not match the present, that does not ever stand a chance of becoming shared, and that marks the boundary of the couples' capacity to share. The husband and wife may accept every detail in each other's story; what neither can accept is that the other's story is the true one, for neither story has the capacity for becoming a joint story.

This disunited past is related to how the present is seen. For the husband, significant living is found in a 'man's world', in fighting to win, in surmounting danger, and in the comradeship which a common enemy and shared risk bring. To the extent that both husbands believe this, civilian life lacks lustre and the home cannot be a centre of anything other than domestic security. The war did not in itself make them believe it, nor does that belief in itself decide how they are to view the war. But the war happened, and offered them an experience of significance which they had not encountered anywhere else; it is little wonder that they can think of looking nowhere else for significance for themselves than in reminiscence. Past and present conspire to prevent the two men adjusting to a new reality. That is true for their wives also. At the critical time when their husbands were away they were expected to maintain a home life that was perforce severely disrupted and the comradeship which their husbands so much treasure was denied them. Their value was related only to their ability to keep house and home together, and it still is. They cannot enter the man's world about which their husbands reminisce, and can find no new sphere in which meaning might lie for them. Their past and present are also locked together in a conspiracy which ensures that the future will be no different; the best that can be hoped for is that past and present will continue. Their experience of the past and attitudes in the present ensure that for husbands and wives alike the future will hold nothing really new.

The second example is a more contentious situation. This conversation is taking place at a street corner in Liverpool. Two people, both Irish, are talking about the events of the day called in Londonderry 'Bloody Sunday'. Their conversation is earnest, and they talk about the sheer brutality of the British army, its total disregard for the lives of the people, its pro-Protestant bias. It was certain, they say to each other, that it was the army who fired first, that the crowd was unarmed, that there would have been no breach of the peace if the troops had not started it all in the first place. A fellow-countryman passes along the road, overhears the conversation, and shouts an obscenity at the pair. They round on him. He says (among other things) that they have got it all wrong. The army was not at fault, or, if it was, it is simply that it does not take enough action against terrorists and gunmen. The crowd in Londonderry consisted of large numbers of people carrying guns, and if the army had not done what they did there would have been far more bloodshed. The passer-by is joined by some of his friends, and they also join issue with the original pair. They point out that an impartial judge had investigated the whole thing, and had found quite clearly that the army had not been at fault. But that, according to the other two, is just what you would expect a British judge to discover. 'We've had them in Ireland for years,' they say, 'and all they do is support Unionist injustice.' The others rejoin that if they believe that they will believe anything. The argument becomes very heated, and eventually develops into a full-scale fight which the police have to come and break up.

The argument was about the shape of the past. It related to what happened at a particular town on a particular day. But clearly for both sides the truth of their own particular version mattered. So much did it matter that, unlike the previous example, it would be hard to discover any single detail in the two versions of the past that matched. Truth was determined by the way in which things were said, not just about that day and that particular bit of the past, but about a whole range of other deeply contentious past events such as the Battle of the Boyne, the siege of Derry, the repeal of the Corn Laws and the Government of Ireland Act. Parts of the past have different names in the vocabularies of the two sides; they have learned this vocabulary not so much in history lessons at school as in the social mythology of the places where they live and were brought up. The ordinary criteria of investigation about the past by scholarly historians and wigged judges decide nothing, for everything is decided by a view of the world fashioned entirely by the community to which each side sees itself belonging in the present. The deep disagreements about the shape of the past will continue; they will not be solved by 'impartial' historical and judicial investigation, if that means inquiry by people who do not investigate on the basis of any of the convictions and concerns of the two sides. The disagreements about the past will be solved only when descendants of the two sides have overlaid the contentious past with a common one that has taken over from it the role of shaping their view of the world. It is that new, shared, past which will then determine the version that comes to be accepted of what happened on 'Bloody Sunday', and at the Battle of the Boyne and all the rest. They may even come to feel about it as most now feel about the Crusades or the battles of the Reformation, that to see what happened in terms of one side being good and the other to blame is far too simple. The new generation may condemn both of the present sides for their intransigence, or on the other hand they may understand it as the result of certain economic and social pressures at a particular time; they may understand, accept and forgive. They may even at certain points admire. We cannot tell the future shape of the past, because it will be moulded by the future shape of the commitments and loyalties of human beings just as is the present shape of the past.

It is thus difficult to disentangle the judgments made about the past from the commitments held in the present. As Williams says,

> Across the water in Northern Ireland, we see what being a satisfactory member of a national society can involve. The conflict in Ulster is between two nations, two national identities, and in order to qualify as a true-hearted citizen of either nation, one has, to put it mildly, to lose a certain degree of one's humanity. The pressures brought to bear on individuals to abandon their own personal identity in order to conform to the prejudices and phobias of the two respective national groups is obviously enormous. And it is not a case of individuals being forced to do what they do not want to do (though that must often be so). What happens is that individuals are successfully persuaded that they are Ulstermen and Irishmen first and people second. A man feels that he just is his nation.[37]

This is no doubt part of the truth, but only a part. Being part of a nation is not simply a loyalty; it also involves accepting certain versions of the past at critical moments. The continuous conflicts between the two communities and the heated disagreements about what happened at certain key points in history are bound together, and their solution is based likewise on the elusive combination of the discovery of a common past and a present solidarity with each other. At the point where that is discovered, the unsolved mysteries of 'Bloody Sunday' may be solved, but the likelihood is that responsibility will be placed not on one side or the other of those who were then involved, but on a situation and a history within which both sides were somehow trapped. Thus a new view of that portion of the past will emerge from the need to forge a common future. In the meanwhile, however, two communities find their identity in hanging on doggedly to views of the past which can only give meaning at the expense of those who are held to be in the wrong. The past is death-dealing not because it is past but because it has allied itself with the prejudices of the present in a destructive attempt to purchase life through hostility. Here what is under discussion is history not as it is investigated with a dispassionate concern for what happened, but as it is appropriated by particular groups of people with a passionate concern that it should have happened in the way it has been believed. This kind of history is not one which can be highly valued in historical circles, nor among those who are trying to bring communities together, but it is a kind of history that exists wherever people are looking for the meaning and shape of their lives, and are contending precisely about what that meaning and shape are.

This phenomenon, of making a certain part of the past integral to the present manner in which we shape our world, is not merely to be found in the reminiscences of old soldiers or in the quarrels of Ulstermen. It is part of what is involved in belonging to any kind of group, family or community; without shared memory community seldom occurs. A person with no past in which he has an investment is not the ideal historical investigator nor the best possible high court judge. He is primarily a disoriented human being, who actually belongs nowhere; he remembers nothing as actually belonging to him, and so is incapable of entering into the essential humanity by which history is made. For the past is not the succession of events; it is also the succession of commitments made on the basis of memories that are either shared or not shared.

So far, the examples chosen have exhibited something of the mechanisms involved in the relationship between present commitments and understandings of the past, but where the results have been divisive and destructive. Yet this would be a very one-sided picture. The discovery of a shared past is one of the most potent forces for unity, and a major feature of an emergent community is the creation of shared traditions. A biblical analogy may be cited of an event which, though lying in the past, none the less determined the shape of the life of a community, and the analogy may be all the more pertinent because the event in question was held by the early Christians to have prefigured the resurrection of Christ. This is the exodus from Egypt, at least according to the analysis of it given by some Old Testament scholars.[38]

Research into the remains of Palestinian civilization before 1000 B.C. and also analysis of the Old Testament traditions themselves have led some to the conclusion that while some of the Israelites may indeed have made the journey from Egypt to Canaan, the vast majority did not. They were already there, but in the position of serfs in the Canaanite city kingdoms. There is evidence that a relatively small number of the tribes could have come from Egypt, and that the rest were those of the serfs, the *habiru*, who had rebelled against their Canaanite masters and set themselves up as a tribal amphictyony independent of the city states where they had originally been subjects. The rather diverse positions taken up by the various literary strands in the Pentateuch and the books of the Kings suggest that those who had had their origin in the Canaanite kingdoms had a very different view of the advantages or disadvantages of kingship from that held by other members of the amphictyony. Their recollections of their corporate past were different. Nevertheless, they came to accept, in the end, one story as giving the clearest account of their origins, the story of the exodus. Despite the fact that this was not, factually, a true account of how all of them had their beginning, it was the account of how all of them chose to see their past, the story which they would all remember and pass on as the true past of their society.

There was one reason for this which was of overriding importance, which was that this account of their past was one that offered a guarantee of the values by which their whole community had in fact resolved to live. The story of the law-giving at Sinai became an integral part of the exodus narrative, and with the development of the law of Israel and Judah over the subsequent centuries, Moses, the leader of the exodus, became its natural speaker and the wilderness its natural location. 'A wandering Aramean was my father' (Deut. 26.5) became the justification for each man's offering of his first fruits, even though it may not have been factually true, and 'You shall remember that you were a servant in Egypt' (Deut. 5.15) became the prophetic cry that had the power, whatever may have been its historical basis, which could remind the community of the values by which it had chosen to live and the event which gave those values their backing. Equally in the New Testament period, the resurrection story was believed and appropriated through the experience of life in a community which lived by the values that event proclaimed and, at the same time, acted as a standard of judgment by which the community could be recalled to the values by which it was pledged to live. 'If you then have been raised with Christ, seek the things that are above' (Col. 3.1).

We commonly believe far more history than we can verify. We do so in part because the assumption of common memories is something that gives reality to membership of a community. There is nothing especially or necessarily good about this; communities are of varying types, their internal and external relationships differ, they can be inclusive or exclusive, and they can do good or harm. But, within the life of any community, the role of shared memory is crucial. The coherence of belief which is found in the New Testament community, and its ability to connect past, present and future, are present in other communities also, such as in the cases just described. Meaning and value are experienced within the life of a group or a society when the stories which are told in that community match the values by which it lives.

So resurrection faith is like other kinds of communal believing; it rests not merely on what is able to be verified historically but also on the matching which is discernible between the implications contained in the story the church tells and the values by which it lives. Had there been no matching there could have been no faith. This is the way in which present experience gives access to a past which is then able to be the bearer of meaning and judgment about the future life of the community of faith. So a contemporary resurrection proclamation cannot take its stand either on individual hopes for survival beyond the grave alone or on the discernment of death-resurrection patterns in personal experience alone. What we are looking for are the characteristics of a community which could tell the resurrection story and match it with its life; only such a community could credibly claim that what happened to Jesus contains within it the destiny of mankind.

3

MORE LOOKING THAN FINDING

While believers go on believing, even if in ways which seem to leave out some important elements of the original resurrection faith, a scholarly debate goes on about the nature of the evidence and its meaning. The debate takes place at a time when the whole aim of the pursuit of historical study has undergone a massive change: from the period of Hegel, Comte and Marx,[1] all of whom believed firmly that the study of history could yield some general laws of human destiny by which the lives of individuals and whole societies could be regulated, we have emerged into a period where concern among historical scholars is mainly with refining their methods and taking more care in the examination of their sources. It is not merely that the search for general laws of human destiny has proved remarkably difficult; more alarming to the Western mind has been the experience in this century of the devastation and suffering that can be brought about by those who claim to know the purpose of human living and declare themselves as the ordained agents of that purpose, whose opponents have no rights and whose supporters are justified in using any available method to retain and extend their power. Karl Popper speaks for the feeling many have about the grand claims made for the study of history when he dedicates his attack on the 'universal law' concept of history-writing to the millions whom he claims to have died as a result of the belief held by their society in immutable laws of human destiny.[2]

The story of the changed understanding of history is one of a continuing attempt to come to terms with the availability of more and more tools for research under the impact of the scientific revolution. The initial attempt to liberate the study of the development of mankind from religious dogma led to an understanding of history as purely cyclical, as Vico or Herder maintained[3] or else, as Kant held[4], possessed of a purpose inscrutable to the human reason. Against such doctrines, which offer no inspiration to reforming spirits, the end of the eighteenth century brought an understandable rebellion, and the histories of human destiny emerged, written by such as Condorcet and Buckle, as well as Hegel and Marx.[5]

Despite the recent attempts of Arnold Toynbee to rehabilitate the idea of a purposive understanding of history,[6] in general we are in a period where the debates are about the methods and aims of history-writing rather than the direction of events. Information about the past and archaeological and other sources have become available at an accelerating rate, with them has appeared the increasing possibility of understanding particular occurrences or, as Collingwood would suggest, of entering into the minds of the protagonists so as to discover more clearly why they acted as they did. Issues of destiny have increasingly been left to the theologians, but they too have found their own material increasingly difficult to handle, and the relation of faith to history has become the subject of increasing contention.

Of particular interest in our quest here are the attempts to liken historical inquiry to other kinds of search. Aron likens the historian more to a judge seeking the cause of a particular crime than to a scientist seeking general laws,[7] while A. C. Danto and W. B. Gallie regard him primarily as a story-teller, more concerned with producing a plot that is plausible than the predictable working out of general laws. Because of the role of the story in the handing on of the Christian tradition, theologians have been particularly concerned, in form criticism, with the function which particular stories performed in the life of the church.[8]

The implications of this historical debate for the search for the resurrection are vital. If on the whole historians are now sceptical about attempts to derive laws of human destiny from particular events, it is bound to be more difficult to enter into the language of resurrection which, as was said at the outset, is the language of ultimate destiny and the goals of existence. If historical method is becoming more and more refined and the tools of biblical criticism sharper, it is not going to be any easier to say anything about what happened after the death of Jesus that can command any kind of certainty, let alone a certainty of the sort required to sustain faith. And if our concern is to tell a plausible story of Easter, how shall we hold together such varied accounts and how shall we know if the story we are telling is not only plausible but also true? Our concern in this chapter is to see what theologians have made of the resurrection in the context of a debate that ranges widely over history, philosophy and theology. Their methods and presuppositions have been extremely varied, but our concern in examining this debate is to see whether we can find any assistance there in the task of looking for a resurrection which restores the connections referred to in the first chapter, between past, present and future, between individual and community, and between event and meaning, connections which have been increasingly severed, as we have seen in the last chapter, in the mind of the ordinary believer.

The Greater Attraction of Theology

A cynic could be forgiven for concluding that in the historical discussion of the resurrection of Jesus he was being asked to call 'tails' against a double-headed coin. As the attempt to adduce historical evidence for the event of the raising of Jesus becomes more and more difficult, there comes a point in the discussion, often quite suddenly, when he is told that the very essence of the resurrection of Jesus is that it cannot be proved as a historical event, for it depends for its acceptance on faith.

This dilemma has to be pointed out because it is there to be reckoned with by anyone seriously examining the present state of the historical and theological debate. It is a dilemma, it is true, which has been exacerbated by the relatively modern attempt to apply the techniques of historical criticism to the biblical records, but in principle it is inherent in the documents themselves. The reader is confronted there with what is clearly a call to faith in Christ as risen from the dead; that call goes far beyond mere assent to the proposition that a certain rather unusual event had taken place in the recent past. And yet it is also clear that the New Testament writers were in every case anxious to make clear that the risen one of whom they were speaking was risen indeed. In the examination of the evidence in the next chapter a stress will become apparent on the conviction that something real had taken place to cause the earliest disciples to believe that Jesus who had been crucified was now alive. It will also appear, however, that there are a number of theological motifs which are customarily allied with the resurrection, and are mentioned in conjunction with it. These themes were part of the resurrection faith, and without them the conviction that Jesus had been raised cannot be understood. It was in fact that inseparable combination of a belief that something had happened and belief in certain theological implications which followed that both constituted resurrection faith and made it possible. That faith was held on the strength of a matching which was experienced by the earliest believers between the personal and corporate consequences which were proclaimed as following from the resurrection and the life-style of the community which was proclaiming it. The resurrection of Christ as event was experienced through the present realities of mission, forgiveness and newness of life.

The theological implications of the resurrection have certainly received considerable attention in the current debate. The idea of resurrection as central to the Christian faith has led to the writing of a number of books which lay stress on one or more of the implications of the resurrection, in a way that is almost always extremely evocative and usually grounded in the biblical text. Williams, for example, elucidates most persuasively the implications of resurrection faith for the contemporary Christian:

> We have spoken of Christians being raised up here and now with Christ, and of how His risen life is to permeate the world order and the physical universe, making them new with God's glory. We have seen how if Christians are to be raised with Christ they must first die with Him, approriating His self-surrender to the Father as their own. We have tried to show that by this means the severances wrought by time and distance are overcome so that nothing which men are or do here on earth is lost or left behind. We have spoken of the risen manhood of Christ as providing the perfect reconciliation between the claims of the individual personality and those of society. What, in short, we have tried to do is to show the landscape of human life irradiated by the sunshine of the resurrection.[9]

In a rather different style, and concentrating rather more specifically upon a particular theological motif, Markus Barth and V. H. Fletcher dwell on those aspects of the resurrection accounts which speak of justification and forgiveness.[10] Barth's survey and exegesis of those resurrection passages which bring these ideas to the fore, in their historical and legal context, leads into Fletcher's application of these ideas to a 'politics of the resurrection', and some account of the kind of church life and world order which would bear witness to a resurrection faith such as Barth has described. Both halves of the book are in their way exceedingly relevant to the provision of a modern exegesis of the resurrection faith, and particularly of one that speaks to the public as well as the private areas of man's life. The connection between the two halves, however, is not very clear, and Fletcher's section on 'The Constitutive Event' describes the theology of the event rather than the event itself.[11]

One of the best known English books on the resurrection is A. M. Ramsey's *The Resurrection of Christ*. In it he devotes a great deal of attention to the questions posed by modern historical criticism, exposing some of its presuppositions and offering a minimal account of the assumptions which Christians need to hold in order to examine the narratives. Yet it is not clear that these minimal assumptions really allow for the application of rigorous methods of criticism.

> If the evidence is pointing us towards a miracle we will not be troubled, for the miracle will mean not only a breach of the laws that have been perceived in this world but a manifestation of the purpose of the creator of a new world and the redeemer of our own.[12]

His examination of the gospel evidence leaves a distinct feeling that some of the difficulties inherent in the narrative are disposed of somewhat too simply,[13] and it is the theologies of the accounts and their contemporary interpretation that are the strongest parts of the book.

Some theologies of the resurrection point the reader towards the future, through a stress on the eschatological significance of the idea of resurrection. For Jürgen Moltmann, the major implication of Christ's resurrection is that the promises of God were fulfilled and therefore can be accepted as reliable in the present. What the resurrection does is to reinforce the categories of promise and fulfilment as the ones by which human history is to be understood. There is therefore held out to man 'the future of Jesus Christ', a future in which the 'reconciling synthesis of cross and resurrection can be hoped for solely in the totality of a new being'.[14] The raising of Jesus the crucified from the dead is, for Moltmann, the licence we have to speak of Christ not merely as the one whom we follow in the present, but also as the one who will bring in his kingdom. Thus the power of the resurrection of Christ lies in the fact that it is the fulfilment of the promises of God, and thus the sign that all human history is under the promise of God. This is most powerfully stated, and its implications for Christian doctrine and mission declared with great force; but it will be necessary to ask at a later point how closely it can be shown to be linked with a careful handling of the historical material.

The idea of resurrection as the sign of man's future is also the note struck by Lloyd Geering in his *Resurrection – a Symbol of Hope*. For him resurrection is an idiom traceable in the history of religion in general, and in the biblical record in particular, which has formed the way in which mankind has expressed both individually and corporately its hope for the future. It is that hope which is the Christian's strength.

> When the Christian confesses that God raised Jesus from the dead, he is testifying to the source of spiritual strength which enables him to overcome lethargy and temptation, to continue in the bearing of the cross, and to become involved in the pain and suffering of the world with an attitude of hope.[15]

Whether this is a full account of what the Christian is confessing is doubtful; but the persuasiveness of Geering's book lies in the theological theme which he relentlessly pursues rather than in the extreme historical thesis which he advances.

Even though Willi Marxsen makes one of the most careful examinations of the whole New Testament evidence, it is in the theological implications he draws out that we see most clearly the intention of his study and also what it is that he thinks the resurrection proclamation is really about.

> [By confession of faith in the resurrection] we acknowledge that in finding faith we have experienced Jesus as living and acting; we acknowledge the presence of Jesus' past — which is all that is meant by the acknowledgment of the Holy Spirit. But we are not acknowledging any one of the concepts apart from the confession of faith; for it is only within a confession of faith that it is possible to speak meaningfully, theologically, of the resurrection of Jesus; just as it is only by the Holy Spirit that a man can call Jesus Lord.[16]

It is necessary to point here, as with Geering and some other theologies of the resurrection, to a tendency for those concerned primarily with expressing a theology of the resurrection to reduce it to a single motif, to the exclusion of a number of others. For it is surely right to ask whether 'the presence of Jesus' past' really is '*all* that is meant by the acknowledgment of the Holy Spirit'. We shall see that if the historical quest is considered alongside the theological one the theological implications are shown to be much more complex.

For Walter Künneth as also for Wolfhart Pannenberg, the resurrection has its importance in the central place it occupies in the formulation of a Christology. Both see the resurrection as a vindication of the eschatological perspective of Christian faith, which affirms that Jesus Christ is *Kyrios*. It signifies the end of the age and the judgment of the world, the commissioning of the church to be the Body of Christ, and the sending of the Spirit. It is also for Künneth the beginning of the new creation and the consummation of this age,[17] while Pannenberg affirms:

Only in connection with the end of the world that still remains to come can what happened in Jesus through his resurrection from the dead possess and retain the character of revelation for us.[18]

While it is not surprising that G. W. H. Lampe's Easter address is mainly concerned with theological implications rather than the historical basis of the resurrection, it becomes clear in subsequent discussion with MacKinnon that he considers himself to have been speaking not only of the implications of the resurrection but also of its definition.

> For Easter speaks about God. It is not a story of a return of a dead person to this life. It has nothing in common with what a surgeon might do if he got a heart moving again after it had stopped. It has nothing to do, either, with the idea that there is some part of our being that is inherently immortal; some entity that we might call a soul. No . . . The Easter experience tells us that God *is*; that faith in God won't let us down; that Jesus' way of life, his trust in a God of love was justified; that a life of faith in God, and so of love and acceptance of other people, was vindicated for him and can be vindicated for us too. God has said that last word about it; and that word is 'Yes'.[19]

So there is no lack of theologies of the resurrection. The biblical records have been interpreted with care and attention, and accounts of their meaning for today have been given which certainly stir the imagination and, inasmuch as they are faithful to some of the diversity of material that clusters around the New Testament writings about the resurrection, command acceptance. And yet there remains a question upon what basis these various theological implications are to be accepted and by what criteria choices are to be made among them. From what do they follow, and against what are they to be judged? Are they theological implications without anything to imply them? There is every reason to agree with Evans' conclusion that the most impressive theologies of the resurrection, even those which purport to shed light on the difficult general question of the relation of theology to history, show themselves far happier with the theological than with the historical content of the resurrection traditions.[20]

Yet the less attractive, detailed, historical questions can hardly be evaded, even if many, like H.-G. Geyer, would wish that they could:

> The question of the *significance* of the resurrection of Jesus must be regarded as the primary problem. For the question of *fact* is only meaningful as a *consequence* of the question of its significance, while the problem of the significance of the resurrection of Jesus, if rightly understood, can only be that of its meaning in its original context.[21]

On the strength of this assertion, Geyer makes light of 'the question which largely dominates present-day discussion, that of the fact of the resurrection, and whether it actually took place in space and time'.[22] This seems a most questionable judgment, both sociologically and philosophically. The fact is that, in any contemporary Christian apologetic, the question of the status of that event on which the whole faith claims to be based is central, and this sociological fact about the present-day world is not hard to understand philosophically. It is a matter of logic that however relevant the theological implications of the resurrection may be for an understanding of its meaning, the truth of a proposition cannot be deduced from the truth of its implications.

It is certainly the case that faith in the resurrection of Jesus Christ may arise simply from the preaching of a convinced believer and from the quality of the individual and corporate life of Christians — of say a Paul or a Barnabas; yet D. P. Fuller is right in saying:

> There are times . . . when it is needful to check the historical foundations of the message of a Barnabas in a more direct way than by argument that his message must be true since his life cannot be explained by causes within the world.[23]

As he says, there is need for some independent verification of the message for two reasons: first, it is necessary in order to check that the theological implications being drawn are the correct ones, and secondly, if the church wishes to maintain that its faith has links with history, and to defend those links both to those outside the church and to those within it who are affected by the modern questions of historical reliability and objectivity, the historical quest must be undertaken.

What has been discerned in the writings of many theologians, including some who have been mentioned already, is the tendency to blur the distinction between that which is implied and that which offers the implication, and further, to assume that by some theological sleight of hand the matter about which the true/false decision has to be made, that is to say the resurrection of Jesus Christ, can simply be made synonymous with a series of theological affirmations of which the resurrection can function as an evocative symbol. Certainly the view that a symbolic interpretation of the resurrection is the only viable one today requires examination; there are good grounds for thinking that this view might be correct. What is important, however, is that if the historical aspect of the resurrection is being abandoned in favour of a straightforwardly symbolic interpretation, this should be quite clearly stated. Even if, as will appear, the evidence is very complex and certainty about it is impossible, some answer about the matter of historicity has to be given.

C. F. D. Moule declares that there are three kinds of option represented in the current historical debate about the resurrection.[24] There are those who would assign the resurrection entirely to the realm of faith, subjective in character and independent of any means of historical verification. On the other hand are two groups of people who would assert the need for belief in an 'objective' resurrection: there are those who feel able to make some comment on the nature of the transition between Jesus' death and his life, and there are those who, while asserting that there was a real transition, remain agnostic about the nature of that bridge. To these categories may be added a fourth, namely those who, like Pannenberg and V. A. Harvey, regard the resurrection not as something to be fitted into the contemporary understanding of the historical, in accordance with some prior definition of what that is, but as something which is itself normative of the true nature of history.[25]

The Impossibility of a Historical Resurrection

Those who have argued that the resurrection cannot be approached on the basis of scientific methods of historical research have done so on two basic grounds. First, they have maintained that the results of such research, far from lending support to an account of the resurrection event, simply reveal a picture of the greatest possible confusion. The second point they make is a theological one, namely, that in principle resurrection faith cannot be of the kind that can be confirmed or refuted by historical methods; commitment to Jesus Christ, on this argument, is something which cannot rest on such uncertain foundations. In practice these two arguments, though distinct, have gone hand in hand; those who have wished to give to the resurrection message a primarily existential relevance have tended also to regard the evidence for a resurrection 'event' as the most unreliable.

In his early writings, Karl Barth took a position similar to that taken more recently by Rudolf Bultmann. In *The Resurrection of the Dead* he states that the resurrection of Jesus is not a fact open to historical investigation, but rather a divine fact which could only be grasped by revelation. Even those texts which appear to be attempts to prove the fact of the resurrection, such as I Corinthians 15.1 - 11, were not to be understood as proofs, for they are themselves articles of faith which express the miracle of revelation. The vision of the five hundred brethren at once is not, according to Barth, an attempt to prove the resurrection by reference to numbers, but is included from a desire to show that the benefits of the resurrection were not even lost to 'some who have fallen asleep'.[26] Bultmann took a less extreme view, at any rate about the verses in question. Even though he agreed with Barth that the resurrection could not be established by historical methods, he none the less admitted that this could be what Paul had been aiming to do in his citation of the evidence in I Corinthians 15. There is, however, no doubt for Bultmann that the Easter 'event' is not recoverable by us through historical investigation; it is rather the expression, in the imagery current in New Testament mythology, of the significance of the death of Jesus. The cross and the resurrection are one.

> The resurrection itself is not an event of past history. All that historical criticism can establish is the fact that the first disciples came to believe in the resurrection. . . . The historical event of the rise of Easter faith means for us what it meant for the first disciples — namely, the self-manifestation of the risen Lord, the act of God in which the redemptive act of the cross is completed.[27]

It is possible to question the assurance with which Bultmann asserts that the resurrection of Christ *meant* for the earliest disciples the various theological doctrines he mentions, even if it is certainly true that it implied them. At this point, however, it is important to note that his view about the resurrection falls entirely within the essentially neo-Kantian understanding that knowledge is of two kinds: the attainable by the exercise of the human reason, and that which belongs outside the use of the reason, attainable only through commitment. It is basic to his thinking on this and other aspects of the demythologizing of the New Testament that religious truth must be of the second kind. Even though this basic presupposition of Bultmann's is shared to a remarkable extent by Barth, the latter is appalled by the logic of it, and in his later *Church Dogmatics* he insists that the realm of revelation and the realm of space and time can and do meet, even if the criteria of historical research cannot always be satisfied. In his later view, therefore, Barth approximates much more closely to the last group who will be discussed in this chapter, those who hold that there is a category of sacred history which is historical even if not amenable to historical research.[28]

It has already been said that a rejection of a historical approach to the resurrection can begin from one of two points: it can have a theological/philosophical starting-point, or a historical one. The view represented by Bultmann, and by Barth in his earlier days, is one which places the resurrection beyond historical research on grounds of theology, for it would contradict the nature of the Christian relevation if the resurrection of Christ were accessible by any means other than faith. This point of view has two consequences: first, the attempt to prove the resurrection historically is abandoned, while, secondly, and for our purposes more importantly, the resurrection remains just as central to the Christian proclamation. Geering's view, however, illustrates the great difference that is made if the resurrection is regarded as inaccessible to historical research not because of a theological presupposition but because on inspection the evidence not only fails to be sufficient to prove a 'historical' resurrection, but indeed supplies strong grounds for believing that such was not what the New Testament writers were wishing to present anyway. The result of his investigation, an example of the relentless pursuit of the logic of an argument, is a resurrection which is neither historically provable nor theologically central.

> Our study has shown, in addition, that not only do the New Testament writers show some diversity in the way in which they talk about the resurrection of Jesus, but they are not all equally dependent on the use of the idiom for the proclamation of the Christian message.... If in the present, or in the future, Christians wish to confess Jesus Christ as Lord, without resorting to the idiom of resurrection, then we must acknowledge that there may be valid reasons for doing so.
>
> Nevertheless there are at least three good reasons why Christians may continue to use the idiom of resurrection to confess their faith concerning Jesus. The first is this. The more basic any term has been in the proclamation of the Christian Gospel, the more reluctant we should be to dispense with it, for, by its very use, it serves to demonstrate the continuity of Christianity from age to age. This is one of the great values in the continued use of the ancient creeds. (It must be acknowledged, of course, that few, if any, when they come to recite the creeds today, mean exactly the same as their fourth-century Christian forbears did.) Basic words and concepts, even when the changes of cultural milieu necessitate some re-interpretation, help to preserve the essential continuity of the living stream of Christian tradition. No-one could deny that the resurrection idiom has appeared to play a basic, and almost indispensable, role in Christian proclamation.

The second reason is that the idiom is peculiarly apt and forceful in communicating the particular truth about Jesus which Christians wish to confess. There are other words and concepts which could replace it in certain areas of its usage, such as 'vindication', 'exaltation', 'ascension', etc., but because the Easter message is essentially concerned with the death of Jesus, we would be hard pressed to find another idiom which acknowledged the significance of his death equally as well.

The third reason is that though the idiom of resurrection has pursued a long and varied path, in all cases it has been used as an expression of hope, enabling an otherwise closed future to be regarded as open-ended.[29]

Geering's examination of the New Testament evidence is exceedingly thorough, and at the end of his argument there is no uncertainty at all about whether the phrase 'the resurrection of Christ' has for him any historical reference point. It has not. What Geering sees as the most plausible reconstruction of the Easter appearances and of the empty tomb is that they are the developed reflections of the disciples on the significance of the death of Jesus. Resurrection is consistently described as an idiom, and the conclusion at which he arrives is that it is an idiom which might or might not, though at the moment it seems that it does, serve usefully to speak of the hope that is in us. It has on its side a long tradition and a peculiar forcefulness; but as Geering does not hesitate to say, it also has a grave ambiguity, and is peculiarly a part of the religious heritage that has collapsed under the strain of the modern world-view.

Geering points out that his rejection of a resurrection of Jesus in space and time arises not only from the abrasive character of the modern world-view, but because an inspection of the narratives of the resurrection themselves requires such a conclusion. The views they take about the resurrection experiences are so diverse, and the accounts of the empty tomb argue so strongly for the gradual development of a legend, that, on the strength of the biblical documents alone, we are left with no possibility of belief in a resurrection that took place objectively in space and time. This discovery is one which Geering greets without any apparent sense of loss. On the contrary, he sees it as great gain.

In actual fact, however, what appeared to be a loss turns out to be a distinct gain. As the Christian comes to abandon his belief in the empty tomb and 'bodily resurrection', even though he once regarded it as a sure and certain proof of the truth of Christianity, he may experience an exhilarating sense of freedom.[30]

He says of the old tradition of the bodily resurrection that has collapsed:

> It forever tries to turn our attention back to some supposedly historical event which took place at the tomb on Easter Day instead of the present reality of the risen Christ. Unless the Christian can affirm the presentness of the risen Christ (as Paul did in Galatians 2.20) then it matters little what happened at a tomb some nineteen centuries ago.[31]

Although it does not base itself on either existentialist philosophy or on neo-Kantian presuppositions about the nature of knowledge, there is no question that Geering's position has marked similarities to Bultmann's. The sheer straightforwardness of the argument and the unqualified way in which it is put forward present the dilemma facing theologians today with unusual clarity. Yet it would seem that several questions are left unanswered by this kind of analysis. The details of the historical analysis of the tradition of the empty tomb can be left to be examined in chapter 4, but there are many who would find the tradition too pervasive to be accounted for merely as a legendary development. There is a further historical question to be asked about Geering's analysis, in that his conclusion seems to depend very heavily on the assumption that resurrection was an idiom known to Jesus' contemporaries, with a long and identifiable tradition behind it; this also is discussed in chapter 4. Furthermore, Geering's tying of the phrase 'bodily resurrection' to the stories of the empty tomb seems to foreclose on other options concerning what the 'objectivity' of the resurrection might have been like.

What must be questioned at this point is the value of the kind of resurrection faith which is left when it is said that 'unless the Christian can affirm the presentness of the risen Christ . . . it matters little what happened at a tomb some nineteen centuries ago.' Granted that a Christian is able to affirm the presentness of the risen Christ, does it then matter what happened at a tomb nineteen centuries ago? And if he is not able to make any affirmations about what happened at the tomb, what meaning is he going to be able to give to the expression 'the presentness of the risen Christ' anyway? Is there going to be some alternative way of describing the reality to which he is drawing attention, of which he can say that the resurrection is an idiomatic translation? It is necessary to ask, further, about the theological significance of the admitted presence of a belief in a space/time element in resurrection in the New Testament. It is generally said that the theological importance of the affirmation of a bodily resurrection lies in its proclamation that the purpose of God is known in the realm of space and time, and not in some world outside and beyond this. What then becomes difficult to see is how that affirmation can continue to be made without speaking, in more or less specific terms, about something God did in this world.

Otherwise, without in any way attacking the coherence of Geering's position or at the moment challenging his evaluation of the historical evidence, it remains uncertain whether a release from a space/time resurrection is likely to be such a liberating experience after all. It may turn out that with Geering's conclusion there is a sense of bereavement which will have to go along with the sense of liberation. Hope in general, and a belief in a providential concern for mankind in general, could be poor substitutes for the specific proclamation the New Testament writers were able to make that God had declared a particular man to be righteous by raising him from the dead.

The impossibility of conceiving of the resurrection of Jesus as a miraculous event is also held by Marxsen. Like Geering and Bultmann, he expresses the view that the language of resurrection arose from the disciples' reflection on the total ministry of Jesus, and assumes that the idiom of resurrection had a sufficiently well-established place in the religious life of the New Testament period to lend itself naturally as the language in which the disciples could express their commitment to Christ. This assumption may turn out to be the point where their position is most vulnerable to criticism on historical grounds. Marxsen also holds that historical research can only go back as far as the rise of the Easter faith in the disciples.

> Now in our historical inquiry into the background of our texts, we do not come upon the fact of Jesus' resurrection; we come upon the faith of the primitive church after Jesus' death. This belief, or the expression of it, is a verifiable reality. At the same time we find the assertion that this reality had come into being through a miracle. And the miraculous nature of this reality was expressed through the concept of the resurrection. When I therefore say that talk of the resurrection of Jesus is an interpretation, this is not to deny its reality. It only means defining precisely where the reality lies.
>
> The same is true today. If I experience my finding of faith as a miracle and if I express this miraculous event by saying 'Jesus is risen', I cannot by so doing say any more than the early church said when it used the phrase.[32]

The assumption that the idiom of resurrection was ready to hand for
use by the disciples as an interpretative tool with which the disciples
were able to express their faith is held by Marxsen, together with the
assumption that there is a rigid distinction between fact and interpretation.

> We can say quite confidently that it did happen that witnesses saw
> Jesus who was crucified. We must express it more precisely. Wit-
> nesses claim, after the death of Jesus, to have seen *him*, and it is just
> this vision which they express in different ways, partly already with
> incipient interpretations of what they saw. On the basis of this
> vision, which witnesses claim to have happened to them, they then,
> by a process of reflective interpretation, arrived at the statement:
> Jesus has been raised by God, he is risen. *At that time* they naturally
> also took the view that they were speaking of an event which had
> really taken place. They were now convinced that the resurrection
> of Jesus had taken place.[33]

Marxsen goes on to say that we are in an even more indirect position
in relation to the evidence than the earliest disciples were. But on closer
examination this last quotation presents considerable difficulty. When
he refers to the 'claim' of the witnesses as a more 'precise' way of
expressing the matter, this is surely an understatement. If it can con-
fidently be stated that it did happen that witnesses saw Jesus who was
crucified, that is to affirm a resurrection in history; if all that can be
affirmed is a claim by witnesses to have seen him, then the issue that
arises is how the disciples were in a position to decide that it was Jesus
whom they were seeing, and how it could be decided whether they saw
him or not. This has the appearance of a historical question, and the
theologians discussed in the next section are those who take the view
that the material in the New Testament is adequate to provide some
answers to such questions.

The Possibility of a Historical Resurrection

As has already been said, it is not possible to group together all those
who believe in an objective resurrection, for there are among them
considerable differences as to the nature of the objectivity which they
impute to the resurrection event. Moule's distinction between those
who are willing to name the kind of transition between Jesus' death
and his life and those who are not is a useful one to make, although
even then it seems that there are some who are prepared to say more
about the transition than others.

Thus it is clear that Lampe is among those who would wish to say very emphatically that something objective happened as a result of which the disciples had an enduring and intense conviction that their Lord was alive; but he rejects the account of the empty tomb on both historical and theological grounds, and therefore has little to say about what this 'objective' factor in the resurrection might be.[34] His historical reason for rejecting the empty tomb is that the evidence for it is late and inferior, and his theological reason is that the resurrection of Jesus cannot be fundamentally different from that which is in store for every Christian. Thus Lampe would be unwilling to accept with Bultmann or with Geering that the historical material is quite irrelevant, and yet he has treated it sufficiently critically to leave his reader unclear what it is that is still being retained.

J. A. T. Robinson maintains a much more explicit, even if guarded, position, which puts him on the other side of Moule's divide, in that he is prepared to say a good deal more than Lampe about the nature of Christ's transition from death to life. In his article, 'Resurrection in the New Testament',[35] he makes two points very strongly: first, the empty tomb material is far too strong in the tradition to be dismissed as legendary accretion,[36] if only because there is no evidence that anything other than a bodily resurrection was ever preached by the church, and also because the production of the body of Christ would have been a substantial answer to the Christian apologetic. The first point, however, cannot be decisive, as Robinson makes clear; belief in the empty tomb, however persuasive the evidence might be, is not belief in the resurrection. That rests on his second point, the appearances; and here again he is far more confident than many would be about the status of the evidence. He stresses the distinction made between those who had actually been witnesses of the resurrection and others who could only speak of its power. He is also prepared, as few others would be, to list as parallels different resurrection appearances as they are described in different sources. The vital point in the proclamation is not that the appearances become more physical as time goes on, but that very great stress is laid on the fact that the risen one is identical with the one who lived and worked and was crucified.

Robinson's theological conclusion from this is spelled out in the section on the resurrection in *The Human Face of God*.[37] He repeatedly stresses both that the historical evidence is such as can be used to work out a coherent historical picture of the first Easter, and on the other hand that the discovery of such a historical picture can never be decisive. He quotes with approval both Neville Clark's observation that the role of historical research cannot possibly be the verification of the Christian faith, though it could conceivably be its falsification,[38] and R. Gregor Smith's comment that we must be free to say that the bones of Jesus may still be lying around somewhere in Palestine.[39] Christian faith, according to Robinson, takes its stand certainly on the fact that the appearances were not 'purely subjective hallucinations (the equivalent of seeing pink rats) or purely private'[40] and on the fact that the empty tomb stories did not originate in 'deliberate deceit by the disciples, or [on the basis] that the women went to the wrong tomb and no one bothered to check, or that Jesus never really died, or that his body was not buried but thrown into a lime-pit'.[41]

There are however ways of being mistaken that are not as gross as seeing pink rats or as going to the wrong tomb and not bothering to check. If historical research is only admitted to have even the power of falsification if it can unearth such gross error, its role is limited indeed. What Robinson appears to weight too lightly is what historical research has already shown. This has nothing to do with error, but a great deal to do with the influence of the particular presuppositions and evangelistic intentions of individual New Testament writers. It is not simply that writers use what had happened in the service of particular theological motifs, but that saying that something had happened was one of the theological motifs; and the descriptions we are offered all bear very clearly the stamps of divergent kinds of resurrection faith. It may be that the different narratives contain common patterns, a certain 'hard core'; but this is not in itself a sufficient reason for asserting that it is a hard core of fact rather than of belief. It is easy, if one wishes to prove a case, to assume that the divergences arise from theological considerations while the points of agreement arise from factual ones. What is puzzling, and Robinson gives little help here, is why a series of traditions each of which is anxious to show that the resurrection is part of the process now called history should have taken so little care (from a modern point of view) in establishing what that link with history was.

This point is well made by Don Cupitt in his discussion with Moule,[42] where he contends that faith in the resurrection is ultimately a matter of theological reflection on the life and death of Jesus, and not of the acceptance of a series of experiences of seeing Jesus or the empty tomb. He points out that resurrection faith was in reality born very much of talking through reflections on the life of Jesus, and that the religious experiences depended for their acceptance on that reflection, and on the doctrinal presuppositions which the individuals concerned held. The Emmaus story is a clear example of what he means; two disciples reflect on the meaning of the Old Testament scriptures and of what they have just experienced in the death of the one whom they hoped might be the redeemer of Israel, and it is in the midst of such reflections that they encounter the experience of the risen Christ. Just as visions of Buddha are only vouchsafed to Buddhists, and of the Virgin to Catholics, so the experience of seeing the risen Christ could only be received by those whose conceptual framework, theological reflection and experience of the world had prepared them to be recipients of it. Whether Cupitt is right in assuming so readily that resurrection was one of the things that early Christians would have been prepared for is a matter to which it will be necessary to return later, but certainly the doctrinal reflection in which they engaged, and the conclusions to which the earliest Christians had come about Jesus, have given to the narratives their present character and shape, and it may prove exceedingly difficult to discover what the stories would look like without them.

In reply, Moule finds that Cupitt's account does not do justice to the difficulty of accounting for the rise of the resurrection faith in the earliest disciples. Some transcendent cause, he says, is the only explanation which will serve to account for that. He points to the number of people who held the resurrection faith, and the tenacity with which they held on to the belief. He is doubtful whether the belief that an individual has through resurrection entered on the life of the new age could possibly have been derived from the Old Testament or from Pharisaic Judaism; indeed it was the resurrection faith which appears to have distinguished Christians from other Jews and caused their exclusion from the synagogues.

What is beginning to emerge here is that the difference of conclusion about the role of historical research in relation to faith may derive from the different concerns of the historian and the philosopher. The historian wishes to discern the cause of the rise of the resurrection faith; he examines the evidence and reaches the conclusion that the attribution of the rise of that faith to unaided reflection by the disciples will not do. Not only is it very unlikely that such reflection on its own could have produced the gospel accounts, but those accounts seem to insist on a great deal more than that. The philosopher, on the

other hand, is concerned to see what justification there could be for
holding the resurrection faith; to him the results of historical research
are in their essence altogether too tentative, and provide answers that
could never serve as the substance of anything like religious belief.

This may provide some account of Robinson's position. As a historian of the New Testament he is convinced that the evidence cannot
be made to square with the possibility that the bones of Jesus may be
around in Palestine; as an apologist anxious to commend Christian faith
he wishes to be free (or his hearer to be free) to believe that they are.
Whether the bones of Jesus could be somewhere in Palestine at the
present time without either deceit or error on the part of the earliest
Christians is, however, exceedingly doubtful, and deceit or error would,
in Robinson's view, make the resurrection faith incredible. It is hardly
likely that such a position as he advocates will succeed in doing justice
either to the earliest Christian apologetic, which appears to have been
willing to take its stand at various points precisely on the fact that
something had happened, or to the needs of contemporary apologetic
in a world which continues to ask what took place. It might be wel-
come if historical and apologetic questions could be kept apart, but to
the extent that this was done any real link between history and faith
would have been severed. All that will be achieved is the appearance of
being content to use history as a support for the Christian faith until
the going becomes rough.

At this point it is necessary to mention those who belong more
clearly to Moule's second division, that is those who are willing to name
the bridge between Good Friday and Easter. D. P. Fuller, after an examination and rejection of views of the resurrection that do not take
their stand on history, builds his own position entirely on that taken by
Luke himself, whose approach he regards as the most relevant to the
modern historical dilemma.[43] The Lucan argument, he says, is that the
events of Acts, which are what the unknown Theophilus would have
experienced in the life of the church, can only be explained if the truth
of the resurrection of Jesus Christ is assumed. It is the Gentile mission
that gives the final proof that the apostolic teachers were inspired and
that the events which the gospel records were true. We might well
accept that this line of argument might have operated to some degree,
and at a later stage, among converts. Further than that, we may well
agree with Fuller that the evidence of the New Testament is so varied
that this is the only kind of argument that can be offered, and that, as
the resurrection is nowhere described, we can only argue from the

effects to the probable causes. What Fuller in fact does, however, is to base his argument on the Lucan narratives as they stand, even though it is precisely some elements of these accounts which even the most conservative critics might find most questionable; and this prevents him from seeing the weakness of his position as a historical argument. The argument from the life-style and success of the Christian church to the truth of the resurrection may appear compelling; indeed, it will emerge in later chapters that this may in essence be the only position left to take. Nevertheless, this can hardly be called a *historical* argument as such, and it says nothing at all about what it is in the many confused and conflicting traditions and narratives which the New Testament offers that the life-style of Christians might constrain the reader to accept. Luke has not bridged the gap between faith and history, because it is transparent that the Lucan accounts are as much based on faith and theological insight as any others, if not more so.

Three other attempts to give an even stronger account of the essential harmony and reliability of the historical evidence which can be derived from the New Testament may be mentioned. The first two approach the resurrection stories with what can only be called the skill of novelists, as the titles *Who Moved the Stone?*[44] and *The Passover Plot*[45] testify. The third, *A Lawyer among the Theologians,*[46] approaches them with the eyes of a lawyer. The first two arrive at opposite conclusions: both after a remarkable weaving together of detail from the accounts themselves and from the authors' knowledge of the social life of the times. The former concludes that the New Testament evidence is substantially true; the latter that it is false and that in fact Jesus never really died. All gaps are beautifully filled in, and the whole fitted together into a story that is in some ways rather more exciting than the originals from which they were taken. This excitement is due to the way in which the behaviour of all the characters is described and their actions accounted for; even God, who in *Who Moved the Stone?* is left as the primary agent, turns out to behave like a particularly ingenious human being, who leaves nothing to chance.[47]

When J. N. D. Anderson, the lawyer, steps among the theologians, it is with the intention of acting more as a judge among those who, in his submission, have acted far more like prosecuting counsel. Many of his criticisms of the way in which theologians have conjectured are undoubtedly valid, and he is at his best in exposing many of the prejudiced assumptions about the documents. He invites his readers to treat the New Testament as they would any other kind of evidence, to accept that many of the details which are not filled in are such as could only be elicited if there was a chance to interrogate the witnesses, and to deduce, as the only reasonable conclusion, that what the New Testament writers affirm to have happened, namely the raising of Jesus, is what in fact happened. In so doing, he attacks critical theologians on the grounds of their scepticism and applies to the New Testament writers the ethical standards which are now expected from those who stand in the witness box and give evidence under oath. The tone of his defence of the authors invariably suggests that he is defending not only their conclusions but also their character, and at the point where he begins his own constructive account of what he thinks the documents point to, he clearly discards the robes of the judge and replaces them with those of counsel.

> How many facts of history – or for that matter, how many adulteries or murders – can be proved by the testimony of unimpeachable witnesses to having actually seen the event or act concerned? Some of the best and most convincing evidence is, in reality, based on a combination of testimony and virtually inevitable inference, or on a concurrence of circumstances which are often much less open to fabrication than the memory of some fallible witness. And this is particularly cogent in regard to the case in point, where the supranatural breaks in on the natural, and the eternal world impinges on the world of space and time.[48]

A great deal is required before the raising of Jesus from the dead can be regarded as a 'virtually inevitable inference', and if it is intended to be something available for all mankind to believe than it is perhaps more legitimate to ask for reliable witnesses. To the extent that a virtue is made of the reliance on circumstantial evidence, it must surely be said that there is another example here of the double-headed coin against which the sceptic is being asked to call: if evidence exists it is to be used; if none exists, the conclusion is even stronger.

The difficulty with both the detective novel and the lawyer approach to the evidence is that no real argument is offered against what is assumed by modern critical scholarship. For biblical scholarship is not founded upon an immovable scepticism, but on the positive discovery that the New Testament writings are of a particular kind, intended to offer a proclamation and not to provide material either for detectives to work on or lawyers to try. And it is clear that both Frank Morison, the author of *Who Moved the Stone?*, and Anderson are aware of this, for both, and particularly Anderson, develop clear theological convictions about the meaning of the resurrection. It is to the extent that they do not hold their theological conclusions together with their historical ones that they fail to give a coherent account of the evidence. This incoherence arises because the narratives are removed from the convictions which any perusal of the documents shows to underlie them. It is possible, though difficult, to use the evidence as though it was just that, evidence at a trial, and thereby to construct an account of a kind. Yet if the price of doing so is to sever the connection between the account that results and the new life that sprang from the original proclamation, many will consider the price far too high. For when the attempts to harmonize the various traditions are abandoned it is not just because they are not easy to piece together as history, but because their theological content also is different, and therefore the attempt to harmonize them destroys their meaning. The result is a good story, at its best, and the writer of that story may in addition hold certain convictions about life; but what will appear when the traditions are examined in chapter 4 is the way in which narrative and belief are held together, and that wholeness will be lost in the attempt to fit the jigsaw together. That is perhaps the reason why both Morison and Anderson, like so many others before them, have wished to rely most of all on the historical evidence supplied by the transformation of the disciples between Good Friday and Easter. Certainly that transformation is one of the pieces of the New Testament picture which needs to be explained. Nevertheless, the problem remains that the transformation can be shown to have taken a variety of forms in the different authors whose works constitute the evidence. The New Testament record has not merely become more difficult to prove under the pressure of historical criticism, but also more difficult to decipher.

A serious examination of the faith of the various witnesses, within the critical assumptions of our time, has been made by J. A. Baker, who nevertheless considers it possible to tell the story of the development of the Easter traditions in such a way as at least to commend the resurrection of Jesus as the most likely explanation.[49] He too makes a virtue of necessity: not only does the failure of the New Testament to provide proof conform to Paul's experience in Athens, but it was also the way in which the earliest Christians understood the parable of Dives and Lazarus. The acceptance of the moral challenge of Jesus is alone what makes the resurrection credible. He points out that the stories do not at all argue for the authors' having used the cultural expectation of a resurrection to clothe what was in essence theological reflection. What he manages to discover, even though he affirms the essential reliability of the empty tomb traditions, is a pattern which underlies the stories of the resurrection appearances, which were, he says, the basis of the faith of the New Testament church. The women go to the tomb, but apparently do not meet the Lord; there is a proclamation by a messenger to the women, an encounter of Jesus with a few chosen individuals and a decisive meeting with a few principal disciples. From this basic tradition, the other developments can be explained. The decisive appearances all carry with them the command to preach the gospel throughout the world, while the empty tomb stories point the disciples to the conviction that the one who appeared to them is the one who was crucified, for the resurrection of Jesus is not the reversal of the cross, but its lifting up to the realm of meaning for all mankind. This is also the meaning of the story of Jesus' encounter with Thomas. Behind this perception must lie an event in its own right which changed the disciples' understanding of the cross.

Baker's writing undoubtedly retains the unity between the historical and the theological, and the result therefore is a 'preaching of the resurrection' which stands in the tradition of the church's preaching of Easter. What is less certain is his contention that he has somehow achieved this by penetrating through the particular traditions and developments to a central tradition that underlies them all. The frustrating aspect of the New Testament documents is the absence of a recipe for a single Easter faith. It is, however, possible that this diversity might itself provide, and the next chapter will endeavour to show that it does so, the key to a contemporary Easter proclamation.

A further indication that Baker may not have taken this diversity seriously enough is the point to which it takes him at the conclusion of his chapter on the resurrection. He refers to the essentially eschatological significance of the raising of Jesus:

> In the life and work, the crucifixion and rising again of Jesus, the end is already here, and once set in train cannot but run its course. Our own perspective of cosmic history is so incomparably more vast than theirs that the actual timing of the end ceases to concern us, and we look instead to the personal implications of the belief.[50]

Here an unwillingness to allow for real diversity in the New Testament witness, and an insistence that it must have, in the end, one single message, leads either to the abandonment of many of the issues with which the New Testament had to contend or to the demand that we must assimilate our thought patterns to theirs. Thus the change in our cosmological perspective leads to an abandonment of any concern for the timing of the end, and to an exploration only of the personal implications of the belief. The resurrection faith can only be a statement about the world if we allow ourselves and our cosmology to be assimilated to the eschatological world-view of the New Testament. We might, that is to say, be wrong; so Baker remarks in a footnote to the passage just quoted. But it is surely possible that an attention to the diversity of the New Testament witness and a willingness to accept that diversity might eliminate the need to make a choice between our cosmology and the concerns of the New Testament writers. This would be the positive side of Evans' conclusion about the diversity of the historical evidence and the difficulty of using the narratives of the gospels for the purpose of arriving at a single account of the Easter event.

> For what have to be combined are not a number of scattered pieces from an originally single matrix, but separate expressions of the Easter faith. Each of these is complete in itself; each has developed along its own line so as to serve in the end as a proper conclusion for an evangelist of his own particular version of the gospel. Behind and within all the traditions, of course, is the conviction that Jesus of Nazareth continues to be and to operate, and that in him past, present and future are somehow related; but the mode of this continuation is differently conceived in the four gospels, and in each case is closely related to the theology of the particular gospel concerned.[51]

This does not, of course, mean that the attempt to give some account of the Easter event is to be abandoned; there remains a task to be done, even if it does not seem likely that the one undertaken by Morison or Anderson will succeed. 'Whatever the Easter event was, it must be supposed to be of such a kind as to be responsible for the production of these traditions as its deposit at whatever remove.'[52] It is not surprising that some have thought that this exploration could only be done if our whole conception of history were revised, and it is to the consideration of this possibility that we now turn.

Saving Knowledge

In his earlier writings,[53] Barth had maintained that the resurrection of Jesus was not a historical event, and his words on the subject could well have been written by Bultmann. He had called Easter the 'non-historical happening by which all other events are bounded, and to which events before and on and after Easter Day point.'[54] But by the time of the

Church Dogmatics his standpoint appears to have changed. He criticizes Bultmann's view on the ground that it removes the objectivity of the resurrection, making it a purely subjective matter; what the New Testament is concerned to maintain is that it is 'the fact that the risen Christ can be touched which puts it beyond all doubt that He is the man Jesus and no one else'.[55] It was Jesus, the man himself, who rose from the dead; the physical elements in the New Testament accounts are vital to the making of this point.

The difficulty about this later view of Barth is that while he steadfastly maintains that the resurrection was an event in the physical, historical world, he also denies that it is open to historical verification.

> It is sheer superstition to suppose that only things which are open to 'historical' verification can have happened in time. There may have been events which happened far more really in time than the kind of things Bultmann's scientific historian can prove. There are good grounds for supposing that the history of the resurrection of Jesus is a pre-eminent instance of such an event.[56]

This is not to say that Barth rejects all use of the tools of historical criticism on the gospel narratives. Some of the passages he regards as legendary, while in some details he pronounces them vague and confused. This is taken as confirmation of the fact that the disciples were describing an event beyond historical understanding and surpassing description, rather than an event which was not fully within history. In the same work, Barth explicitly locates the resurrection within history, but in a different sense; it is now part of a 'second history of Jesus'.

> Jesus has a further history beginning on the third day after his death, and therefore after the time of his history had clearly come to an end. In temporal sequence it is a second history – or rather the fragments of a second history – of Jesus.[57]

But what does the word 'history' mean in this context? Barth is undoubtedly right in much of his criticism of Bultmann, and particularly in suggesting that it might well be possible for an event to be within history and yet not amenable to scientific methods of criticism; but he sheds no light whatever on what alternative criteria for the use of the word 'historical' there might be.

Much more of an attempt at discovering the relationship between faith and history is made by Paul Tillich, who in his *Systematic Theology* takes as his starting-point, as do Barth and Bultmann, the essential unity of cross and resurrection. 'They cannot be separated without losing their meaning.'[58] Yet he draws attention to a number of qualitative differences between them. Whereas the accounts of the cross point to an event 'that took place in the full light of historical observation, the stories of the resurrection spread a veil of mystery over the event'.[59] Here he begins to part company with Bultmann, in that he declines to accept that the resurrection is simply a symbolic interpretation of the cross without any kind of objective reality.

We observe in Tillich the same assumption as is made by other scholars who wish to isolate the resurrection event from accessibility to historical research, namely that the resurrection idea is a 'familiar mythological symbol', and in particular that in the circumstances in which early Christianity began, it obviously suggested itself.

> In the moment in which Jesus was called the Christ and the combination of his messianic dignity with an ignominious death was asserted – whether in expectation or in retrospection – the application of the idea of resurrection to the Christ was almost unavoidable.[60]

The questionableness of this assumption will concern the early part of the next chapter, but in any case Tillich is careful to observe that the prevalent symbol of the resurrection is transcended in its application to Jesus in the way that the concrete picture of Jesus 'transcended the mythical pictures of the mystery gods'. He omits to say specifically that it also transcended the understanding of the resurrection which could be gleaned from late Judaism.[61] This transcendence of existing categories suggests to Tillich that 'a real experience made it possible for the disciples to apply the known symbol of resurrection to Jesus, thus acknowledging him definitely as the Christ.'[62]

Although Tillich acknowledges that the 'factual element' in the story of the cross shows more clearly through the documents than it does in the case of the resurrection, he considers the problems, and the relationship between history and faith, as fundamentally the same in both cases. Just as historical research can never bring a person to accept the symbolic meaning of the cross, so

> Historical research is justified in trying to elaborate the factual element [in the resurrection narratives] on the basis of the legendary and mythological material which surrounds it. But historical research can never give more than a probable answer. The faith in the Resurrection of the Christ is neither positively nor negatively dependent on it. Faith can give certainty only to the victory of the Christ over the ultimate consequences of the existential estrangement to which he subjected himself. And faith can give this certainty because it is

itself based on it. Faith is based on the experience of being grasped
by the power of the New Being through which the destructive
consequences of estrangement are conquered.[63]

Tillich at any rate does give some account of what that faith is which
alone, in his view, can enable a person to believe the resurrection after
historical research has done its best. It lies in the overcoming of estrangement through being grasped by the New Being, and therefore it is a
highly personal matter both in its content and in its results. 'It is the
certainty of one's own victory over the death of existential estrangement which creates the certainty of the Resurrection of the Christ as
event and symbol.'[64]

Tillich's view of the mechanism is thus that historical research can
establish that a 'real experience' was required for the disciples to come
to the certainty that Jesus was the Christ (and therefore that he must
have been raised). The believer then has faith because of his own awareness of having overcome existential estrangement. This faith gives him
certainty not only that existential estrangement has been overcome in
Christ, a victory he expresses in the symbolic language of the resurrection, but also that the experience of the disciples was real, that is to
say, Christ did in fact surrender himself to the 'ultimate consequence
of existence, namely, death under the conditions of estrangement',[65]
this is what makes both cross and resurrection necessarily both factual
and symbolic, both event and symbol, for 'without the factual element
Christ would not have participated in existence and consequently not
have been the Christ'.[66] Thus, in contrast to Bultmann, Tillich maintains that the existential consequences of belief in Christ demand an
essential historical content to belief. But a number of questions remain
concerning the nature of the factual content that is required. It is clear
from what he says that the historicity of the crucifixion of Jesus is
required for faith, but far from clear what content has to be given to
the raising of Jesus for it to have taken place 'in existence'.

What is creative about Tillich's kind of account of resurrection faith
is that it draws attention to the kind of matching process which is
necessary between the personal experience of the believer and the
experience of the disciples as it is discernible in the New Testament.
But here again we must question whether the terms in which he describes that process are adequate to the proclamation which the New
Testament offers. That is, of course, to question the entire dependence
of his theology on existentialist reinterpretation, which is beyond our
scope here. Yet in relation to our particular quest, we shall have occa-

sion to ask, in the next chapter, whether the kind of existential, personal reorientation which is for Tillich both the meaning of the resurrection faith and its main content is actually all that the New Testament is concerned to offer when it speaks of the resurrection.

Yet his view of the limitations of historical research as a way of establishing faith is not dissimilar to that which has been regarded as orthodox within the church. That view is that Easter certainly took place within history, but belief in it cannot be attained by using historical research, for belief can only be in the last resort an act of faith.[67] To believe means at a certain point to surrender the historian's craft in favour of an act of faith. It is not perhaps unfair to suggest that the later position taken by Barth results, as in some measure does Tillich's view, from a reluctance to embrace fully a logic which was fully seen and accepted by Bultmann. Faith is still, for both Barth and Tillich, the means by which the resurrection is believed through the proclamation of the word; that is so even if what is proclaimed is in some undefined sense 'within history', for what is wanted is a historical resurrection without paying the price of openness to historical criticism.

Künneth's position is not dissimilar. The critical event for him in the awakening of faith in the disciples or in the contemporary believer is the proclamation of the word of the resurrection, and neither the appearances nor the empty tomb have any capacity to awaken faith except in so far as they are the bearers of the kerygma of the risen Lord. This means that knowledge of the resurrection of Jesus is always believing knowledge, and that it 'excludes all attempts to arrive at an understanding of the resurrection that are foreign to faith'.[68] Not only does it exclude the discovery of faith by means of speculation on the basis of some mystical reflection or contemplation of a religious *a priori*, but, more than that, it specifically excludes the critical approach of the historian.

> On the one hand [the critical historical approach] is governed by the erroneous assumption that by eliminating the standpoint of faith it can exercise its cognitive functions free of presuppositions, while on the other hand it is concerned to give an impartial account of the historic situation as it was apart from faith. . . . This inevitably leads to the usually convulsive attempts to explain the resurrection of Jesus somehow or other — which, however, means to project it into the objective plane, and to find a place for it within the previously given concepts and ideas and subject it to them. Yet if the knowledge of the resurrection is open only to faith, then every method that is detached from faith must in principle lead to failure.[69]

This exclusion of historical criticism does not mean that the historian has no role in the understanding of the resurrection narratives, but that that role is limited to elucidating the confessional nature of the various documents. For the documents are written on the basis of the saving knowledge of the resurrection, and judgments about them cannot be undertaken with the aim of finding whether the narratives are true but only of discovering whether the confession is appropriate.

> Understood as confession, the narratives as a whole have the validity of a statement of faith: any possible gradation of the sources as of primary or secondary importance finds its criterion not in historical considerations but in measuring the appropriateness of the content of the confession. Giving due consideration to the confessional character includes also the possibility of criticism. We have then to ask whether the statement in question adequately expresses the proper sense of the confession and thus of the knowledge of faith, or whether it obscures it.[70]

Thus the link between the resurrection and historical research is effectively cut. The resurrection itself stays within history, an objective happening, yet inaccessible to historical research. For the historical question of truth there is substituted the theological question of appropriateness, and 'the believing confession of the resurrection of Jesus demands as a precondition of knowledge that our methodological principle should be trust.'[71] There can be only one result of such a view: that is the abandonment of any attempt to fit the resurrection into a given understanding of history, and in its place the fitting of our understanding of human history to our given faith in the resurrection. If, for example, we conclude that the resurrection narratives assume an eschatological view of history and of the passage of time, then our understanding of time must be assimilated to that which our belief in the resurrection of Jesus demands.[72]

This is a robust proclamation of the need for a total change in thinking, and an exposition of a theology of the resurrection which makes very clear demands upon those who hear it. Once accepted, such a proclamation offers criteria for both thinking and living, but if we ask instead whether it offers any grounds for accepting it we are likely to conclude that what is offered is a proclamation of the word which is either to be taken or left. There can be no question about what the implications of accepting such a view of the Easter proclamation would be. It would not merely be historical research which would have shown itself incapable of bringing any person nearer to belief in the resurrection; any kind of natural theology would also, in traditional Barthian manner, have to be rejected. It would not merely be a looking at the past that could offer nothing to confirm faith, but also a looking at the present or the future. To seek for anything which any person not already a believer could be shown as a sign of the continuing activity of God would be to seek in vain. Historical research could take us back to the kerygma, but whether the cause of the kerygma was what the kerygma says it was would be beyond the scope of human inquiry.

Pannenberg appears, on the other hand, to take the view, expressed in his essay 'Did Jesus Really Rise from the Dead?',[73] that the resurrection narratives can be used for the purpose of arriving at a coherent account of the event of Easter. The difficulties and divergences are on the whole treated lightly, the evidence for the empty tomb is broadly accepted, the appearances are discussed and any idea of their having been 'subjective visions' is discounted. He admits the difference in the thought-pattern of the time in which the documents were written and says that the resurrection can only be understood within the framework of apocalyptic expectation. This difference of thought-pattern, however, appears to affect how Pannenberg considers the resurrection is to be understood and not whether it is to be believed.

His thesis is much more extensively argued in his christological work, *Jesus – God and Man*, where the same rather uneasy alternation is to be seen between the view that the evidence of the New Testament is sufficient for the resurrection to be believed as a historical event, and the other view, that the resurrection of Jesus necessitates a total revision of our concept of the historical to bring it into line with the apocalyptic world-view which was prevalent in New Testament times and which alone would allow the resurrection to be understood as historical.[74] Hidden within this call to what is essentially a rejection of those ideas which have made modern historical criticism possible are some fairly conservative attempts at resolving the difficulties in the traditions[75] together with the well-tried argument that the rise of the early church is the strongest argument for accepting not only the 'event' which the disciples accepted but also the thought forms within which they understood it. The concept of the historical has thus been considerably blunted.

> Then the resurrection of Jesus would be designated as a historical event in this sense: if the emergence of primitive Christianity, which apart from other traditions is also traced back by Paul to appearances of the resurrected Jesus, can be understood only in spite of all

critical examinations of the traditions if one examines it in the light
of the eschatological hope for a resurrection from the dead, then
that which is so designated is a historical event if we do not know
anything more particular about it. Then an event that is expressible
in the language of the eschatological expectation is to be asserted as
a historical occurrence.[76]

What Pannenberg is doing is in effect to adopt the double-sided argument which he attributes to Paul in I Corinthians 15. There, according
to Pannenberg, Paul 'called the expectation of a resurrection of the
dead the presupposition for the recognition of Jesus' resurrection'[77]
and used the resurrection of Jesus in order to commend the general idea
of the resurrection of the dead, in particular to Gentiles who would not
bring the idea with them from their cultural background. He admits,
however, that the resurrection of Jesus is not sufficient by itself to
prove the general concept of the resurrection.

> The expectation of the resurrection must already be presupposed as
> a truth that is given by tradition or anthropologically or is estab-
> lished philosophically when one speaks about Jesus' resurrection.[78]

Two points should be observed: Pannenberg's argument presupposes
not merely that the expectation of the general resurrection of the dead
was present within the cultural environment of first-century Christianity, but that it was sufficiently strongly present to enable it to be
used as an argument to persuade Jews of the truth of the claim that
Jesus had been raised.[79] Secondly, he appears to require that a pattern
of argument which he admits would not have been strong enough to
persuade Gentile Christians of the first century, because the general
resurrection of the dead was not one of their expectations, should
nevertheless avail sufficiently to persuade twentieth-century historians
to revise their criteria of judgment. When it is asked what additional
reasons might encourage such a person to revise his thinking in the
manner required, Pannenberg's appeal is to the phenomenology of
hope, to the question whether life is understandable without any hope
beyond death. This hope is not confined to the issue of personal survival beyond the grave, but relates to the whole of human life and
behaviour.

> Man is not restricted in his behaviour by definite environmental
> signs whose perception sets off instinctive reactions. Rather, he him-
> self must first determine the direction of his impulses. In this he
> never achieves more than a temporary concretion of his striving. The
> whole of his impulses point beyond every given situation and press

toward further, better fulfilment. Thus man must always seek further for that which could grant the fulfilment of the totality of his impulses, for his destiny, while animals live out their destiny without question. Now it belongs to the structure of human existence to press on, even beyond death, that search for one's own destiny, which never comes to an end.[80]

This hope can be perceived not only in Jewish apocalyptic but in a whole range of human philosophies and anthropologies. This is sufficient cause

> to indicate that the expectation of a resurrection from the dead need not appear meaningless from the presuppositions of modern thought, but rather it is to be established as a philosophically appropriate expression of human destiny.[81]

Not only that; the congruence of modern thought about man with the driving motivation of Jewish apocalyptic, in man's hope beyond death, is such as to enable us to engage with the primitive Christian perception of Jesus' resurrection.

The question whether man's general hope of life beyond death is a suitable starting-point for understanding the primitive Christian proclamation was considered in chapter 2; what is relevant here is that it appears that Jesus' resurrection was not in fact understood as the fulfilment of some general hope of life after death, or even of the specifically Jewish hope of a fulfilment of human history in a general resurrection, but as the fulfilment of some expectations and, by implication, the non-fulfilment of others, which were thereby declared to be wrong. The thrust of the message of the resurrection of Jesus, as it was expressed for example in the early chapters of Romans, was that whereas the promise associated with Moses (the law) had not been fulfilled, and indeed was powerless to achieve the salvation of man, the promise of justification through the grace of God had indeed been accomplished through Jesus. The difficulty of any argument for the resurrection of Jesus from general human expectations is that it appears that in the original proclamation what was preached had the power to make judgments about and among those expectations.

Moltmann, in tackling the problem of the relation of faith to historical research, also questions modern historical criteria, but takes much more account of this need for discrimination. He acknowledges that for Paul Christ was not the fulfilment of all promises.

> [Paul's] reason for going back to Abraham as the 'father of the promise' in contrast to Moses and the law lies in the fact that for Paul

the Christ event is not a renewal of the people of God, but brings to life a 'new people of God', made up of Jews and Gentiles.[82]

Yet Moltmann is quite clear that this depends on the prior affirmation of an event in the history of God's promise, but this affirmation is only

> in harmony with the texts in so far as they themselves speak of an event which can be dated. But it is alien to the texts if, and in so far as, the historical form of the question implies a definite anterior understanding of what is historically possible, and one which since the birth of the modern age does not coincide with the understanding which those texts themselves have of the historically possible as being the divinely possible. The concept of the historical, of the historically possible and the historically probable, has been developed in the modern age on the basis of experience of history other than the experience of the raising of Jesus from the dead — namely, since the Enlightenment, on the basis of the experience of man's ability to calculate history and to make it.[83]

There can be no question that the resurrection of Jesus must be held to be a historical event, but to do so requires a questioning of the criteria of modern historians. This means approaching the resurrection narratives on some other basis than their coherence with our understanding of the past, their internal difficulties and contradictions and the intrinsic probability of what they record,[84] and that basis is the orientation which the narratives themselves have towards the future, the eschatological horizon which they open up as part of the history of promise and fulfilment.

> It has its time still ahead of it, is grasped as a 'historic phenomenon' only in relation to *its* future, and mediates to those who know it a future towards which they have to move in history.[85]

Moltmann's exposition of the resurrection of Jesus leads to a profoundly stirring account of the church's mission as the outworking of resurrection faith not merely in salvation for the individual or for the exclusive sect, but as the leaders of a continuing 'exodus' in society at large. In this he works out practically what he has earlier concluded about the pattern of the church's thought about history.

> But the church — including theology — is neither the religion of this or that society, nor yet is it a sect. It can neither be required to adapt itself to the view of reality which is generally binding in society at the moment, nor may it be expected to present itself as the arbitrary jargon of an exclusive group and to exist only for believers. As the church is engaged with the surrounding society in a struggle for the

truth, so theology, too, has a part in the mission of the church. It must engage with views of history and historical world-views in a struggle for the future of the truth and therefore in a battle for the reality of the resurrection of Jesus. If in contesting and exploding the modern historical concepts of reality we are wrestling for the mysterious reality of the resurrection of Jesus, then that is no mere wrangle about a detail of the distant past, but this reality becomes the ground for questioning also the historical means of attaining certainty about history. It is a struggle for the future of history.[86]

Here is delineated very clearly and cogently the nature of the struggle, but what is less clear is whether Moltmann has actually engaged in it or (to use his own metaphor) rung the bell which will signal the time for others to go and wrestle. He as much as anyone confirms Evans' view:

The reader of the gospels or preacher of the gospel is likely to be able to appreciate and use this eloquence [of the risen Lord] to the extent that he is not over-preoccupied with historical considerations.[87]

Faith and History

The reconsideration of the relationship between the commitment of faith and the knowledge which is obtainable by the methods of historical research has proceeded in a less kerygmatic style among English and American scholars. They have been concerned chiefly with questions about fact and interpretation, the nature of historical judgments and their relation to the believer's commitment to Christian doctrine.

R. R. Niebuhr[88] takes his stand on the fundamental uniqueness of all historical events. Theology in his view — and he has secular counterparts in writers such as Popper who has already been mentioned — has accepted with too little question the model provided for historical research by the natural sciences. Where it has not done this, it has accepted the view that there is such a thing as a *Heilsgeschichte*, a history of salvation which is divinely directed and runs alongside and parallel to the ordinary tide of events, *Historie*. Such views, he argues, are altogether too mechanistic and regular in their understanding of history. History is neither a succession of predictable causes and effects nor is it a unitary plan made in heaven and moving relentlessly forward. It is rather a succession of independent, arbitrary and irrational events, each of which has to be approached for its own sake and, by means of the human memory, on an individual basis. Of such events the resurrection of Jesus is the paradigm; far therefore from assimilating it to previously formulated canons of historical judgment, it can itself be the event which illuminates how all others are to be perceived.

If this view of the historical process could be defended it would undoubtedly have great attractions. It would mean that there was no natural order which was being violated by a claim of miraculous intervention and no need to submit the difficult New Testament evidence to detailed scrutiny. But this is not quite the conclusion that even Niebuhr reaches. He is as willing to discount as other liberal writers such stories as that of Jesus eating fish, and even the empty tomb narratives, as later and legendary additions to the original tradition,[89] and this he does evidently on conventional historical grounds. It is thus only the resurrection itself, not the traditions or beliefs which were held about it, that is immune from the scientific historical approach. He is clear that the traditions must contain elements that are open to the exercise of historical judgment − the corporeality of the appearances,[90] the identification of the risen one with the Jesus who was crucified − and yet at the crucial point he allows the resurrection to escape that net by asserting that its problematical nature is such as belongs to all events (except the late addition of the empty tomb stories?), and that belief in the resurrection is not refutable by the criteria of scientific history; what has been overcome if the resurrection is true is not the natural order but the rule of death.[91]

There are two difficulties here, which are closely related. The first is that Niebuhr offers no criteria for deciding the point at which the use of scientific history ('historical reason') should end and recourse be had to the intrinsic uniqueness of events. The second difficulty arises not only in Niebuhr but in the writings of those others who have tried to isolate the resurrection from the uncertainties of historical research. It lies in the assumption that the primary difficulty about the resurrection traditions lies in obtaining sufficient evidence to justify belief in the truth of what they say. This is, however, far from being the only difficulty that the traditions occasion. The prior one is the question of what the resurrection which they offer for belief amounts to. If we take seriously, as Niebuhr is clearly willing to do, the role of historical research in isolating the different kinds of resurrection faith contained in the narratives, this question is unavoidable. An appeal to the uniqueness of the resurrection, and of all historical events, offers no way forward here, because it is the nature and not just the plausibility of the unique event which is in question. It is hard to avoid the judgment that what Niebuhr has done is to assimilate the whole of the historical process to the irrationality which he admits would alone make the traditions of the resurrection acceptable; he forswears an irrational leap out of history only at the cost of making the whole of history a series of irrational leaps. This is only another version of that opting out of the historical process at the crucial point to which we referred when considering the traditional view of the relation of faith and history.

A brave attempt to solve this question by reinterpretation of our understanding of history is offered by Alan Richardson.[92] His major contention is that all history-writing is to some extent relative, and determined by the perspective of the writer. Thus the Christian in writing history does so from a Christian perspective and is thereby no different from those who write from other perspectives. Using the terms of Ramsey's account of the nature of religious language,[93] he speaks of the Christian's investment in historical events as lying in his capacity to see them as 'disclosure situations'. The story of the people of Israel, for instance, is not unique in any way that differs from the essential uniqueness of all nations' histories, but there is a uniqueness in the faith that arose when Israel attended to the 'moral truth which had been prophetically discerned in Israel's historical experience'.[94]

This may indeed be a valid account of the Old Testament, but does it get any further forward in dealing with the twin difficulties of deciding what is offered for belief and how to know whether what is offered is true? Certainly Richardson is not arguing that one meaning is as good as any other, for he resists strongly the idea that the meaning of any event is simply what the particular interpreter cares to make it. But given the difficulty, indeed the impossibility, of reconstructing the 'bare facts' of any of the great biblical disclosure situations, it is hard to know by what criteria it would be possible to determine which interpretations are true and which are not. And since for Richardson there is no distinction between facts and interpretations, that in turn means that there are no agreed criteria for the determination of the facts.

This is clearly his position with regard to the resurrection of Jesus, as can be seen from his handling of the evidence about it.[95] What Richardson does here is to make a very strong case that the New Testament documents cannot be understood except on the basis that their writers believed Jesus to have been raised from the dead. He appears to regard this as an argument for the resurrection as an event, when he has in fact only succeeded in arguing for the (not very controversial) point that the raising of Jesus was believed by all the New Testament writers. What he appears to want is all the advantages of a Bultmannian position,

in which all that history can do is give us access to the rise of resurrection faith in the earliest disciples, while continuing to claim that the
resurrection is thereby shown to be a fact of history. He has shown
only that it is a fact of interpretation. As to the question what the
resurrection is, which, as already stated, is a question prior to that of
how it is to be substantiated, we are clearly no further forward at all.
The resurrection is a fact only in the sense in which the word 'fact' is
used by Richardson, namely, it is an interpretation, and, it must be
added, a series of differing interpretations at that.

Nevertheless the idea of perspective has had a very strong appeal for
one of those who have most thoroughly examined the debate. Harvey
achieves much in *The Historian and the Believer* by analysing a number
of questions that appear to some of the protagonists in the debate as
single and simple. For example, he is able to demonstrate that one of
the major errors most commonly made is to assume that there is a
single account to be given of historical method and its presuppositions.
In fact the variety of the arguments which can be used to support the
occurrence of a particular event is almost as great as the variety of the
events themselves. The 'morality of historical knowledge' consists in
assessing the arguments which are used, and such arguments are complex in their form. There is no single method to be conformed to in
attempting to give an account of the traditions about the resurrection
of Jesus. This is not to offer a convenient escape; on the contrary, the
fact that the resurrection is so unlikely an event means that the kinds of
justification which will be required for it will be to that degree stricter.

With regard to the question of the relation of faith to history, once
again Harvey performs the service of reminding his readers that there
can be no single answer to it. The earlier contention of Barth that faith
cannot be dependent on the uncertainties of historical research is no
more true than the opposite, the contention that Christianity must take
the full risk of the ambiguity of the historical.[96] The question at issue
is not whether Christianity is independent of all historical judgments or
totally dependent on what the historian is able to uncover, but whether
there are not particular historical affirmations which Christians require
to make, and where historical uncertainty therefore weakens faith. The
question then is which particular assertions these are and what kinds of
justification such assertions would require.

He is clear that certain events are paradigmatic, that is to say, they
have the power to raise questions of the meaning of living – he cites the
death of President Kennedy as an example[97] – and suggests that the

historian is able to analyse the various 'memory-images' contained in the documents concerning Jesus so as to discern that Jesus was just such a person. In the light of that discovery it is also possible to test whether the Christ who is affirmed to be Lord of all is worthy of this trust. Christianity therefore is the conviction that the particular questions raised by the life and death of Jesus are also the questions to which human beings at all times have to address themselves in searching out the meaning of existence. To say, however, that that conviction itself can be determined by something that is accessible to historical research is to undermine the essence of faith, and also to provoke a confrontation with the morality of historical inquiry, which depends on the independence of the historian.

Harvey is basically confident about the results of historical inquiry into the records about Jesus. From the memory-images of Jesus offered by the New Testament can be determined sufficient about the character of Jesus for it to be possible to decide whether his proclamation about the meaning of existence is the one in which trust should be placed. And this, according to Harvey, is the real issue. It is not an issue which can be decided on the ground of belief in some additional historical event, the resurrection, which somehow 'proves' that what the believer wishes to say about Jesus is true.

> The Christian church emerged with the confession that Jesus was the Christ, which is to say that he was in fact the revealer. And because his life was a revelation, the proclamation necessarily took the form of representing the pattern of his life as the disclosure of the divine righteousness. . . . It is in this context that the resurrection-ascension belief must be interpreted. This belief . . . is not an additional *credendum* to the conviction that Jesus was the revelation. . . . In the resurrection belief — Jesus is 'raised to the right hand of God' — Jesus is confessed to be what he really was, the decisive witness to and awakener of faith. Whatever we believe to be the historical occasion for this resurrection belief — a resurrected body or a visionary appearance of some sort — the point is . . . these appearances are not regarded as making faith any easier, and those who do not experience them are put at no disadvantage. It follows that all men are 'without excuse'. Christian faith is not belief in a miracle; it is the confidence that Jesus' witness is a true one. This faith is not made easier or more difficult by the occurrence of a miracle. . . . The resurrection-faith is that Jesus is, in fact, the Word, that this image does, in fact, provide the clue to the understanding of human life.[98]

So resurrection faith is the holding of a perspective which affirms that the key to life is revealed in the person of Jesus. For many people, the resurrection may be that, but we must ask again whether Harvey's conclusion is not somehow distorted by a failure to give adequate attention to what the documents themselves actually say. For if this account of the resurrection faith is intended to be a description of what Paul's resurrection faith, or Matthew's or John's, amounted to, then it must be judged inadequate. For as will be shown in the next chapter, the raising of Jesus from the dead, while it certainly involved the belief that Jesus' life and death contained the clue to the meaning of existence (though this belief itself is expressed in a variety of ways which cannot all be simply reduced to that), involved more than this. The miracle is not, of course, a proof of what the church taught and believed about Jesus; but it certainly was in itself part of what the church believed about Jesus.

In any case, it has further to be asked whether the historical evidence about the life of Jesus is not itself as difficult to grapple with as that about the resurrection. If the Easter faith in fact informs the whole presentation of the narrative of the life of Jesus, does not the application to it of the historical method imply that this same method can also be applied in some way to the 'event' that it presupposes? Harvey preserves a role for history in filling in, as it were, the details of the Christian proclamation, but only, it would seem, at the cost of denying it a role at the central point where a response of acceptance or rejection has to be made about it. At that point we are left reflecting on whether Jesus is the key to human existence, and that is what is meant by the question whether he is raised from the dead.

F. G. Downing, in his survey of the historical problems surrounding *The Church and Jesus* argues that history is not even able to sustain the role of clarification which Harvey requires of it. If, as he points out, there is a problem in discovering the historical Jesus, there is a prior problem of the discovery of the historical early Church.

> What material is there that claims explicitly or incidentally to describe the period of the primitive Church, and how far are the claims beyond reasonable dispute? What may be thought to have been produced *in* the period, though not referring to it and so be indirect evidence for it (the Gospels perhaps)?[99]

Downing pursues these and many other questions and comes to the conclusion that not only is research unlikely to build up an agreed picture of the historical Jesus, but it is also unlikely to offer a single picture of the life of the early church. His discussion of the New Testament materials concerning the resurrection faith[100] and of what has been made of it by recent theologians leaves one with a devastating impression of uncertainty. Yet Downing is persuaded that more of this and not less is what is required. His major criticism of Harvey[101] is that after a careful separation of the historian and the believer, his attempt at the end to join them together again by allowing the historian a role in clarifying the memory-images of Jesus (which Downing calls 'the final slightly desperate arguments') attributes too great a degree of certainty to the historian's discoveries as well as saying too little about the contribution that those discoveries have made and can make to the life of faith.

What Downing sees as the only possibility in the historical quest is that there should continue to be the maximum production of as varied a selection of pictures and accounts of the history of the church and Jesus as possible, and the only arguments and reconstructions which he would wish to rule out are those which claim for a particular account either of the life of Jesus or of the belief of the church a security which would justify their protagonists in excluding a whole range of other accounts from consideration. It may be observed that, on the basis of the account Downing himself gives of the materials and of the debate, there is little risk, if the debate continues at all, that anything other than variety could possibly ensue.

Yet at the end of the day, it is proper to ask whether Downing is not interested in the debate primarily because it is interesting and not because it has anything to offer as a support for faith. This seems to be the meaning of his concluding words:

> If a man accepts the prior commitment that here the saving love of God has come through to us most powerfully, there is no other course open than to continue the debate. To come closer to the facts is to come closer to the gift. . . . The quest to come, as nearly objectively as possible, closer and always closer to the facts immediately and less immediately involved in this gift of love that we believe we have received must . . . be an urgent imperative, integral to that commitment of faith itself — difficult and inconclusive, but imperative.[102]

So the commitment must be prior, and history is then the consequence, the activity which follows out of interest and obedience. It may be asked whether this is not in the end simply a repetition of Harvey's position: if you believe that Jesus is the key to human existence, then you must try to find out all you can about him. But nothing you find out about such a matter as the resurrection of Jesus could cause you to undertake that commitment.[103]

Conclusion

Much of the theological debate that has been surveyed above has produced a situation where, in some more or less disguised way, the position of Bultmann or the earlier view held by Barth is where most of the protagonists come to rest. There is also the distinct impression that the certainty declared about the historical character of the resurrection of Jesus is in inverse proportion to the amount of attention that is given to the New Testament material itself. There could be many reasons for this; it is in the interests of those who wish to maintain a very sceptical position to show how the New Testament records justify this, just as it is in the interests of those who wish to maintain their certainty about the resurrection to demonstrate their enthusiasm for the philosophical questionings of contemporary man and also the fact that they do not base their position on a mere biblical fundamentalism. Yet the impression remains: a greater attention to the biblical material seems allied to a greater historical scepticism, and to the sense that it is not only difficult to say what actually 'happened', but it is even scarcely possible to make any judgment about what the content of the faith of the earliest disciples was.

To elucidate the point that in essence so many end up in a Bultmannian frame of mind, it is perhaps necessary to point to the readiness of the holders of the various positions outlined above to have recourse to a notion of faith which remains almost wholly undefined. Either history can conduct men to the edge of belief in the resurrection and then they must leap, or else they must leap first because history will get them nowhere. The appearance given by such writers as Pannenberg and Moltmann that they have retained a fundamental role for history disappears when it is observed that their understanding of history is one in which the leap of faith has already been taken. Certainly to the extent that their theological conclusions from resurrection faith have more to do with a God who gives meaning and purpose to human history, and not merely to the personal choice of the individual, as Bultmann would say, they may be judged truer to the overwhelming weight of the views held by the New Testament writers. But that does not mean that their conclusions provide a solution to the issue of how resurrection faith can be grounded in what has been (and therefore can be) and not merely in what the individual person chooses to commit himself to. Faith rests for them where it does for Hugh Price, who after an examination of Romans 8 says:

The question that these verses raises is a personal one, and not the question which bothers Christian apologetics: 'Did Jesus rise from the dead?' It is the question: 'Does the Spirit of him which raised up Jesus dwell in me?' And I think this question is what was important for St Paul. That is the question which the resurrection raised for him. And that we may say is what it means.[104]

As Mitchell rejoins, this view of the matter, which takes history, if it takes it at all, to arise simply as the expression of a personal commitment, in effect prises the resurrection away from history altogether.[105]

If it is true that this is where most of the theologians involved in the current debate come to rest, a chief contributory cause is the immense difficulty of handling the New Testament material. This can be seen from the attempts to give even a 'minimal', let alone a 'fuller' or 'full-blooded' interpretation of the resurrection which were offered in the course of the debate from which the comment of Price, quoted above, is taken.[106] To speak either of the 'adequation between the person of Jesus of Nazareth and this at-least-personal factor (which met the disciples in and through their world and in the understanding of Israel's history),[107] as being all that the resurrection is, or of 'the empty tomb, the body which could eat and the hands which could be handled and yet was under such control of the Risen Lord as to be able to pass through doors and to disappear at will',[108] is to do justice only to some part of the New Testament evidence, and efforts to unite them into a statement of a single resurrection faith would seem to be doomed to failure.

Yet it belongs to theology to attempt to give some rational account of what faith is, however difficult that may turn out to be. Unreasoned commitment is not a virtue in itself, and in any case it has become clear that a major area of disagreement and difficulty is to decide what it is we are being asked to commit ourselves to.

It is not intended to register disagreement with those who find that the New Testament evidence cannot yield of itself a single and coherent account of what the resurrection faith is and is to be. There is surely no possibility that by working harder at it, or by a more ingenious use of the tools to hand, there will be established what the heated debate of our period has failed to discover. Yet it is the case that something that is called believing in the resurrection continues, and many who do believe in it are not unaware that there are vast and unresolved historical difficulties in doing so. Many of them also have sufficient commitment to theology as a rational discipline to wish to offer some explanation of what is, in a short-hand way, called faith, but which is frequently described as though it were desperation. Further, many of those who believe something they call the resurrection faith would be unwilling to concede that there is in the last resort no real relationship between the experience they have of the world and the critical faculties they bring to bear on those experiences, on the one hand, and their believing on the other.

Such people have existed from the beginning. Most of those who were believing the Easter faith, or the various versions of the Easter faith which have come down to us, by the time the New Testament was being written also had a historical problem. It was necessary for some decision to be made about what others were saying they had seen and experienced. They were perhaps unaware of the abrasive qualities of historical criticism, but there is nevertheless enough diversity and record of controversy from the New Testament period to suggest that a number of difficult questions were already being asked.

It is possible that the difficulty of giving some account of resurrection faith would be eased if an attempt were made at matching the experience of those who first heard at second hand about the raising of Jesus and believed and those who now have to make or have already made a decision about it in our time. This will involve examining more than what is narrowly called the evidence, but it will involve at least that. What it certainly means is that the resurrection faith has to be seen in its relationship with other areas of belief and practice where people express where they stand in relation to the world and how they understand it. In his essay in the debate already mentioned, Ninian Smart is concerned to ask, 'What are the Dimensions of Belief in the Resurrection?' He hints at the kind of harmony we may hope to discover.

> This harmony, this power of suggestion from one aspect of the faith to another, may seem like the organicness of a work of art. There is, no doubt, an analogy. The doctrine of the rather bodily resurrection of Christ seems to me to bring out the beguiling and dramatic softness of relations between different elements of the Christian faith. I would therefore draw the conclusion that a full analysis of the faith must be a good deal richer than the accounts that any of us [in the debate] have so far produced.[109]

Smart's concern is the relationship of resurrection faith to such things as worship and ethics. He perhaps still spreads his net too narrowly, for the basis on which men have stood and stand in assenting to the resurrection is not merely their religious understanding. Smart describes the dimensions of religious experience, but there are a greater number of dimensions to history than this, for history is about what people think has been, what can be and what will be, and, before they can ask where they fit into the story that history tells, whether there is a story to tell at all. It appears that people have believed, and do believe, much more than what has been called 'the evidence' would justify. That in turn suggests that a further search for evidence would be valuable, and may indeed be a more attractive option than mere commitment.[110]

4

LOOKING AT THE NEW TESTAMENT

The task which emerged at the end of the second chapter was that of finding the kind of community which could, by the way in which its life matched the story it was telling, commend the resurrection of Jesus as something which connected past, present and future, an event which conveyed something of the destiny of mankind and could be perceived in the present experience of the community. We have found the theologians whose work has just been examined all conveying something of the meaning of the resurrection but at the cost of separating elements which we are attempting to reconnect with each other. This has been contrasted repeatedly with a New Testament witness which held these various elements together, and it is time to examine in some detail the way in which this was accomplished.

It is natural that we should assume that the situation facing the New Testament church as it sought to proclaim the resurrection was vastly easier than ours, because the actual witnesses were there. In fact this was not so; from a very early point the resurrection was being spoken of by people who could not have claimed to have had first-hand experience. We shall be examining the evidence not primarily to trace the development of the resurrection traditions[1] but in order to see how the resurrection was commended, to what experience of the tellers and the hearers it was related and how it came about that something of which a very few people claimed to be witnesses came to be accepted by many.

A word must be said at the outset about the difficulty of using the New Testament documents for this purpose. For despite the apparent centrality of the resurrection of Jesus for the earliest Christians, what this central pillar of the faith was made of is scarcely described, let alone set out in any systematic way. It is set out in a series of documents of very varied purpose and nature, and it is often necessary to argue from effects to the supposed causes of those effects by the use of circumstantial evidence. This difficulty is well illustrated by one of the Pauline expositions of the resurrection:

> For if we have been united with him in a death like his, we shall certainly be united with him in a resurrection like his. We know that our old self was crucified with him so that the sinful body might be destroyed, and we might no longer be enslaved to sin. For he who has died is freed from sin. But if we have died with Christ we believe that we shall also live with him. For we know that Christ being raised from the dead will never die again; death no longer has dominion over him. The death he died he died to sin, once for all, but the life he lives he lives to God. So you also must consider yourselves dead to sin and alive to God in Christ Jesus (Rom. 6.5 – 11).

Clearly Paul is here relating faith in the resurrection of Jesus to profound ethical and personal results in the life of the Christian community; but did the resurrection create those changes or was it merely a way of talking about them? And in what sense was it believed that the life of the church was really a re-enacting of the death and resurrection of Jesus, a being united with him in a death like his, and to what extent was what had happened to him judged to be unique and 'once for all'? This is just one example of the kind of exegetical question that arises before it is possible to know what was believed as the content of the resurrection faith.

Further difficulties concern the weight to be given to any argument from the considerable number of issues and beliefs about which the New Testament is silent, or about which conflicting views are recorded. Is it to be supposed, for example, that the fact that there is no account of the actual moment of resurrection in any of the canonical gospels means that no such account existed in the New Testament period or that no beliefs were held about it? Is it to be concluded that those whose convictions have been recorded, Paul and the evangelists, reflected widely held convictions which were generally regarded as normative from before or soon after the books of the New Testament were written, or were they at that time rather untypical, and perhaps even unpopular, views which only later came to command respect? How is the fact that Luke 24.33f. records an appearance to the disciples in Jerusalem to be evaluated, given the explicit statement recorded in Matthew 28.7 that Jesus would appear to them in Galilee?[3] Does Paul's silence about the empty tomb in his account of the resurrection tradition (I Cor. 15.3 – 11) mean that he had no knowledge of any traditions about it?

These are all questions which have to be raised whether we are trying to establish the nature of the resurrection event or simply what the earliest Christians believed about it. Three relevant points can be made at the outset. First, there is no unity in the descriptions offered of the resurrection appearances, even though there are various matters about which the writers show evidence of a common viewpoint. Secondly, despite this lack of uniformity in description, the evangelists and Paul are all concerned to speak about something which should be called 'factual'. Thirdly, despite this factual content, there are a number of theological themes which seem to recur when the resurrection is mentioned. The factual and the theological seem to have formed part of the resurrection faith from the beginning.

The disentangling of the 'theological' and the 'factual' elements in this faith will never be completely possible, for the distinction belongs to a specifically modern consciousness. Yet such a separation has to be attempted if the contemporary question of the nature of the resurrection faith is to be tackled. The question we are asking is what was the role of belief in the resurrection in the faith of Christians of the New Testament period. In the course of separating the historical from the theological — a separation undertaken here strictly in order to see how these elements which have become separated in modern understandings of the resurrection can be reconnected — it will be necessary to gather the material relating to the resurrection under various theological headings, such as the new justice, mission, and new life. These headings have been selected not because of their particular modern interest, but because they seem to be the ones which arise when the raising of Jesus is mentioned in the New Testament. In so gathering the material we shall have in mind some pressing questions: is the joining of the Easter message with these theological themes a mere coincidence, or was the idea of resurrection sufficiently associated with those themes to make them its natural partners? Was the idea of resurrection so well established as the bearer of these themes in New Testament times that the stories of the raising of Jesus could be said, as some of the theologians we have examined suggest, simply to be a way in which those theological messages could be conveyed in the culturally provided clothing of the age? In that case talk of the resurrection *event* need not detain us. Or do the theological themes which appear in conjunction with the resurrection undergo change as a result of that conjunction? In that case the resurrection of Jesus can be said to have a life of its own which needs investigation.

The Resurrection and the New Justice

There are factors which point in the direction of regarding the resurrection stories as no more than the clothing in which the earliest Christians wrapped their faith; mention was made in the previous chapter of a number of theologians who so regard them. Yet, as C. F. Evans points out in *Resurrection and the New Testament*, this issue is not settled by the discovery that there are a number of mythologies, Greek, Persian, Jewish, in which resurrection figured at the time of the New Testament. What makes the thesis that the early Christians were simply using existing mythology to express their faith hard to sustain is the great change of meaning and importance which happens to the idea of resurrection under the impact of the Christian proclamation. From being an idea which appears in, but is eccentric to, a number of different religions and cultures and has as many different meanings as are the settings in which it appears, the resurrection becomes for Christians, as we shall see, a belief that is radically transformed and utterly central. It is to this change that we shall be drawing attention in this chapter.

Although resurrection is not at all an idea which might be derived from reflection on the Old Testament, it does begin to make its appearance during the Maccabean period as a direct response to the experience of persecution.[2] In II Maccabees there begins to emerge, over and above prophetic notions of divine justice and retribution, the view that those members of Israel who have remained steadfastly loyal to God even under stress of persecution and the suffering of torture and death are able to proclaim a hope of resurrection and eternal life for themselves.

> And when he was at his last breath, he said, 'You accursed wretch, you dismiss us from this life, but the King of the universe will raise us up to an everlasting renewal of life, because we have died for his laws' (II Macc. 7.9).

This 'renewal of life' is a reward for faithfulness, but it is more than that. It accomplishes something for the whole people through the ending by the righteousness of faithful Israelites of the suffering which is the result of Israel's sin. Justice and atonement are the twin motifs of this understanding of resurrection.

> You have not yet escaped the judgment of the almighty, all-seeing God. For our brothers, after enduring a brief suffering, have drunk of everflowing life under God's covenant; but you, by the judgment of God, will receive just punishment for your arrogance. I, like my

brothers, give up body and life for the laws of our fathers, appealing to God to show mercy soon to our nation and by afflictions and plagues to make you confess that he alone is God, and through me and my brothers to bring to an end the wrath of the Almighty which has justly fallen on our whole nation (II Macc. 7.3⁵ – 38).

So this resurrection is peculiarly a vindication and a judgment; just as their loyalty serves to atone for the sins of Israel, so the apostasy of those who give in involves them in a resurrection to condemnation. This close association of the emerging concept of resurrection in late Judaism with some concept of divine judgment is immensely important. Sometimes both righteous and unrighteous are raised, the former to eternal life and the latter to condemnation. 'And many of those who sleep in the dust of the earth shall arise, some to everlasting life and some to shame and everlasting contempt' (Dan. 12.2). Sometimes, on the other hand, as in I Enoch 83 – 90, resurrection is conceived as something offered only to those who have been righteous. But in every case where the idea of resurrection appears in Judaism it is related to the theme of the final judgment of God when the righteous will receive the reward of their faithfulness and the unrighteous their due punishment.

There are signs in the New Testament that one of the meanings attached to the resurrection of Jesus was that of the seal set on his righteousness. This must, for example, be the significance of the contrast made by Peter when he speaks, while on trial, of Jesus as the one 'whom you crucified, whom God raised from the dead' (Acts 4.10). It is also the implication of the metaphor of the builders: 'This [Jesus] is the stone which was rejected by you builders, but which has become the head of the corner' (Acts 4.11). The raising of Jesus declares who was in the right and who in the wrong; it is an event of judgment. Given the relationship between resurrection and judgment in later Judaism, it might well be said that the proclamation that Jesus had been raised was 'a way of saying' that Jesus had been shown to be the righteous one over against those who had condemned him. This might be regarded as evidence that the accounts of the raising of Jesus are simply ways in which material from the cultural background is pressed into the service of a theological message.

The rise of belief in the resurrection in late Jewish circles has to be seen as part of the development of their belief in the kingdom of God. In those terms any failure to achieve in visible form a kingdom ruled by him, whether during the sixth-century exile in Babylon or in the period

of occupation and persecution in the second century BC, presented a
theological crisis. It is against the background of such crises that the rise
of apocalyptic thinking, with resurrection as part of it, has to be
understood. The question to which it is a response is not 'What happens
beyond the death of the individual?' or even 'Is there a world beyond
this one?', but rather 'How can we continue to believe in a righteous
God who is all-powerful when it is clear that his purpose and the
accomplishment of his kingdom are constantly being frustrated?'
There could be no question of sacrificing the belief that God was able
to fulfil his purpose or the conviction that that purpose was righteous;
yet as attempt after attempt in their history failed to re-establish his
visible rule in Israel, recourse was had to projecting even further into
the future the time when his kingdom would be established. Apocalyptic is the end of that process of projection at a point where the future is
deemed to have an end in a moment when the total rule of God will
be established once and for all. Whatever interpretation is given to the
idea of resurrection, it always retains the connotation of the time when
God's righteous rule would be established, with an end to unrighteous-
ness and injustice.

Yet the motif of judgment contained in the idea of resurrection in
late Judaism is not merely used in the New Testament; it is also remarkably changed in its content. In the first place, in comparison with the
meaning which resurrection has in late Judaism, the idea of judgment
which appears in the New Testament takes a most unexpected turn.
For example, the argument of Paul in Romans is not merely that the
death and resurrection of Jesus vindicate his claim to be righteous, or
even that, in the manner of the Maccabean martyrs, the unrighteous-
ness of Israel will be expiated by his suffering, but that they are also
the source of righteousness for all, despite their sin, and regardless of
whether they are Israelites or not.

That is why it depends on faith, in order that the promise may rest
on grace and be guaranteed to all [Abraham's] descendants – not
only to the adherents of the law but also to those who share the
faith of Abraham, for he is the father of us all, as it is written,
'I have made you the father of many nations' – in the presence
of the God in whom he believed, who gives life to the dead and
calls into existence the things that do not exist (Rom. 4.16 – 18).

The resurrection of Jesus is thus a fulfilment of the specifically
Abrahamic promise and offers blessing to all the nations whether or not
they live under the Mosaic law. The judgment pronounced by the

raising of Jesus is one that declares the law itself to have been in the wrong and thereby opens up the promise of God to the Gentiles, as is argued in Galatians.

> Christ redeemed us from the curse of the law, having become a curse for us — for it is written, 'Cursed be every one who hangs on a tree' — that in Christ Jesus the blessing of Abraham might come upon the Gentiles, that we might receive the promise of the Spirit through faith (Gal. 3.1.3f.)

So the judgment associated with the resurrection of Jesus does not merely produce a vindication for Israel or for the righteous, but is the source of righteousness for all.

If the relationship of the resurrection faith to the idea of resurrection in late Judaism is to be fully evaluated, two further important and related differences are to be noted. It has already been pointed out that the resurrection was part of apocalyptic thinking; it concerned the projection into the future, and then beyond the future to the end, as it were, of all futures, of the visible rule of God. To some extent, the Christian belief in the forthcoming resurrection of all believers partook of the characteristics of that belief. The remarkable fact, however, given that background, is that Christians were prepared to assert that Jesus had been raised and that thereby the forthcoming rule of God had been established, but in a visible community. This new community of Jew and Gentile, the church, is the result of the raising of Jesus by the God who 'gives life to the dead and calls into existence the things that do not exist'. Secondly, and following from this, the resurrection of Jesus was 'before the end' and therefore held out a future before the end came. We can agree with M. E. Dahl that 'the resurrection hope looks forward to a mode of existence different from the present one, which is, nonetheless, anticipated in the sacramental fellowship of the Church'.[3] Or, as Moltmann puts it,

> Christian eschatology differs from Old Testament faith in the promise, as also from prophetic and apocalyptic eschatology, by being Christian eschatology and speaking of 'Christ and his future'. It is related in content to the person of Jesus of Nazareth and the event of his raising and speaks of the future for which the ground is laid in this person and this event.[4]

And the particular future for which the ground is laid in the raising of Jesus is in contrast with the apocalyptic tradition.

> It is not that the secrets of what awaits world history and the cosmos at the end of time are disclosed in advance according to a

heavenly plan – 'what shall befall thy people in the latter days' (Dan. 10.14) – but the universal future of the lordship of the crucified Christ over all is spotlighted in the Easter appearances.[5]

Thus the character of the judgment as presaged in apocalyptic, its content, timing and criteria are all changed under the impact of what is nevertheless described in apocalyptic terms, the raising of Jesus from the dead.

If on the other hand it is suggested that the vocabulary of resurrection was available to the earliest Christians not primarily from Jewish sources but rather from the mystery religions, further differences and changes can be noted. It is immediately evident that the motif of judgment, prevalent, as has been pointed out, in the New Testament witness to the raising of Jesus, is entirely absent from the resurrections of gods and demigods in the ancient mystery and fertility religions. The myth of Isis and Osiris has a great deal to say about the desire of ancient peoples for the renewal of their crops each spring, as Isis' tears are mingled with the waters of the Nile, or as Osiris' limbs come to life in the fields with the new season's crops.[6] But it has nothing to say about the essential New Testament hope for the establishment of God's rule over his people.

Nor would it appear that the New Testament writers took over, in any very straightforward way, Hellenistic conceptions of the immortality of the soul, even to the extent that these had penetrated into Judaism. The New Testament has no parallel for what appears in Wisdom:

> But the souls of the righteous are in the hand of God,
> and no torment will ever touch them.
> In the eyes of the foolish they seemed to have died,
> and their departure was thought to be an affliction,
> and their going from us to be their destruction;
> but they are at peace (Wisd. 3.1 – 3).

Thus the New Testament proclamation tends to accept only with the utmost discrimination the materials offered by the surrounding culture for the expression of the faith of the earliest Christians. The relevance of that material to a study of the New Testament lies not so much in its capacity to give, at any rate on its own, an adequate account of the origin of that proclamation as in what it reveals of the meaning of the proclamation which emerged.

If it is said that speaking of the resurrection of Jesus was a way of using the cultural furniture of the age to express the truth of faith, and even to express the truth, which it undoubtedly does express, that God's judgment had been shown forth, some explanation would have still to be given of how this kind of concept came to be associated with the particular kind of judgment which the New Testament wishes to say has been placed in Jesus' hands through the resurrection. Had this understanding of resurrection been introduced in order to interpret the gospel to a Jewish audience, it would have to be said that it had been introduced with a view to causing the maximum confusion about its import. For it was now being used not with a view to speaking of the rewards which await those who loyally abide by the precepts of the law despite the consequences, but of stating that in the case of Jesus the law, by condemning him, had come to stand on the wrong side, and that therefore those who had failed to achieve the righteousness of the law had hope through the miraculous righteousness of faith. As to the likely comprehensibility of resurrection language to Gentile audiences, there seems little reason to disagree with Luke's suggestion that mention of the raising of the dead caused the Athenians at best to be confused and at worst to scoff (Acts 17.32). Inasmuch as the resurrection was an idea current at the time of the New Testament, the values associated with it were, in the proclamation of the earliest Christians, completely overturned.[7] It is not an unreasonable assumption that it was historically something to do with Jesus that caused that overturning to take place; what is certainly the case, as the extracts quoted from Romans and Galatians testify, is that the resurrection declared that God had focused his judgment of Israel and of the world in Jesus. Thus in Acts Paul concludes his sermon at Athens with words which are critical to an understanding of resurrection faith in the New Testament:

> The times of ignorance God overlooked, but now he commands all men everywhere to repent, because he has fixed a day on which he will judge the world in righteousness by a man whom he has appointed, and of this he has given assurance to all men by raising him from the dead (Acts 17.30f).

The Resurrection of Jesus and Mission

Judgment was not the only theological idea associated with the resurrection of Jesus in the thinking of New Testament Christianity, nor was it the only idea which was radically changed by being so associated.

One of the ideas most frequently connected with the resurrection is that of mission, and it also assumes characteristics which would not have been associated with mission prior to the coming of Christ. Indeed, unlike some of the other concepts which will be considered in this chapter, there is nothing especially automatic about a connection between resurrection and mission as there might be between, for example, resurrection and life. Nevertheless, mission is implied even in the passage which represents the earliest recording of the resurrection tradition.

> Now I would remind you, brethren, in what terms I preached to you in the gospel. . . . For I delivered to you as of first importance what I also received, that Christ died for our sins in accordance with the scriptures, that he was buried, that he was raised on the third day in accordance with the scriptures, and that he appeared to Cephas, then to the twelve. Then he appeared to more than five hundred brethren at one time, most of whom are still alive, though some have fallen asleep. Then he appeared to James, then to all the apostles. Last of all, as to one untimely born, he appeared to me also (I Cor. 15.1 - 8).[8]

This passage is introduced in a context which suggests that the 'facts' are being rehearsed in order to argue against those of the Corinthians who denied the resurrection of the dead. And yet quite a different strand appears in the argument, one concerned with function and mission.

For the Corinthians the resurrection is, according to Paul, what guarantees that their conversion was not in vain (I Cor. 15.2), and the point is explicitly stressed a few verses later:

> . . . and if Christ was not raised, then our gospel is null and void, and so is your faith; and we turn out to be lying witnesses for God, because we bore witness that he raised Christ to life, whereas if the dead are not raised he did not raise him (I Cor. 15.14 - 16, NEB).

A double point is being made; the resurrection of Jesus is both the guarantee of the faith of the believers and the sign of the authority of the witnesses. Thus Paul, in adding himself to the traditional list of those who had experienced appearances of the risen Lord, immediately goes on to say what the vision had resulted in for him:

> I persecuted the church of God and am therefore inferior to all other apostles – indeed not fit to be called an apostle. However, by God's grace, I am what I am, nor has his grace been in vain; on the contrary, in my labours I have outdone them all – not I indeed,

but the grace of God working within me. But what matter, I or
they? This is what we all proclaim, and this is what you believed
(I Cor. 15.8 – 11).

There is therefore a close connection between the vision of the risen
Lord and the function and mission to which Paul felt himself called
and equipped; there is a connection in Paul's thinking, that is, between
the resurrection of Christ, mission and grace.

On the basis of this passage alone, therefore, a strong link can be
seen between resurrection and the function and mission of the believers
in general and of the apostles in particular. The resurrection is 'what we
all proclaim'. The resurrection of Christ was that which gave to certain
people their distinctive function and role within the Christian community, and indeed the role of the twelve and the existence of a group
called apostles are so closely related to the resurrection of Christ that
one can scarcely be mentioned without the other.[9]

If we turn to the other New Testament evidence, interesting confirmation of this link between mission in general, and apostleship in
particular, and the resurrection of Christ can be found in a number of
places. There is, for example, Peter's speech calling for the election of
another to take Judas' place among the twelve.

> So one of the men who have accompanied us during all the time that
> the Lord Jesus went in and out among us, beginning from the
> baptism of John until the day when he was taken up from us – one
> of these men must become with us a witness to his resurrection
> (Acts 1.21f.).

Matthias being chosen is assigned, according to Luke, 'a place with the
eleven apostles'. The question of the existence of a distinction between
the twelve and the apostles (as Paul implies in his list) need not concern
us here, what does appear is that Luke wishes to say that even if having
been with Jesus during his ministry was an essential qualification for
being numbered among the twelve, witnessing to his resurrection was
the primary function of the group.

In the gospels, the link between resurrection and mission is quite
inescapable. This is so even in the fragmentary, if not actually incomplete, ending of Mark, where the messenger greets the women with
an instruction to 'go tell . . . Peter that he is going before you to Galilee;
there you will see him, as he told you' (Mark 16.7). Even this short
reference given the association of Galilee with the Gentiles, provides an
indication of the missionary import of the resurrection.

In Matthew, this note is sounded even more strongly; after giving the same account as Mark of the message given to the women, the author records a single appearance to the eleven in Galilee, and the purpose of this account of Jesus' appearing is summed up in what the risen Lord is recorded as saying:

> All authority in heaven and on earth has been given to me. Go therefore and make disciples of all nations, baptizing them in the name of the Father and of the Son and of the Holy Spirit, teaching them to observe all that I have commanded you; and lo, I am with you always, to the close of the age (Matt. 28. 18 – 20).

Luke records a different timetable, in that mission for him involves the Pentecost story at the beginning of Acts, and the conclusion of what he sees as a definite period, limited to forty days, of resurrection appearances. It is only after this point that there is any question of leaving Jerusalem. The Marcan hint of an appearance in Galilee is therefore absent, but it is perhaps all the more remarkable in view of this that even in the appearance in Jerusalem there is a strong missionary note.

> 'This', he said, 'is what is written; that the Messiah is to suffer death and to rise again from the dead on the third day, and that in his name repentance bringing the forgiveness of sins is to be preached to all nations. Begin from Jerusalem; it is you who are the witnesses to it all' (Luke 24.46 – 49, NEB).

Similarly, at the beginning of Acts, we read:

> So when they had come together, they asked him, 'Lord, will you at this time restore the kingdom to Israel?' He said to them, 'It is not for you to know times or seasons which the Father has fixed by his own authority. For you shall receive power when the Holy Spirit has come upon you; and you shall be my witnesses in Jerusalem and in all Judaea and Samaria and to the end of the earth' (Acts 1.6 – 8).

So although mission might be thought to have been adequately covered by Luke as a theological theme in the rest of Acts, it is specifically joined to the accounts of the appearances of the risen Jesus.

This link is also strikingly present in John. In the first appearance to the twelve, Jesus is recorded as saying,

> Peace be with you. As the Father has sent me, even so I send you. . . . Receive the Holy Spirit! If you forgive the sins of any, they are forgiven: if you retain the sins of any, they are retained' (John 20.21 – 23).

The words, 'As the Father has sent me, even so I send you', are especially important, since a designation of the Father throughout the gospel is 'he who sent me'. In these words the disciples are therefore told two things: first, Jesus is putting himself in the same relationship to them as his Father had had to him, and secondly he is giving to the twelve a function and status similar to that which had been his in his ministry. And it is this development which is associated with the resurrection of Christ as John understands it.

The notion of the resurrection as primarily something to be proclaimed is borne out also by what is said at Jesus' appearance to Thomas. It is made clear here that the primary sense of a 'witness' of the resurrection is that of one who testifies to it. Being a witness did apparently involve being one who had seen the Lord, and yet this is not what is focused on. So Jesus says to Thomas, 'Because you have seen me you have found faith; happy are they who never saw me and yet have found faith' (John 20.29, NEB). It seems that having seen the risen Lord determined function rather than status; it was an experience of being sent.

The twenty-first chapter of John presents interesting problems of its own, especially in relation to how it came to be appended, as it seems to have been, to the rest of the gospel. Marxsen considers that this story, although designated Jesus' third appearance by the editor, and although it includes the beloved disciple, in fact seems to be the account of a first appearance to Peter, mentioned by Paul in his list in I Corinthians 15.1 - 8 and, though without further description, in Luke 24.34.[10] Certainly the chapter is remarkable for the way in which the resurrection is related to the function of Peter in the church's life; first the disciples are told a way in which they may catch a great haul of fish, which they contrive to do without the net breaking. The fact that this occurs in Galilee, together with the strong reminiscence of what is recorded in the synoptic gospels as the *pre*-crucifixion call of Peter, gives this story a powerful missionary meaning. This is further expanded as Peter receives his instruction to 'feed my lambs' as well as hearing the prediction that he will be led 'where you do not wish to go' (John 21.18), interpreted as a prophecy of his martyrdom. So the story is a further link between the resurrection and the function and missionary purpose of the church and of Peter within it.

Whatever then may be the differences between the various accounts of the appearances of the risen Christ, and even though the tradition given in I Corinthians cannot be harmonized as to factual content with all or even any of the gospel accounts, there is an astonishing unanimity about at least this particular implication of the resurrection of Jesus. There are differences in the way mission is conceived: Luke is the one, it appears, most concerned to bring out the apostleship of the twelve, as for instance in Luke 24.48; Acts 1.8, while Matthew (e.g. 28.20) construes mission as the proclamation of Christ's new law.

The resurrection then certainly involves mission: but is the proclamation of the resurrection simply a way of expressing the conviction that the church, and within it Peter, the twelve and the apostles, had a mission, and a gospel to proclaim? The answer to this must surely be negative. The kind of mission which results from the resurrection, and which includes it as an essential part of the proclamation, is not something which could simply have been read off from the resurrection idea itself. It is integrally related to the judgment of God, to the person of Jesus and to the universality of the gospel; in that sense the resurrection did not only speak about mission; it was understood as creative of it.

The Resurrection of Jesus Christ and his Exaltation as Lord

We have already noted how, in Mathew 28.18, the risen Lord greets his disciples with the words, 'All authority in heaven and on earth has been given to me'. There are many passages about exaltation which appear to take no account of the resurrection, passing, as it were, straight to his appointment as Lord. There are two ways in which exaltation is spoken of without mention of resurrection. There are passages which talk in eschatological terms, but say nothing about how the end will come about, such as the reply of Jesus to the high priest: 'I am [the Messiah], and you will see the Son of man sitting at the right hand of Power and coming with the clouds of heaven' (Mark 14.62). There is, on the other hand, the thought of Hebrews, where the exaltation of Christ as the high priest does not appear to be related to the resurrection, but rather to the sacrifice which he has made. 'He did not confer upon himself the glory of becoming high priest; it was granted by God, who said to him, "Thou art my Son; this day have I begotten thee" ' (Heb. 5.5, NEB).

The fourth gospel seems to regard Christ's exaltation as resulting directly from his death, and not from the resurrection. Thus as Judas leaves the room Jesus is recorded as saying, 'Now the Son of Man is glorified, and in him God is glorified; if God is glorified in him, God will also glorify him in himself, and glorify him at once' (John 13.31f.). The same line of thinking is made more explicit in the previous chapter (12.28 – 33).

> Father, glorify thy name. Then a voice came from heaven: 'I have glorified it, and I will glorify it again.' The crowd standing by heard it and said that it had thundered. Others said, 'An angel has spoken to him.' Jesus answered, 'This voice has come for your sake, not for mine. Now is the judgment of this world, now shall the ruler of this world be cast out; and I, when I am lifted up from the earth, will draw all men to myself.' He said this to show by what death he was to die.

Thus it would appear that the concept of exaltation had an independent existence; it is not bound to the concept of resurrection for its meaning.

Nevertheless, there are passages where the two concepts are very closely linked. For example, the exaltation of Christ as Son, as the successor of David, is sealed by the resurrection in Peter's sermon at Pentecost:

> But God raised him to life again, setting him free from the pangs of death, because it could not be that death should keep him in its grip. For David says of him:
>
> 'I foresaw that the presence of the Lord would be with me always, for he is at my right hand so that I may not be shaken,
> therefore my heart was glad and my tongue spoke my joy;
> moreover my flesh shall dwell in hope,
> for thou wilt not abandon my soul to death,
> nor let thy loyal servant suffer corruption.
> Thou has shown me the ways of life,
> thou wilt fill me with gladness by thy presence.'
>
> Let me tell you plainly, my friends, that the patriarch David died and was buried, and his tomb is here to this very day. It is clear therefore that he spoke as a prophet, who knew that God has sworn to him that one of his descendants should sit on his throne. . . . The Jesus we speak of has been raised by God, as we can all bear witness. Exalted thus with God's right hand, he received the Holy Spirit from the Father, as was promised, and all that you now see and hear flows from him. For it was not David who went up to heaven; his own words are: 'The Lord said to my Lord, "Sit at my right hand until I make your enemies your footstool." ' Let all Israel then accept as certain that God has made this Jesus, whom you crucified, both Lord and Messiah (Acts 2.24 – 36, NEB, quoting Pss. 16.8 – 11 and 110.1).

The resurrection here functions as the sign that Jesus has been chosen as the successor of King David, and thus that the eschatological kingdom of God has been realized in him. The two concepts are very closely linked in a passage in Ephesians, where the exaltation of Christ is shared with those who commit themselves to him.

> I pray that your inward eyes may be illumined, so that you may know what is the hope to which he calls you, what the wealth and glory of the share he offers you among his people in their heritage, and how vast the resources of his power open to us who trust in him. They are measured by the strength and the might which he exerted in Christ Jesus when he raised him from the dead, when he enthroned him at his right hand in the heavenly places, far above all government and authority, all power and dominion, and any title of sovereignty that can be named, not only in this age but in the age to come. He put everything in subjection under his feet and appointed him as supreme head to the church, which is his body and as such holds within it the fullness of him who himself received the entire fullness of God (Eph. 1.18 – 23, NEB).

There are places also where the two concepts of exaltation and resurrection are not explicitly linked, but where it appears that the concept of exaltation is used instead of resurrection, almost as though the two ideas are interchangeable. An example of this is the hymn in Philippians, where it is said of Christ that

> Bearing human likeness, revealed in human shape, he humbled himself, and in obedience accepted even death – death on a cross. Therefore, God raised him to the heights and bestowed on him the name above all names, that at the name of Jesus every knee should bow ... (Phil. 2.8 – 10, NEB).

The lordship of Christ, to which he is exalted by God, is among the first of the things which we find Christians confessing. It has been argued that the earliest traditions represent the appearances of Jesus as having the character of visions of the Lord of glory, and that it is for this reason that Paul is able to make no distinction between the appearances to the twelve and the appearance to himself on the road to Damascus.[11] Such exaltation would place Jesus with God in the final state of his glory; it was all that could be said of him and the most that could be said of anybody. It would state that Jesus was the one who was agent of God's final rule over all things. Inasmuch, therefore, as the church was concerned to make such an eschatological proclamation about Jesus, lordship offered itself as the best available concept.

It therefore requires to be explained why, with such a concept readily to hand, the church none the less found it necessary at several points to retain the concept of resurrection alongside it when, as has already been said, resurrection was altogether more ambiguous and less likely to elicit an immediate response. The appearance of the two concepts together merely accentuates the puzzling aspect of the persistence of resurrection. 'If you confess with your lips that Jesus is Lord and believe in your heart that God raised him from the dead, you will be saved' (Rom. 10.9).

It will not be sufficient simply to say that the stories of the raising of Jesus were so dominant in the minds of his disciples as to require that they be recorded and the concept retained irrespective of its difficulty. What has also to be answered is how the two concepts came to be linked in the way they were, and yet to have retained at other points their independence of each other. The answer to this must lie in a certain weakness in the concept of exaltation as a medium for the proclamation of the gospel, and certain distinct contributions which the idea of resurrection had to make to the better understanding of it. The language of exaltation is entirely metaphorical; this is so even where in Luke's hands it acquires a spatial character in the stories of the ascension. The exalted Lord has to be described in language which is stretched to the limit, as the one who is 'at the right hand of God' or 'glorified' or 'seated far above all heavens'. Such language functions well as the language of submission and of worship; it would also have functioned well as the vocabulary of a Christian mystery religion. It is language which lifts the worshipper up, leaving the world far behind.

Compared with this the language in which the resurrection appearances are described is language which is singularly lacking in the imagery of glory. Where resurrection is specifically referred to, we are dealing with the unusual, with the odd, to be sure; but we are not dealing with the Son of Man of Jewish expectation returning on the clouds of heaven, nor with the returning demigod of the mystery cults. On the other hand, we are not dealing with a returning human being either. The risen Lord of the appearances is not like Lazarus walking out of his tomb restored to that past life which had been interrupted by death (John 11.44) or like the son of the widow of Nain (Luke 7.11ff.) or the daughter of Jairus (Mark 5.22ff.; Luke 8.41ff.); all these had been raised to life but would die again. In each of these cases the story makes clear that while it concerns a miracle, it is a miracle which leaves the human status of the person raised unaltered. In the case of the resurrection of Jesus, the narratives show a person who, in being raised, was also exalted to his kingdom and raised to the life of the new age. Yet this exaltation by resurrection is recorded in a way that does not deny the truth of the continuity that exists between the risen and exalted Christ and the Jesus whom they had known in his ministry and death.

It was in the risk of denying that continuity that the language of exaltation had its chief limitation. The Jesus of the ministry would then either have become the avenging Messiah of traditional expectation or the other-worldly hero of gnostic cults. Either would have isolated the one who was to be worshipped in the life of the Christian community from the person who had ministered and then been crucified. The idea of resurrection, linked inescapably as it is with the idea of the cross, makes it certain that the church is to preach a Lord who was crucified and no other. The resurrection is what safeguards the scandal of the cross. It can be replaced in passages such as the hymn in Philippians where the exaltation is clearly stated to be exaltation from the cross, but otherwise it had that essential role to fulfil. Thus the stories of the resurrection of Jesus point both backwards to the Jesus of the ministry and the death, and forwards to the fulfilment of God's purpose which the raising of Jesus had anticipated.[12]

Yet it could only fulfil that role because, as was pointed out in the previous section, it was a radical reinterpretation of the idea as it was available to the disciples from their surrounding culture. It was not merely that the one who was raised happened to be Jesus, but that the manner of the raising corresponded to the character of his ministry and the nature of his death. The idea of resurrection was available and might well have been an equivalent of the exaltation; certainly the desire to proclaim Jesus exalted as Lord was part of what drove the disciples into the proclamation of the resurrection. But retained alongside it, the resurrection idea, and particularly the resurrection as it was applied to Jesus, tied the exaltation of Jesus to the particular manner in which the New Testament writers wished to declare that God had his dealings with men.

This does not, of course, answer the question how the disciples came by this revised concept and what made them hold to it. It merely explains one significance of their having done so. Whether the resurrection of Jesus as they described it was believed to have been itself what created this new understanding, or whether it only proved it or merely expressed an understanding formulated on other grounds, remains to be asked. But such questions can for the time being be allowed to rest; for our major concern is not with those who in the first instance came upon the resurrection themselves and proclaimed it to others, but primarily with those who, in the second generation as it were, were asked to believe it on the testimony of others. What they were asked to believe, so it would seem, was tied to something which held together the Lord for whom they were seeking and the Jesus who had ministered and died.

The Resurrection and the Life – the Johannine Concern

It is hardly surprising that 'life' should be one of the ideas most commonly associated with resurrection in the New Testament, for the connection is in a sense obvious. Given that it was preached at all, it is natural that it should have as one of its results, as the New Testament Easter faith understood it, the offering of new life to all believers. 'We were buried with him by baptism into death, in order that as Christ was raised from the dead by the glory of the Father, we too might walk in newness of life' (Rom. 6.4). This connection is made with particular force, however, in the fourth gospel, where life, $z\bar{o}\bar{e}$, is one of the most recurrent themes, and a great deal is made at many points of the contrast between death and life, and of the significance of eternal life. This also would not surprise the reader of a book designed to commend the Christian gospel to an age in which the offering of life would be one of the most obvious meeting grounds with the current quest. The consciousness of the Hellenistic world asserted that the most significant thing about the world was its mortality, its being destined for death, and naturally, therefore, that for which people most longed was the offering of the key to a life that was eternal. So many of the passages relating to the notion of life simply attribute to Jesus what might reasonably be expected to be attributed to anyone about whom the kind of claims made about Jesus in the fourth gospel were being made. So Jesus is the bread of life (John 6.35, 48), he is water springing up to eternal life (4.14) and he speaks to his disciples the words which bring eternal life (6.63, 68). What he offers to all his hearers is eternal life (John 3.15f., 36; 10.10, 28).

What is perhaps more surprising, and needs to be noted in connection with the main question being pursued here, is that the theme of life is linked on more than one occasion with that of resurrection, and this latter concept is not considered to have been included in the word 'life'. The idea of resurrection would not, as has been said, do anything to commend the gospel to Greek hearers, and in fact would be likely to be understood if at all by only a small minority of Jews. There is, first of all, a passage which relates resurrection to life and speaks with a strongly Maccabean voice.

> As Son of Man, he has also been given the right to pass judgment. Do not wonder at this, because the time is coming when all who are in the grave shall hear his voice and come out: those who have done right will rise to life; those who have done wrong will rise to hear their doom. I cannot act by myself; I judge as I am bidden and my sentence is just, because my aim is not my own will, but the will of him who sent me (John 5.27 – 30, NEB).

Here there appears to be the straightforward attribution to Christ of the kind of view of resurrection which was noted earlier as current in late Jewish circles, without the slightest modification. It is the resurrection of eschatological judgment which is being spoken of. But it is possible that this is not really the point that is being made. Apart from the narrative descriptions of the resurrection appearances themselves, there is one other passage where there is an explicit reference to a link between the concepts of resurrection and life, and that is in the encounter between Martha and Jesus just prior to the account of the raising of Lazarus.

> Martha said to Jesus, 'Lord, if you had been here, my brother would not have died. And even now I know that whatever you ask from God, God will give you.' Jesus said to her, 'Your brother will rise again.' Martha said to him, 'I know that he will rise again in the resurrection at the last day.' Jesus said to her, 'I am the resurrection and the life; he who believes in me, though he die, yet shall he live, and whoever lives and believes in me shall never die. Do you believe this?' She said to him, 'Yes, Lord; I believe that you are the Christ, the Son of God, he who is coming into the world' (John 11.21 –27).

In v. 25, 'I am the resurrection and the life', there is some manuscript evidence to suggest that the last three words are a later addition. If this is so, the motive of the addition is likely to have been the rather surprising words of Jesus (incomprehensible from a Hellenistic point of view), 'I am the resurrection.' Even, however, with the longer text, it has to be asked why a concept so difficult to John's readers as resurrection must undoubtedly have been is included at all. Part of the answer no doubt lies in the desire to present Jesus as the fulfilment of the hopes of Jewish eschatology; Martha says, 'I know that he will rise again at the last day' and Jesus replies, 'I *am* the resurrection.' That is to say, the resurrection is now in the present, and need no longer be hoped for in the future.

Yet this is not a sufficient answer. The juxtaposition in the fourth gospel of highly philosophical concepts like 'life' with elements which emphasize a highly physical, not to say crude, aspect is extremely common. It could be said that this begins with the words in the prologue (1.14), 'The Word became flesh' and continues in the discourse following the feeding of the multitude, where Jesus says, 'Unless you eat the flesh of the Son of man and drink his blood, you have no life in you (6.53). It is one of the major purposes of the fourth gospel to make that juxtaposition, and it is a prominent feature of the account in ch. 11 of the raising of Lazarus. This account follows immediately upon the conversation with Martha just mentioned, and is full of detailed references to the physical aspects of the situation; we are told that the grave was a cave with a stone rolled against it (v.38), that Lazarus had been buried four days and that there was therefore likely to be a stench (v.39), and that Lazarus came out dressed in the graveclothes (v.44). In this, the last of the 'signs' of the fourth gospel, it is emphasized that the life which Christ offers is to be found appearing within the world of the physical and not simply beyond it. The word 'resurrection' is perhaps a cruder one, a less universal image, than the word 'life', and thus serves to make clear that what is being spoken of is not just some ongoing and eternal kind of life, but the power of God to overcome death itself.

Yet even on the most conservative interpretation of the account of the raising of Lazarus, it could not in itself have been the event which created this new theological understanding, for the understanding of new life within the world of the physical was clearly new to Jew and Greek alike. The account points forward in several places to John's later description of the first Easter morning, and makes contrasts which are as significant as the likenesses. The stone has to be rolled away (v.41), the man had been dead four days (v.39), he is thus assumed to have 'seen corruption', and when he is raised he emerges tied in the graveclothes (v.44) in contrast to the situation after the raising of Jesus where the graveclothes are found lying in a place by themselves (20.6f). This story is no more than the anticipation of the raising of Jesus, and the ideas which are used to describe it are those which have clearly come into use as part of the proclamation of the resurrection faith. Lazarus himself is raised to die again; his mortality is still with him. What is being said in the raising of Lazarus is that Jesus is understood as the fulfilment of the hopes of Judaism for the raising of the dead and of the hopes of the Greeks for the overcoming of mortality. These are what the raising of Lazarus signifies; they are not completely fulfilled in it or created by it.

Thus 'life' as offered by the Christ of the fourth gospel is life tied to the person of Jesus and to existence in the physical world. Inasmuch as Jesus offers life, he does so, according to John, through and in 'the flesh'. The resurrection idea fulfils the role of safeguarding, as it did in the case of Christ's lordship, the link with the person of Jesus which decides and displays the kind of life — as also the kind of lordship — which the church is proclaiming. When the search for life is answered by the risen Christ it is answered in terms which at the same time redefine the quest.

The importance of this is further illustrated by the presence of the resurrection narratives within the fourth gospel at all. For that gospel more than any of the others makes actual narration of the resurrection, from a literary and theological point of view, strictly redundant, as if all the writer wishes to say is that Jesus brought life. As he dies on the cross, he cries out 'It is finished' (19.30), and throughout the gospel the glory of God, his exaltation of Jesus already, are to be seen shining through the ministry and suffering of Jesus. Yet the resurrection stories are there, and turn out to be part of the means by which the evangelist ties life to the same Jesus whom the disciples had known and followed. To that extent life is not merely offered by Jesus; it is explained, demonstrated and changed.

Resurrection and the New Future

The New Testament claims in one way or another that Jesus is the fulfilment of Jewish hopes for the future. The ways in which the resurrection faith is related to such hopes are, however, highly significant, and indicative of the theological reflections of the early church. Thus, it is hard to read the passion narratives without becoming aware at almost every turn of the connections which are being made between what is there going on and the writings of the Old Testament. Every available opportunity is taken to relate the destiny of Jesus to the destiny of Israel. Quite apart from the numerous quotations from, and echoes of, the Old Testament, the imagery of passover and the style of acted prophecy are everywhere present in all the evangelists' accounts. Yet in the case of the resurrection, this element is almost wholly absent.

Certainly the church claimed from the beginning, and indeed continues to claim in the language of the Nicene Creed, that Christ's resurrection was 'according to the scriptures'. Paul says in his earliest statement of the Easter tradition that Christ 'died for our sins according to the scriptures, that he was buried, that he was raised on the third day according to the scriptures' (I Cor. 15.3f.). Furthermore, the unknown stranger who encounters the two disciples on the road to Emmaus declares:

> 'O foolish men, and slow of heart to believe all that the prophets have spoken! Was it not necessary that the Christ should suffer these things and enter into his glory?' And beginning with Moses and all the prophets he interpreted to them in all the scriptures the things concerning himself (Luke 24.25 – 27).

Yet these scriptures are scarcely cited at all, and are indeed remarkably difficult to unearth. Two examples which can be found are from Hosea and from Jonah. In Hosea 6.2 we read:

> Come let us return to the Lord;
>   for he has torn, that he may heal us;
>   he has stricken, and he will bind us up.
> After two days he will revive us;
>   on the third day he will raise us up,
>   that we may live before him.

But this is nowhere cited in the New Testament. The evidence that it was used in the rabbinic literature to apply to the general resurrection would not be sufficient to justify Evans' suggestion that its use may have been early, and have left its mark on the tradition 'at a level deeper than explicit quotation'.[13]

The only other sign which would associate 'according to the scriptures' with the resurrection tradition about the 'third day' is the saying concerning the 'sign of Jonah', but comparison of the Matthaean version (Matt. 12.40), which contains the words

> For as Jonah was three days and three nights in the belly of the whale, so will the Son of man be three days and three nights in the heart of the earth,

with the Lucan indicates that the former is a later development, perhaps made by the evangelist himself. The only other citation of scripture with reference to the resurrection is that of the Psalm 16.10 'Thou wilt not let thy Holy One see corruption' (quoted in Acts 13.35).

This failure to cite scripture is attributable to two factors. The first is that, with the resurrection being hardly an Old Testament concept at all, there was in fact none to hand. It is significant that in the Lucan passage quoted above (from the Emmaus story) it is implied that the scriptures showed how he 'must suffer and so enter into his glory', and the resurrection is not specifically mentioned. What had to be justified, and what could be justified from scripture in the mind of the earliest Christians, was the proclamation of a *suffering* Messiah, but texts to show resurrection were simply not available. The second factor is that, in so far as the resurrection was associated with the Messiah, it was associated with his messianic function and was not something the Messiah himself would be expected to undergo. His coming would bring about the resurrection of the dead; he himself would not need to rise again because he would not die.

Thus it was the suffering of Jesus that required to be justified from scripture; the resurrection could not be justified because there were no texts available, and because the raising of Jesus, while it accorded with those scriptures which could be interpreted to mean that the Christ would suffer, specifically disappointed Jewish messianic expectations as such. This massive contradiction of what was expected is further shown by the fact that the raising of Jesus in the New Testament is for the disciples the 'firstfruits of the harvest of the dead' (I Cor. 15.20,NEB) and thus something that was to have a succession of events after it. This was not a possibility within Jewish hopes. Either the resurrection was entirely in the future, something to be waited for as the final fulfilment of God's plan for the world, or, when it happened, it would be that after which there would be no future at all, for it was part of the end of all things. So the resurrection of Jesus, which had happened and yet which was to be followed by a future and pointed towards the future which awaited all believers, was not what could have been expected as the fulfilment of the promises of the Old Testament.

There is evidence that Paul himself is perplexed by the relation of the resurrection of Jesus to Jewish expectations, and as a result there is a certain ambivalence in his teaching precisely at this point. Thus in Romans 6.5, Christians are said to *have* been united with Christ in his death, while their unity with him in his resurrection is a strictly *future* occurrence. Yet some of the future resurrection is already there in the present. They are dead indeed to sin, but alive to God (6.11). Even now, they walk in 'newness of life' (6.4). According to his thinking in Colossians, the resurrection of Christians has already taken place: 'If then you have been raised with Christ, seek the things that are above' (Col. 3.1).

In so far then as the resurrection of Jesus was held by the early Christians to declare that the promises of God are fulfilled, great care was required. This is illustrated by the way Paul argues from and to the resurrection both in Romans and in I Corinthians. What is for him at issue is not God's faithfulness in general, but the highly specific way in which he fulfils what he promises. It is not only that the very miraculous nature of the resurrection of Jesus made it a very good example of God's faithfulness, but also that there was something in the very pattern of the event, as Paul apprehended it, that made it a serviceable picture of the nature of the divine faithfulness and therefore of what Christians are entitled to expect.

Thus the argument in Romans for God's faithfulness in justification is developed in ch. 4 by reference to the faith of Abraham and its implications for the believing community.

> For [Abraham] is the father of us all, as Scripture says: 'I have appointed you to be a father of many nations.' This promise then was valid before God, the God in whom he put his faith, the God who makes the dead live and summons things that are not yet in existence as if they already were. When hope seemed hopeless, his faith was such that he became the 'father of many nations', in agreement with the words which had been spoken to him: 'Thus shall your descendants be.' Without any weakening of faith, he contemplated his own body, as good as dead (for he was about a hundred years old), and the deadness of Sarah's womb, and never doubted God's promise in unbelief, but, strong in faith, gave honour to God, in the firm conviction of his power to do what he had promised. And that is why Abraham's faith was 'counted to him as righteousness'. These words were written, not for Abraham's faith alone, but for our sake, too: it is to be 'counted' in the same way to us who have faith in the God who raised Jesus our Lord from the dead; for he was given up to death for our misdeeds, and raised to life to justify us (Rom. 4.16–25, NEB).

The conjunction of God's promise to Abraham, his overcoming of the 'deadness' of Abraham's body and Sarah's womb, his raising of Jesus from the dead, and his counting as righteousness the faith of *all* who believe in him (the many nations of which Abraham becomes father) is no coincidence. God has, according to Paul, brought about in the form of the church a visible fulfilment of God's promise to Abraham, and it is of that promise – and not the promise to Moses, as he later argues – that the raising of Jesus from the dead counts as the fulfilment. In a sense God is fulfilling his promise in a way that makes clear that it is Abraham and not Moses who is the embodiment of God's dealings with

Israel, and that fact has been brought to light by the raising of Jesus from the dead.

This point and its implications for the life of the believing community are spelt out in baptismal terms as a death to sin and a life of righteousness (Rom. 6; 7.4 - 6, 24; 8.17; 14.9). Thus both in fact and in manner the resurrection of Jesus Christ is a guarantee of the future God holds in store for the believer.

> But if Christ is in you, although your bodies are dead because of sin, your spirits are alive because of righteousness. If the Spirit of him who raised Jesus from the dead dwells in you, he who raised Christ Jesus from the dead will give life to your mortal bodies also through his Spirit which dwells in you (Rom. 8.10f.).

Thus it is the confession of the lordship of Christ and the belief that he has been raised from the dead that enables the believer to be confident of his own future resurrection (Rom. 10.9).

The relation between present and future in resurrection faith is at least in part the subject of I Corinthians 15, and the complexities of that relation are illustrated by the debate about its interpretation.[14] Paul's reasons for writing that chapter are not stated, and have to be guessed at, but it has been argued that the chapter is closely connected with a situation that dominates the whole epistle and Paul's dealings with the Corinthian church. This situation is that the church there, or some of its members, have developed a spirituality which would in effect transform the faith into an ecstatic mystery cult. Within such a mystery cult the story of a dying and rising God would have an obvious place, and believers could participate in the present in that dying and rising through the medium of the Spirit. What such a mystery says nothing about, however, is the way in which such a dying and rising again can impinge on the life of the world and the life of human beings in it; indeed it implicitly declares that there is no hope for man within the life of the world but only in forsaking it in order to join the cult.

In the background of the epistle as reconstructed by J. C. Hurd and others,[15] the suggestion is that the Corinthians, having been taught by Paul that they would survive until the second advent of Christ, were unwilling to accept the view that the resurrection had any future aspect. In that context, the words of I Corinthians 15.20 - 28 have a strongly ordered ring.

> But in fact Christ has been raised from the dead, the first fruits of those who have fallen asleep. For as by a man came death, by a man

has come also the resurrection of the dead. For as in Adam all die, so also in Christ shall all be made alive. But each in his own order: Christ the first fruits, then at his coming those who belong to Christ. Then comes the end, when he delivers the kingdom to God the Father after destroying every rule and every authority and power. For he must reign until he has put all his enemies under his feet. The last enemy to be destroyed is death. 'For God has put all things in subjection under his feet.' But when it says, 'All things are put in subjection under him,' it is plain that he is excepted who put all things under him. When all things are subjected to him, then the Son himself will also be subjected to him who put all things under him, that God may be everything to every one.

Moltmann in his section on 'Fulfilment Ecstasy in Primitive Christianity and the *Eschatologia Crucis*'[16] draws out the implications of Paul's insistence that the resurrection had a future horizon of what was not yet fulfilled in contrast to the offering by mystery and epiphany religions of a revelation which authenticates itself wholly in the present. In the view of the Corinthian 'spirituals', 'baptism into the death and resurrection of Christ then means that the goal of redemption is already attained, for in this baptism eternity is sacramentally present.'[17] This would mean that the believer's life on earth consists solely in the demonstration of his new and ecstatic freedom. Against this, the conclusion to which Paul's argument leads is the assurance that 'in the Lord your labour is not in vain' (I Cor. 15.58). This is because he views the resurrected Christ as the firstfruits of what lies ahead for all, which is that the body of mortality is to be clothed with immortality, that what is sown in humiliation is to be raised in glory. And this has been signified by the raising of Jesus. Thus the denial, implicit or explicit, by the ecstatics of Corinth that the body had such a future is ruled out by reason of the event which is believed to be central to Christian faith.[18] The resurrection of Jesus Christ transforms man's view of what future lies in store for him.

Thus the resurrection of Jesus, as it had meant mission and as it meant life, also meant the fulfilment of the promises of God, but in each case the meaning is not one that could be read off from some preexistent idea. In being fulfilled in this way, the promises are transformed in content and in time scale. They are transformed in content by the breadth of the Abrahamic covenant seen as the true revelation of God's dealings with all men; they are transformed in time scale because, far from being the end of all futures, the resurrection of Jesus leaves open, in the way that the pre-existing idea of resurrection did not, a future for all. That means that the resurrection has a fulfilling and transforming effect for Jew and Gentile alike. For the search after the destruction of mortality which was embodied in the mystery religions was united with the Jewish search for a future under God. The resurrection of Jesus offered both in a manner that gave meaning to the present experience of the believer.

> That all-embracing truth in which the creature comes into harmony with God, that all-embracing righteousness in which God receives his due in all things and all becomes well, that glory of God in whose reflected light all things are transfigured and the hidden face of man disclosed – all that is set by Paul within the realm of hope in that future to which faith looks forward on the ground of the resurrection of the crucified Lord.[19]

The Resurrection and the World of Hard Fact

The gulf between modern patterns of thought and those of the New Testament period appears at its greatest when the question is raised what beliefs were held in the early church about the factual basis of the Easter faith. The separation between fact and interpretation is, as we have seen, an essential presupposition of modern historical study, and yet it has no counterpart for those who were writing accounts of what God had accomplished among them. Yet the question has to be asked if any account is to be given in the contemporary situation of the content of the original Easter faith. What did the earliest Christians think, as we should say, had actually happened? Here it is necessary to consider those passages which appear to have no other motive than to insist on the factuality of the resurrection.

(a) Paul

Paul's recital of the original resurrection tradition, which he says he had received and which he handed on, contains the verse, 'Then he appeared to more than five hundred brethren at one time, most of whom are still alive, though some have fallen asleep' (I Cor. 15.6). It has all the appearance, particularly to the modern reader, of an attempt to 'prove' the resurrection of Jesus by reference to a large number of people, some of whom were still alive to be consulted, in order that the testimony he was offering could be checked. As such it would of course be of no direct use now, but, it may be thought, would have had an impressive effect then.

Yet if this verse is intended to offer some kind of proof it is of a very puzzling nature, for it describes an appearance which, and of a kind which, is nowhere else recorded in the New Testament (unless it is a reference to what Luke describes in Acts 2, the event of Pentecost). Furthermore, there are grounds for thinking that Paul's motive in speaking about this appearance may not be to offer proof that the resurrection of Jesus took place. The passage as a whole, as has been noted above, is used to authenticate the mission and function of the apostles and the church, and R. H. Fuller regards this verse as referring to the founding of the church.[20] If that is so, the appearance is recorded in order to offer, as well as authentication of the work of particular apostles, a statement of the origin of the Christian mission as experienced by the Corinthians.

On the other hand, this would not explain the words 'most of whom are still alive, though some have fallen asleep'. These are the words which lend the passage the appearance of offering proof of the raising of Jesus. But if what was said above about the meaning of I Corinthians 15 is correct, that it is directed against the view that the resurrection has already taken place, and that therefore all believers are already living in the end, and that as a result their life can be one of total liberty of the Spirit, these words could have a rather different meaning. For in that case they offer proof not of the raising of Jesus as such, but of the fact that even of those who had seen the risen Lord a number are still alive though some have died, and that the resurrection has not, therefore, brought about the end of all things. For that is yet to come, and the experience of the 'more than five hundred brethren' testifies to the fact that the resurrection is in part still in the future.

The significance of this chapter in general, and of this verse in particular, is widely discussed, and cannot be said to have been determined for certain. Whether or not, therefore, the suggestion made above is correct, it is certainly not obvious that the presence of this statement in the tradition as Paul hands it on reflects a concern to give evidence of the truth of the claim that Jesus had been raised from the dead. None the less, the whole passage I Corinthians 15.1 - 8 indicates that, from the very early date which this tradition represents, one of the features of the resurrection faith was an appeal to the experience of others.[21] What was offered to the new convert was not simply a representation in mythological form of certain theological truths which he was invited to accept, but an understanding of life which was rooted in certain experiences of particular people which served as the key to those new experiences which a person might have upon entering the Christian community. In some sense becoming a Christian was not just a matter of undergoing a certain sort of personal or communal reorientation, accomplished in the manner of a mystery religion by incorporation into and re-enactment of a myth, but involved also taking upon oneself certain experiences which had happened in the recent past, which could not be repeated, and which were known as experiences of the risen Lord.

(b) Mark

In Mark is found the earliest account of the finding of the empty tomb, of which it does not seem that Paul had any knowledge which he felt worth recording.[22] It is not possible to establish that he had no knowledge of it at all, because a number of explanations have been given of his failure to record it, all of which are possible. Certainly if his concern was to establish the experience of the risen Christ by appeal to official witnesses, the discovery of the empty tomb by a group of women would not lend him very much support.

In Mark also the story of the discovery of the empty tomb does not appear to be regarded as any kind of proof in itself of the resurrection. The Marcan narrative does not contain any account of an Easter appearance, but even if there had been an account of such an appearance in Galilee, the words of the messenger to the three women at the tomb would have performed the function of pointing forwards to the account of that appearance and thus connecting the tomb tradition with that of the appearances; as it stands it does not suggest any direct inference being made by the women from the discovery of the tomb to the raising of Jesus. There is no suggestion that the women were confirmed in faith by the discovery, and indeed evidence that they were rendered frightened and puzzled by the experience. Some other explanation has to be given for the recording of this tradition of the empty tomb, as can be seen when its place in the narratives of the other evangelists is examined.

(c) Matthew

The Marcan version of the discovery of the tomb receives considerable embellishment from Matthew, including highly legendary accounts of the rolling back of the stone, an earthquake and the descent of an angel. This is followed by an appearance to the women (only two in Matthew's version), and the story of the bribing of the guard to say that the disciples had stolen the body, the latter as the basis for a slander that 'has been spread among the Jews to this day' (Matt. 28.15). The actual appearance in Galilee is narrated in the briefest possible manner, and the emphasis is upon the missionary import of the raising of Jesus expressed through the command to make disciples of all nations.

Once again, it does not seem that the empty tomb as such is offered as any kind of proof of the resurrection. It requires here not only the words of the messenger at the tomb, but also an appearance of Jesus to the women to interpret it, and in addition a further elaboration to substantiate the claim that the story of the empty tomb was not due to fraud. Here the empty tomb narrative does not function as apologetic for the resurrection, but is itself the occasion of anti-Jewish apologetic, both in the form of the invitation to the women to inspect the grave-clothes and of the account of the bribing of the guards. If anything, this story suggests that the empty tomb tradition could be an embarrassment which (from an apologetic point of view) were better done without. It is also highly significant that the narrative of the earthquake and of the rolling away of the stone by an angel does not include an account of 'the resurrection itself': The empty tomb has to be explained, and the raising of Jesus is offered as the explanation by subsequent inference. The raising of Jesus is not part of the original tradition about the discovery of the empty tomb.

(d) Luke

Of the four evangelists, it is Luke who comes nearest to wishing to offer what we should call evidence of the raising of Jesus, and to plead for it more in the manner of a historian. He asserts that Jesus showed himself alive to his disciples after his death 'by many proofs' (Acts 1.3), portrays the risen Lord as eating on the occasion of one of the appearances (Luke 24.36–43), and effects the use of the discovery of the empty tomb as the first sign to the disciples of the raising of Jesus (Luke 24. 22–24).

Yet even here it is made clear that the finding of the tomb was not itself something which led to the inference of the resurrection. For not only is there still present an angel to interpret the sign to the women (this time with the assertion that the raising had been foretold not only in the scriptures but also in the words of Jesus himself), but also the report of the empty tomb is said to have been incredible to the other disciples.

Returning from the tomb they told all this to the eleven and to all the rest. Now it was Mary Magdalene and Joanna and Mary the mother of James and the other women with them who told all this to the apostles; but these words seemed to them an idle tale and they did not believe them (24.9 – 11).[23]

Later, on the journey to Emmaus, the two disciples tell the stranger:

Moreover, some women of our company amazed us. They were at the tomb early in the morning and did not find his body; and they came back saying that they had seen a vision of angels who said that he was alive. Some of those who were with us went to the tomb, and found it just as the women had said; but him they did not see (24.22 – 24).

According to Luke, neither the women who saw the empty tomb nor the disciples who were told of it were thereby persuaded of the resurrection.

Luke's apparent concern with 'proofs' also renders surprising the way in which he uses the appearance to Simon. It is clear from the Pauline tradition as well as from other evidence[24] that there was a strong tradition that there was a first appearance of the risen Lord to Peter, and that this determined to some extent the position which Peter came to hold within the life of the church. Yet not only does Luke fail to elaborate the story — it would appear he had no description of it — but he introduces it quite awkwardly at the end of another incident (24.33 – 35).

There is therefore some need to ask what it was that Luke thought had been 'proved' by the resurrection appearances. Acts 1.3, where 'proofs' are mentioned, continues with the reference to Jesus' 'appearing to them during forty days and speaking of the kingdom of God'. The account of Jesus' eating with the disciples is preceded by a reference to their doubt and anxiety on first seeing him, because they imagined they were seeing a spirit. What they are offered, by being allowed to touch and to see him, is the assurance that 'It is I' (Luke 24.39). Furthermore, the eating is followed by additional exposition of the words which Jesus had spoken 'while I was still with you' (24.44) and of the Old Testament.

This 'It is I' is the burden of the 'proofs' which Luke offers. The issue is the identity of the one whom the disciples experienced (and therefore whom the disciples were preaching and whom their hearers were experiencing in the life of the church), and it is this which the tomb, the eating and the exposition are all intended to confirm. This identity is a total one, as was necessary for it to be an identity at all;

but the tomb and the eating subserve the identity which is of first importance, that of the words. Jesus spoke after his resurrection of that which he had proclaimed before his crucifixion, of the kingdom of God, and in this way the stories give proofs of the authenticity of the apostles' proclamation. What is remarkable in view of this is the way in which the failure of the individual 'proofs' to prove anything is allowed to come through in the completed narrative. If they prove the resurrection of Jesus at all they do so only inasmuch as they establish the identity between the preaching of the church and that of the earthly Jesus. The resurrection functions for Luke as the crucial link between the Jesus of the gospel and the church of Acts, and the proofs which he offers show only that what the reader decides about the latter will also involve his decision about the former.

(e) John

In John's version again, nobody, with the possible exception of the beloved disciple,[25] is convinced of anything by the empty tomb. There is a good deal of detail about the linen clothes, but it is not until Mary (who is in John the only woman to visit the tomb) meets Jesus that any connection is made between the empty tomb and the conviction that Jesus has been raised. Even then, the encounter with Mary (John 20.11ff.) clearly leaves ample room for doubt and failure in recognition, a theme which reappears with the encounter between Jesus and Thomas (20.24ff.). Here it is significant first of all that Jesus allows himself to be recognized by Thomas through the feeling of his wounds, and secondly that a story apparently designed to offer proof of the reality of the raising of Jesus should end with the words, 'Blessed are those who have not seen and yet believe' (v.24). Inasmuch as proof is being offered at all, it seems to be proof of identity, in this case with the one who was crucified. This appears to be the purpose for which the account of the empty tomb is also used. The Jesus who was raised is the Jesus who ministered among them and was crucified. But this kind of proof is neither to be clung to (cf. 20.17) nor to be regarded as conferring status upon those who receive it. This is the elusive aspect of the Johannine resurrection narratives. That they are present at all in a work where the glory of Christ shines through at every point in his ministry, and particularly in the death itself, is remarkable, as has already been pointed out. The fact that the appearances exhibit such a strong element of mystery and so little that is magical and compelling means that their purpose requires some other explanation than that the author thought they had power of themselves to convince.

The appendix to the gospel, ch. 21, is of the same elusive character. The catch of fish with its missionary implications is followed by an account of a breakfast which bears a strong resemblance to a eucharistic meal. There is no attempt to make clear, let alone to stress, that Jesus the risen Lord ate with the disciples, and the emphasis in the story as we now have it lies rather on authentication of the position of Peter and the beloved disciple in the church than on vindication of the resurrection.

(f) Summary

What comes through from an examination of the resurrection narratives of the four evangelists and of Paul's recital of the tradition of the raising of Jesus is an insistence on certain details about the reality of the resurrection, aimed at confirming the identity of the risen one with the Jesus whom the disciples had known and followed, together with what is from the point of view of historical reconstruction a very strange reluctance to press any kind of proof home. We have noted the numerous discrepancies between the accounts: the differences of location with regard to the appearances, the differences of their order and number, the discrepancy in the number of women visiting the tomb and so on. Certainly there does not appear to have been any common effort in the church to produce some authoritative account of what took place. As was seen in the previous chapter, some theologians find this encouraging.

Moreover, what is the case as between the different accounts is also the case within them. The Jesus who is raised is the Jesus who was crucified; his raising is a reality within the world inhabited by the disciples. Yet the nature of the reality of the resurrection is not described, if by reality is meant that which physically occurred. Clearly the writers were handling certain traditions, about a tomb and about appearances to the disciples; yet in so far as they stress the reality, the corporeality, of the resurrection, this is not for the purpose of historical verification, but of theological proclamation. The reality that it is Jesus who speaks and that it is Jesus who is alive is safeguarded, as is his new-found presence within the real world in which the disciples also live. But the pictures of the resurrected Lord vary no less than the pictures of Christ's ministry vary, with the diverse memories and concerns of the several evangelists. The factuality of Jesus' resurrection is not a proof, nor is it proved; it is part of the message each one has to tell. The various theological motifs which have been shown in the earlier sections of this chapter to be linked with the resurrection seem to be held together by another; namely, that these new understandings were to be attributed to the Jesus who had lived and died and who, in the same world as that in which he had lived and died, presented himself to his closest followers and, with the authority given by God's act in raising him from the dead, called them to continue his mission, proclaim his future and offer his life.

The Resurrection of Christ and Theological Understanding

In our search for the nature of the original resurrection faith, it is now possible to offer some tentative conclusions in connection with the major concern to be found in the present theological debate about the resurrection. That concern is whether the resurrection was believed primarily as a complex of theological ideas, or whether at the core of it there was a belief in something that had happened. Five theological motifs which cluster around the resurrection idea in the New Testament have been described and illustrated: judgment, mission, Christ's exaltation as Lord, the new hope for the future and the new life. It could not be shown that the culture of the New Testament period would provide the evidence needed for assuming either that resurrection language was readily available for the use of the earliest disciples, or that these theological motifs were part of some pre-existent complex. Indeed, in so far as these ideas were current in the Judaism of the period, they suffered very considerable change when they became part of the earliest Christian proclamation.

Further, these theological motifs, although appearing along with the resurrection of Christ, have an independent life of their own; they frequently appear without any mention being made of the raising of Jesus. Christ's exaltation as Lord, for example, appears very often on its own, as has been said. The account in Luke 10.1 - 20 of the sending of the seventy would in theory have been a suitable peg on which to hang an understanding of mission, just as the curing of the palsied man might well have been sufficient basis for the assertion that the new judgment had dawned in which 'the Son of man has authority on earth to forgive sins' (Luke 5.24). The New Testament hope does not only appear in conjunction with the resurrection, and mention has already been made of the way in which the concept of life is used in the fourth gospel, without allusion to the concept of resurrection which, indeed, would have been unlikely to commend the gospel to its readers. The question then arises why it was thought necessary to base these concepts on, or at any rate link them to, that of the resurrection of Christ, when, if persuasiveness were the objective, it would seem to have been better to base them on something less open to misunderstanding and doubt.

On the one hand, therefore, the resurrection is linked to a variety of theological concepts all of which can appear independently of it and therefore do not seem to depend absolutely on it; these ideas appear in the stories of the resurrection and yet can exist apart from them. On the other hand, we have noted features of the resurrection stories which appear to have been recorded with the sole motive of persuading the reader that the stories are factual before any particular implications are drawn from them. These two points together should provide some clue for an answer to the question whether the resurrection of Christ is a concept expressing a series of other convictions, or whether it is, in some sense, a conviction in its own right. The case of the fourth gospel seems the most persuasive one of all. Here it is even more clear than in the synoptics that much of the post-resurrection faith has been projected back into the lifetime of Jesus and into his ministry. The lengthy discourses and their ever-present theme of the exalted Christ would seem to make the crucifixion the logical place for the gospel to end, at the point where 'It is finished'. The whole of the gospel appears to lead up to this point. And yet the resurrection stories remain. It is hardly possible to suppose that they are there purely to stress the theological points which the evangelist wished to make about Jesus and which he had already made many times. A far more likely reason is that although John's theological scheme did not require resurrection stories, they were central to the received tradition of belief. Given that they were, John used them, as he used the other traditions of which he was aware, to proclaim the Christ of his faith. Yet had the tradition not held the resurrection to be central to belief and indeed creative of it, the stories might not have remained. It is not without significance that the Marcan tradition of the transfiguration does not appear in the fourth gospel; rather the implications of it are stated in the prologue and reaffirmed by the glorified Christ who speaks throughout. The fact that the theological implications of the resurrection have been similarly spelled out throughout does not, apparently, dispense the evangelist from including accounts of that which, it is surely right to conclude, he regarded as central to his understanding of Christ.

Despite the failure of the evangelists and Paul to give the kind of attention which we might expect to the verification of the resurrection, it is an almost inescapable conclusion that in the structure of the faith of the earliest Christians the resurrection was believed to have been a reality which led to certain theological implications and not just a way of talking about those consequences. Yet there remains the absence of a coherent, let alone an authoritative, account of what took place, and the question remains unanswered of how the resurrection came to be believed by the large number of those who, from the very earliest days, had not seen the Lord. It is of course possible to deal with this problem by ascribing to the earliest converts a degree of credulity which enabled them to accept stories on evidence which we should find too scanty to support the idea of so miraculous an event. Whether or not this is so, the resurrection of Christ is in fact related at various points to aspects of belief and experience in the life of the early church, in a way that suggests that it was never intended that people should accept the resurrection as a bare fact bereft of its implications. Indeed there is evidence in the conclusion of the parable of Dives and Lazarus (Luke 16.19 – 31)[26] that the early church had good reason to understand that such a miracle could only elicit faith in conjunction with an acceptance of the demands of God. 'Abraham said, "If they do not hear Moses and the prophets, neither will they be convinced if someone should rise from the dead." ' Belief in the fact of the resurrection there certainly was among the early Christians, but it appears to have been felt always to go along with beliefs and experiences of quite a different sort. The five theological motifs to which reference has been made are not merely, it appears, ideas which came to be linked with the resurrection for some reason, but realities to be experienced in the Christian community, without which the factuality of the resurrection of Jesus could make no difference. The story of the raising of Lazarus in John 11.45 – 53 appears to be an acting out of this parable, and the Jews react not with belief, but with fear, and conspire to put Jesus to death. So it is that the bare fact of a resurrection does not elicit faith.

We have therefore to do justice both to a belief in the factual content of the resurrection faith, and to a belief that the resurrection faith was only available to those who had also had a different kind of experience of justification by the new justice, of the sovereignty of Christ and of their participation in mission. All these things were felt to owe their origin to the resurrection of Christ, and yet without them the resurrection of Christ could not be perceived. It is significant that, with the sole exception of the rather legendary embellishments of Matthew's account (embellishments which appear, incidentally, in his narrative of the crucifixion as well as in that of the resurrection) there is no attempt to show the resurrection or the appearance of the risen Christ as being in any sense public events. Even the largest appearance of which we hear, the one to more than five hundred, is shown by Paul's use of the word 'brethren' to have been to believers; it was only seen, that is to say, by those who also had experienced in their lives those realities which the resurrection of Christ was believed to imply.

It is then possible to conclude that no account of belief in the resurrection will do justice to the New Testament material if it either makes the resurrection believable only in a purely factual sense, or makes it depend solely on the rise of faith in the believer. We are dealing here with something which was believed to be an event that focused a whole variety of the beliefs and experiences of a community, and which was also perceived as the origin of those experiences. This event was apprehended as the model by which the whole experience of the believer, as well as what he understood to have been the experience of his master, could be both described and judged. More than this; it was an event which so far formed the model for the life of the believer that the initiation of believers into the church was by means of a rite which was seen as a re-enactment of the Lord's experience.

> By baptism we were buried with him and lay dead, in order that as Christ was raised from the dead in the splendour of the Father, so also we might set our feet upon the new path of life (Rom. 6.4, NEB).

It may be for this reason that the rite of baptism itself had later to be understood as having originated in a command of the resurrected and exalted Lord. 'Go therefore and make disciples of all nations, baptizing them in the name of the Father and of the Son and of the Holy Ghost' (Matt. 28.19).

In considering the experience not of those who themselves claimed to have seen the Lord but of those who responded to their proclamation, it begins to appear that the situation for believers in the first century was not so different from what it would have to be now. There was no direct access to the fact; it could not be 're-experienced' in the way that it had been by the first witnesses. Indeed the claim to be able to repeat those experiences is one which Paul most strongly resists. There was access only to the fact as it had been experienced and believed by others, and as it was being enacted in the life of the believing community. That it still seemed to matter that it was an event in this world had itself enormous theological implications in the struggle of the church to prevent itself from becoming a gnostic sect, committed to salvation for the believer but to continuing despair about the future of the world. Already in the New Testament itself we see the believing community guarding against despair of the world by its insistence that the resurrection of Christ had been in the world and for the world.

The Resurrection of Christ in the Circle of Belief

The conclusion that no account of belief in the resurrection will do justice to the New Testament material if it either makes the resurrection believable in a purely factual sense or makes it only a precipitate of the experience of the believer still leaves open the question, what kind of a thing was belief in the resurrection of Christ. What did those who wanted to elicit that faith in others say about it when they proclaimed the resurrection? What would an Easter sermon to a group of converts or prospective converts have sounded like? What was the content of the resurrection faith, that is, not in some theoretical sense of what the structure of rationality supporting that faith was or in our eyes should have been, but in the sense of how the proclamation of the resurrection actually worked for its hearers?

It has to be said at once that this question cannot be given anything like a complete answer, first because we are supplied with nowhere near sufficient evidence, and secondly because it is asked from the standpoint of a philosophical and psychological self-consciousness which is very much part of our time, but had no part in the thought-pattern of the New Testament period. To be able to distinguish between the rational structure of faith and the way in which faith arose in people is not any part of the equipment which a Paul or a John brought to their tasks, so that we should be endeavouring to discover from material provided for quite a different purpose the answers to a number of questions which would not have occurred to the writers themselves. Thus the resurrection of Christ as an idea shares in the difficulties common to many, if not to all, biblical concepts. To say that the question cannot receive a complete answer is not, however, to say that the search for such an answer might not bring to light some strong hints about the kind of things which contributed to the faith of the earliest believers.

An account has already been given of the features which made up the resurrection faith: the new judgment, the lordship of Christ, the mission of the Christian community, its hope and its offering of life, all bound together by an element we can only call factual, however confused the facts may now appear. It has then to be asked how these aspects were proclaimed and how they were received both separately and together. The evidence available suggests strongly that what made this proclamation credible, and what made up its primary, if often unexpressed, content was the life of the community of Christian believers. This link between the life of the believing community, begun in baptism, and the experience of Christ in his death and resurrection, is clearly brought out, for example, in the passage already quoted, Romans 6.3 – 11 (NEB):

> Have you forgotten that when we were baptized into union with Christ Jesus we were baptized into his death? By baptism we were buried with him, and lay dead, in order that, as Christ was raised from the dead in the splendour of the Father, so also we might set our feet on the new path of life. For if we have become incorporate with him in a death like his, we shall also be one with him in a resurrection like his. We know that the man we once were has been crucified with Christ, for the destruction of the sinful self, so that we may no longer be the slaves of sin, since a dead man is no longer answerable for his sin. But if we thus died with Christ, we believe that we shall also come to life with him. We know that Christ, once raised from the dead, is never to die again; he is no longer under the dominion of death. For in dying as he died he died to sin, once for all, and in living as he lives, he lives to God. In the same way you must regard yourselves as dead to sin and alive to God, in union with Christ Jesus.

Baptism, then, and the life of the believing community, are understood as a re-enactment of the death and resurrection of Jesus in the lives of believers. How did this link come to be made, and how could it possibly be appropriated by those initiated into the life of the church? The visual impact of baptism by immersion would hardly have conjured up death-resurrection imagery on its own; it is far more likely that it was the continuing proclamation of the death and resurrection of Jesus and the concomitant experience of the new justice lived out in the Christian church that gave new meaning to a rite that would otherwise have remained pre-eminently if not exclusively a symbol of cleansing, but which instead came to be the determinative symbol of the beginning of the Christian life, understood as life in Christ.

The explanation of the way in which resurrection came to be linked with so wide a selection of theological ideas and religious experiences must lie in the coincidence of certain other events and conflicts in the life of the community of believers; it was these which enabled the connection to be made. The points already mentioned in connection with resurrection faith, those of the new justice and of mission, appear to be the most important in this connection. The whole issue of the reaction of the Judaizers to the Gentile mission, and therefore of the nature of the justification offered to mankind, presented, as is well known, the earliest and one of the most severe challenges to the unity of the church. The fact that this conflict resulted in the end in what appears to be a victory for Paul's point of view meant that faith in Jesus Christ as Lord became the criterion of, and baptism the rite of admission into, the true Israel. Thus the new community and its mission were themselves seen to be founded upon that radical reappraisal which we have called an overturning of values, or the new justice. The believer was invited to participate in a rite of admission and in a confessional statement, 'If you confess with your lips that Jesus is Lord and believe in your heart that God raised him from the dead, you will be saved' (Rom. 10.9), which, as it were, completed a circle of ideas which then looked 'all of a piece'. The ideas of salvation without the works of the law, of a mission to all men, of the exaltation of the crucified Christ, of the resurrection, of the rite of admission in which the ·death and resurrection of Christ were re-enacted and shared with the believer, all these held together. Resurrection, mission, exaltation, the new justice, life and hope were proclaimed by a new community into which the believer was invited. That community was based upon those ideas and gave admission by means of a rite which summed them up and knitted them together. At the moment of the believer's confession and subsequent baptism, this cluster of ideas and beliefs joined in a mutually confirming circle of ideas, beliefs and experiences.

If this notion of a circle of interrelated ideas, beliefs and experiences is in any way descriptive of the proclamation and reception of the resurrection faith, then the complexity and simplicity of the resurrection faith begins to reveal itself. The circle is complex, because there is no single idea that can be regarded as that which was proclaimed above all the others, as that on which all the others were based. The ideas themselves made sense in the company of experiences available to the believer and of the stories of the encounters which he was told the first disciples had had with the Lord after his crucifixion; when the new believer declared his faith that the Lord had been raised from the dead it was this total complex that was in his mind. Yet the circle of belief is simple, because it seems that what was actually proclaimed, behind and beyond the particular items of the proclamation, was the coherence of a number of elements. The story of Easter was told; salvation in Christ apart from the works of the law was offered; an invitation was issued to participate in Christ's mission and in a community seen to be founded upon a new kind of justice. All these elements cohered in the one gospel which the early church proclaimed.

It was because primitive Christianity had this character and proclaimed this kind of resurrection gospel that its proclamation had durability. For it could outlast necessary changes in any one of its ideas. The identity of the coherence in each succeeding generation is not dependent on the survival within the culture of each of the ideas separately. It was for example possible to bring into the circle of related ideas fresh ones which related to the understanding and expectations of different cultures without destroying the faith itself. Thus Jesus could in the fourth gospel be proclaimed as the Word, still within the coherence given by his resurrection. Or in the pastoral epistles language could be used which has more in common with Hellenistic epiphany religions than it has with the Jewish background from which the resurrection faith came.

> He was manifested in the flesh,
> vindicated in the Spirit,
>   seen by angels,
> preached among the nations,
> believed on in the world,
>   taken up in glory (I Tim. 3.16).[27]

The writer, who is probably quoting a Christian hymn, does not mention the resurrection, and he relies entirely on the imagery of revelation and glorification for the new situation to which he was writing.

Yet this very fact about the resurrection faith which accounts for its durability is also its greatest risk. For the capacity of such a circle of belief to absorb what is new and to be related to new situations is what exposes it to the possibility that radical changes, altering its entire significance, could be introduced almost unnoticed. It is no coincidence that the writer of I Timothy, while himself able to make use of new cultural idioms, has also to devote considerable attention to the definition of what is orthodox. The question is thus raised — and it is crucial to the history of Christian doctrine — whether the coherence of belief must of necessity have a starting point or, to change the metaphor, whether the circle of interrelated ideas and experiences does not by its nature require a centre. Without this, by defining faith as the felt coherence of a number of ideas, have we in effect returned, or made it possible to return, to Bultmann's equation of the resurrection of Christ with the rise of the Easter faith?

It has been shown that within the original resurrection faith there was an important 'factual' element. The description of it as the raising of Christ, with the implications it had for the new justice and for mission, was only possible for people in whose world the expectations of Jewish eschatology played a vital role. That eschatology has been shown to have defined what was meant by proclaiming that Jesus had been raised, but it has also been shown how much it had to be revised to allow the resurrection proclamation to be made. For when Jesus was raised from the dead the first casualty was the idea of resurrection. In proclaiming the resurrection as the resurrection of *Jesus*, the disciples contributed without knowing it to the demise of that world-view in which such a proclamation, in those words, could continue to be understood as they intended it to be. The proclaiming of the resurrection of Jesus meant the end of Jewish eschatology and with it the Jewish idea of resurrection; it was no longer that wholly future event which would right the wrongs of the world; it was now that which had taken place and which defined both the present and the future destiny of the world. With the end of the idea of resurrection as that wholly future event that awaits the world it has been necessary for subsequent generations of Christians to appropriate the idea of resurrection as on the basis of very different meanings.

But because the early Christians described what they had experienced as the ground of their faith, using the language and expectations of their time, as 'resurrection', they ensured that whatever cultural expectations have determined the way in which Christianity has subsequently presented itself, there remains a central starting-point within the coherence of belief. For belief is, by the proclamation of the resurrection, tied to Jesus, and that link has served from time to time to bring to light some of the more catastrophic deviations around which some Christians' beliefs have centred. It is an elusive link because it cannot be defined in advance at what point the proclamation that it is Jesus who has been raised will impinge upon and correct the belief of any generation. It was the conviction of the earliest Christians that the experience they called the resurrection had to do with their expectations about the last things that enabled them to understand the experience at all. It was their conviction that those experiences had essentially and irrevocably to do with something that had happened in and through Jesus that freed them from enslavement to their cultural presuppositions and has allowed others subsequently to find that their expectations have been fulfilled, but with similar judgment and correction, by what has happened in and through Jesus. The language of resurrection, its imagery and its rhetoric, has of course been used from time to time with scant regard for historical questions, but inasmuch as the historical questions arise from the link between the gospel and Jesus, and therefore from the belief that the world has somehow to be understood in terms of what happened to Jesus, resurrection language remains irrevocably tied to the questions about what actually did happen to Jesus. That is the reason why the factuality of the resurrection remains the essential starting-point in the coherence of Christian belief. The difficulty is that while it is the starting point, there never has been a time, and, as has been shown, the earliest days of Christianity were certainly not a time, when the starting-point was accessible without the rest of the circle of ideas. What has been clear in looking at the New Testament, as it was clear in looking both at contemporary expressions of the Easter faith and at the theological debate, is that it is only the matching life of a community that makes it possible for the resurrection to be known. What Smart, who was quoted at the end of the last chapter, calls the many dimensions of resurrection faith were certainly present in the New Testament community; it was the interaction of communal experience with the Easter story that engendered belief and it is for such interaction in our time that we are looking.

5

MANY WAYS OF LOOKING

So many different things have now found a place in our looking for the resurrection of Jesus — the beliefs of the present day, the debates of theologians, the ideas of the New Testament period. A search including so many elements is an unusual kind of search, certainly very different from searches which concentrate all their energies on one method, historical research, personal experience or evidence for survival. This multi-dimensional search is not undertaken out of a desire needlessly to cloud the issues, but because of the particular kind of belief which the Easter faith is.

Belief is varied and beliefs are many. It is possible to believe in the restoration of capital punishment and in fairies, but not in the same sense. Police evidence and the Apostles' Creed are both said to be believed, but again the nature of the believing is not the same in the two cases. A person may say he believes something meaning that he is somewhat uncertain about it, but on the other hand he may mean he is more certain of it than anything else. So we need to ask what is involved in a claim to believe in the resurrection.

Few believers would appreciate the suggestion that the claim to believe in Jesus' resurrection is to be compared with the claim to believe in fairies, and yet their hearers, if they are not themselves believers, might well feel that it is the same kind of claim, that is, a claim to accept the occurrence of some doubtful or at any rate controversial phenomenon. The distinction between the raising of Jesus and the existence of fairies is self-evident to one who believes in the former but not in the latter; to one who believes in neither the difference is not so obvious. Certainly 'believe' is used in this sense when it is recognized that some controversy exists as to the truth of what is being believed; we do not ordinarily say that we believe in matters about which everybody is in agreement, like the Battle of Waterloo or the solar system. In this sense, believing means taking sides in a controversy which is acknowledged to exist, and in a debate which is expected to continue with the marshalling of evidence, or in which no certainty is available. That is why the non-believing hearer, confronted with a claim to believe in the resurrection, associates it with other affirmations made about doubtful phenomena.

The believer, on the other hand, will feel a certain unease about putting the resurrection of Jesus among the category of doubtful occurrences, and this unease would not only be because of a sense, which might well be there, that there was a degree of irreverence about a comparison between the resurrection and fairies. His unease would also stem from an awareness of the very considerable difference in the nature of the belief in the two cases. Part of the difference lies in the nature of the thing being believed in and part from the nature of the believing act itself. Believing Christ to have been raised is believing that there is one to whom ultimate allegiance is owed, and therefore the believing contains an essential element of trust and obedience. The believer senses that belief in the resurrection has about it a quality of finality and of ultimacy, that beliefs about other doubtful entities do not have. He would regard his statement of belief as a statement not of a willingness to discuss an admittedly doubtful matter of fact, but rather of a conviction about something which he would consider verified in his own experience and justified by the effect which it had, or at least which he was hoping to let it have, upon the quality of his own life. He would probably be willing to enter into debate with his doubting hearers, but with a reluctance born of the knowledge that his recital of New Testament evidence was only part of the story, and that the other part could not be spoken because it was not included in the terms of reference of a discussion about a dubious historical occurrence.

That reluctance might well be accepted by the non-believer also, on the grounds that belief in the resurrection of Jesus came within the category of beliefs called 'religious'. Such beliefs constitute a type which is recognized as having certain privileges. It is understood in our culture, and especially by those who hold no religious beliefs, that some people have them and that on the whole there is no disputing with them or accounting for them. It is understood, further, that such beliefs are peculiarly impervious to argument, and that therefore they deserve to be considered immune from that kind of attack just because they appear to be so mysterious. They are thought, on this understanding, to belong to a person's private, inner life which it ill behoves any other person to try and disturb, to the interior area also recognized today as conscience, which deserves privilege precisely because it brooks no opposition, and has to be permitted to continue just because it does continue, in some inexplicable way, to exist. Such a privileged position might well be offered in a debate to the one who believes in the resurrection of Jesus.

Some believers would be happy to accept this privileged position, because they see their belief to be grounded in just that inner area to which privileged status is being accorded. They know that faith is a gift, and that belief in the resurrection has been accepted by some and rejected by others from the very beginning, and for no accountable reason. They would affirm the resurrection as an event, but would consider that belief in it rests primarily on present religious experience, and that it is that present experience which decides how the historical evidence is assessed. They would say that it was a historical event, but not merely that; and their manner of argument would soon make it clear that it was in fact the contemporary experience of resurrection that was the real object of their belief.

This view of the nature of religious belief has been developed by R. M. Hare,[1] who regards religious beliefs as belonging to the category of those beliefs which, while indispensable as presuppositions for our discourse about the world, are nevertheless not verifiable or falsifiable by the normal methods we apply to our beliefs. Such logically peculiar, basic, beliefs he designates with the German word *Blick*. Religious beliefs belong to this category because, although not about facts within the world or events within the succession of history, they are expressions of the way in which the whole of the world and of history are understood by the believer.

But this privileged position is most unattractive. It suggests rightly that religious belief relates to more than some particular thing that is alleged to have happened; but on the other hand it makes such beliefs immune from the tests which we normally apply to convictions that something has happened in the life of the world. This would be to make of faith a belief about the world as a whole which had no specifiable implications about any particular thing within the world. This immunity from attack, therefore, is purchased at too high a price, because it inevitably works in both directions. If belief is not open to historical dispute, neither is disbelief. With immunity goes a loss of encounter with the thought of the hearer and the issues of contemporary life. The security of the resurrection faith is then the security only of a person's private world, and no such security would be adequate recompense for the loss of touch with that strand of the New Testament proclamation which insists that the resurrection of Christ is something which occurred within the world of time and drastically affects what we are to make of that world. Religion, if it is only a presupposition about everything, may cease to be about anything at all, an inner conviction which has no describable reference.

We are not however forced to choose between resting belief solely on the uncertainties of historical criticism and a privileged certainty achieved at the cost of losing all claim to be about anything within the life of the world; it is perhaps only because these appear to be the choices that so many opt for one or the other without considering other possibilities. One such possibility would take into account the fact that belief, in the Christian sense, has always connoted, as well as belief in the existence of something and an inner personal conviction about how things are, the idea of personal trust. *Credo in unum Deum* is not merely a statement of belief in the existence of a doubtful entity or a profession of personal conviction that there is one who surpasses what we can see and touch; it is also the expression of personal trust in God. In the same way, resurrection faith is not belief that Christ has been raised without being at the same time trust in the risen Lord. In speaking of personal trust, however, it is not necessary to limit consideration to the dimension of the individual. The question where trust is to be placed is one which can also be asked about communities, for they also, as has been said, locate their loyalties and commit themselves to certain values implicit in obedience to someone or something beyond themselves. Israel's trust in Yahweh was not primarily an individual matter, nor the sum total of the private convictions of the Israelites; it was the stance by which the life of the whole community was decided, and a trust in one who was the Lord of the whole community's life.

Personal trust, and the trust of the Christian community, in Christ, were certainly part of the resurrection faith in the beginning. The confession that Jesus Christ was *kyrios* and the Easter faith were united in one of the earliest creeds we can trace, Romans 10.9, and in the word *kyrios* the notions of belief and trust are very closely linked. Nevertheless the idea of personal trust is not one which can rescue the resurrection faith from the uncertainties of the discussion of historical evidence, and absolve it from the quest for the discovery of 'what happened'. On the contrary, if it is the trust not only of individuals but also of whole

communities which is being referred to, the historical question is more
evidently of paramount importance. If the lives of individuals and
communities are to be based on personal trust, then the question of
who is to be trusted is clamant. Thus in the conflict between Bonhoeffer and the German Christians about the Nazi resurrection festivals
the issue was important precisely because it was related to the wider
issue of the *Führerprinzip*, the question, that is, of who was to be
given ultimate trust. According to the prevailing ideology, Hitler was
not simply to be trusted personally, but was to be the one around
whom the entire German nation was to find its identity and its central
role in the future of the world. At that point the question raised by
and for faith in the risen Lord was the question in whom trust was
to be placed or, in Dietrich Bonhoeffer's terms, 'who Christ really is
for us today'.[2] This was certainly a question about the present and the
future; it was also one which could not be left in uncertainty, since
upon the answer to it depended decisions of life and death. Yet the
shape of the answer to it depended upon certain historical judgments
about Jesus and his resurrection, and to the extent that the issue was
'Who is it whom we are to trust?', the accurate characterization of the
kyrios and his claim was of ultimate significance.

    Three relevant senses of the word 'believe' have now been described,
and it is possible to draw certain conclusions from this description.
Resurrection faith cannot be the type of belief that is simply a judgment about a doubtful historical event, because the level of personal
commitment required by it is of a different order from the level ordinarily required by positive conclusions about particular happenings. On
the other hand, the type of belief which concentrates entirely on
personal commitment and inner experience fails to do justice to the
nature of the resurrection which is said to be the object of faith, or to
preserve the connection between the risen Christ and the world for
which that resurrection is claimed to have paramount significance.
Even if belief is considered in the sense of personal trust or the primary
allegiance of a community, the discussion is still thrust in the direction
of history as the only sphere where it might be possible to decide who
is to be trusted and upon what grounds.

    What constantly emerges in the resurrection faith of the New Testa-
ment period is the remarkable and inescapable conviction of the earliest
Christians that they were members of a community to which they had
not themselves simply chosen to belong, but which had been called
into being by something which had taken place and which it was their

task to proclaim; the circle of belief was, as has been shown, the nature of resurrection faith and makes beliefs about the resurrection event itself very difficult to isolate. Giving a contemporary account of resurrection faith involves the added difficulty that the faith of the New Testament church claimed to be about what was true for all mankind. Inasmuch as the gospel had not yet been revealed universally, there was an element of privacy about the faith, but nevertheless as a community the church was proclaiming the truth about all mankind, and that truth was essentially public. A revelation of and by God had taken place in the raising of Jesus from the dead, and this revelation which had occurred within the life of the world was about what was to happen to the life of the world. It is because the resurrection proclamation related to what was to happen, to who was *kyrios*, to who was to be the judge of living and dead, that the questions what *had* happened and *to whom* it had happened were of such importance. The very writing of the gospels on the strength of the resurrection is testimony to the fact that it belonged to Christian faith to specify something about the one who was proclaimed as risen. It is the resurrection of Jesus as discovered within history which guards the point rightly stressed by Marxsen[3] that it is Jesus of Nazareth who has been raised and not another. What requires to be developed and given rational justification is a notion of belief which preserves contact with the world and which none the less contains more than a tentative decision about historical questions.

Appropriation – Belief through Others

We are concerned here with the rationality of belief, that is to say with its logical structure and the form of its argument, but we are concerned with it in the first place not in theory or in the abstract but in relation both to what Christians in the first century were doing when they believed Jesus had been raised from the dead, which is a historical question, and to what leads those in the contemporary situation to believe in the resurrection of Jesus, which is a sociological and psychological question. Biographical analyses about how people come to faith do not, of course, settle philosophical questions about how their conclusions are to be justified, but if resurrection faith has given and gives indications of being logically unusual and of not easily fitting into rational categories, it may be profitable to begin by considering the rationality of resurrection faith not as a set of conclusions but as something which some people have and have had, that is as an action or procedure. It has been pointed out that, with the exception of those who originally claimed to have seen the Lord, resurrection faith has always been encountered at second hand; those who were considering accepting it were always dependent upon the testimony of others. If the biographical question is raised, however, about how believers came to faith, considerable support appears to be lent to the views of those who would wish to separate religious belief from decisions about the uncertainties of historical events. For accounts of religious conversions bear little if any resemblance to conclusions reached at the end of prolonged and tentative debates about evidence.

This is not to say that conversions happen entirely *ab extra*, with no signs whatever of a background. There is frequently a period of dissatisfaction with an existing life-style, and an incident or series of incidents which sow the seeds of doubt about current beliefs or faith in new ones. There may be contact with people of profound faith and influential character who through their concern or courage come to have an importance in the life of a person which leads him to consider more seriously the merits of some different position. Some of this is likely to be there; conversions with none of these elements are exceedingly rare. Yet the significance of the conversion event for the individual experiencing it does not lie in the background or the build-up but in the radical transformation which the conversion brings. The particular content of a given set of beliefs may become almost secondary, and the agents who from the outside seem to have contributed greatly to the process leading up to the conversion itself may disappear again into the background. The arguments and deliberations which may previously have taken place turn into distractions from the real object of the new-found faith. It is no longer a matter of opinion but of conviction. Taking such conversion experiences seriously, is any role left in them for historical questioning?

It is instructive in this context to look at one of the most dramatic accounts of a conversion preserved, that of Paul on the Damascus road. This is the classic instance of conversion, in the sense that it produced the most complete reversal imaginable in a man who, as the story is presented both in Acts 9 and in Galatians, forsakes one set of beliefs for another which he was at that time engaged in persecuting. The story shows no traces of a discussion of evidence (Philip's encounter with the Ethiopian enuch in Acts 8.26-40 might look more like such a debate), but is cast in the form of a confrontation with the one about whom any debate now seemed irrelevant. The event is presented as a Christophany, at any rate to the extent that 'the Lord's' voice is heard, with an effect that is literally blinding. The result is a new person who, despite his own frequent resort to various kinds of argument, has little to say about the evidence for Jesus as he was as a man, but a great deal to say about the life-style and understanding of the world that belongs to being a Christian and to being the church in the world. It is highly doubtful whether such a transformation as this could ever have had its basis in any procedure remotely like modern historical inquiry.

On inspection, however, even this very dramatic instance may have a background which is less insignificant than appears at first sight. The mention of the presence of Paul at the stoning of Stephen (Acts 7.58) on the one hand, and the elaborate arrangements made for his care and rehabilitation among the Christians at Damascus (Acts 9.10 - 25) on the other, both suggest that part of the transformation experienced by Paul was a dramatic change in his relationship to the early Christian community. To see this as a necessary result of his conversion is only part of the truth; the separation of event from results belongs with the error of separating a man's beliefs from his whole history, for coming to belief for Paul was a nexus of change in beliefs on a number of topics, change in pattern of life and change in relationship to the church.

Especially significant for the purpose of this discussion, however, is the fact that there appears at the heart of the conversion itself a reference to the specific person to whom he was now to give his allegiance. In Galatians 1.16 the reference is more allusive, but in Acts 9.5 the voice is quite explicit: 'I am Jesus whom you are persecuting.' The historicity of the details of this account are questionable, but what matters here is that in the presentation of this event a specific and historical reference is made. Like the Old Testament theophanies in which God introduces himself by reference to particular historical people or to the events of the exodus, the appearance to Paul is similarly tied to history.

Thus in one of the most remarkably personal of such conversion experiences, there is distinct reference to the communal and to the historical. Paul was not merely transformed, but transformed in relation to the community of the earliest Christians and in his attitude to a person who is named. He now made his own something that involved not only himself but also other believers and the one to whom they attributed the authorship of their faith. In the case of Paul at least, resurrection faith offers a model that is at the same time personal, social and historical. The words which most accurately describe this making one's own of a belief which has a relationship to the beliefs of a whole community, and which is related to that which brought that community into being is 'appropriation'. For what happens when the resurrection is believed in so as to be made somebody's own involves a totality such as the word 'believe' does not normally suggest, and a process involving a number of distinct elements. In particular, it involves the perception by the believer of a congruity between the character of the story to be appropriated, the community which offers the story for appropriation and his own personal needs and experiences. The analysis offered of this personal experience of coming to belief leads naturally therefore to the discussion of the sociological factors in belief.

Such a sociological analysis concerns the role of the community in which the belief is held. In the specific case of belief in the resurrection of Jesus, it refers to the community of the early Christians, which felt itself called into being by the raising of Jesus from the dead and by the consequent need to declare to all men the imminence of the judgment of the whole world by Jesus. In sociological terms this means considering the church as a community which had a sense of mission, but it needs to be made clear that such a description hardly does justice to the way in which this mission was not merely the function of the early church but was integral to its very existence. It did not see itself as a community which was first called into being and then given a mission; it was called into being as mission, for the church was God's mission to mankind, as Christ had been and was. It claimed for itself, or rather claimed to have been given, the fullness of Christ's function. The church was not simply the community which handed on the resurrection faith; it was itself the handing on of that faith.

As has been previously noted, there appears to have been a very close correspondence between the life within the Christian community in the New Testament period and the theology which it developed in order to express its faith. Both the experience and the theology were felt to reflect what it was like to be the community which took its beginning, its life and its future from the resurrection of Jesus. That beginning was not only an eschatological sign, the beginning of the end, but was also an event filled with meaning for the values by which the community and the individuals within it were to live. This was because it not only spoke of the coming resurrection of the dead, but also because the particular one who had been raised could be named and described. The fact that it was Jesus who had been raised excluded some options for a style of community life and required others. It was Jesus whom God had raised and had thereby made both Lord and Christ, and therefore the resurrection community was the community of his disciples. Conversion therefore involved alliance with the new community just as much as it involved personal reorientation and the believing of the Easter story; it meant making one's own the life of a community, appropriating both its story and its values. The theological position that Paul was led to take up, therefore, in which the gospel of the new community was self consciously proclaimed over against the message of the old, was integral to his having been converted by and to the risen Christ.

It is this communal dimension which is lacking in so many contemporary versions of the resurrection faith. It is commonplace to find the story offered for belief in a way that simply allows it to confirm the believer's hope for immortality but does nothing to compel the believer towards the communal realization of the power of the risen one. An attempt may then be made, by those who have some awareness of the corporate nature of the New Testament proclamation, as it were to graft some corporate implications on to a faith which is expected to be believed on other grounds. The resurrection faith is then essentially a private one with perhaps some communal implications, but these remain implications and cannot become integral to the faith itself. Such a style of faith is not only, as has been shown, discordant with the manner in which the resurrection of Jesus was orginally appropriated, but it also lacks credibility, inasmuch as the Easter story was and is only believable on the strength of the existence of a community in which the values implicit in that story are being acted out. What disappears in a proclamation of the resurrection faith which is not fundamentally corporate is not merely some important implications of that faith, or even some vital elements in its content, but the very rationality which the faith originally had. For its implications, even more its content, and most of all its credibility depended on the fact that it was a proclamation within, by and about the community which it had itself called into being.

But we have to ask, on logical grounds, whether the life of a community telling a certain story is a relevant factor in deciding whether the story is true. Do the canons of rationality normally applied in historical study include as a relevant factor the life-style of the community which holds a certain history, and the congruity of that life-style with the values implicit in that history? The answer to this question, in the vast majority of cases, must be negative. Documents, eyewitnesses, monuments and photographs have something to contribute to the task of arriving at the facts, but that a number of people of unimpeachable character believe a particular story ordinarily does not. If we are to maintain that in the case of the resurrection this is a relevant consideration at the present time, we shall need either to establish a unique claim for the resurrection to be considered along different lines, or else to show at what points it is reasonable to use a believing community's life-style as evidence for the truth of the story it tells.

Acceptance of beliefs on authority is a common experience. It is not possible for everybody to find out everything for himself, and from a very early age the evidence of parents' and teachers' opinions is accepted. There can be no question either that this is regarded as reasonable at that stage, or that it depends upon the relationship of trust between parent and child, teacher and pupil. Generally, however, this is bound to be a second-best procedure for forming opinions which, in mature adult life, are best formed, as far as possible, by the person himself in the exercise of his powers of reasoning and observation. If such verification is not possible, then it may still be considered reasonable for a particular belief to continue to be held, provided this acceptance is provisional and has a tentative quality. This is the first difficulty in making resurrection faith apparently depend on the authority of the community proclaiming it; for acceptance of beliefs on authority is reserved in general for situations where we are too young or too inexpert to form our own conclusions. It may be reasonable to accept a doctor's diagnosis because of his superior training; but can a community rightly claim to show that it has expertise in the fundamental questions of the meaning of existence? It would appear, in any case, that the authority of the New Testament church and of its apostles was established through the truth of the gospel they were proclaiming, and not the other way round. The congruence which has been noted between the life-style of the New Testament church and its message is in no way analogous to the basis on which we are now accustomed to accept expert advice. So what account can we give of the way the life of the first Christians affected the credibility of what they proclaimed?

It was pointed out in the last chapter that the raising of Jesus was understood as making a comment on the righteousness of the Jewish community. This means that the response of the hearer would be greatly affected by the relationship in which he felt himself to stand to that community. Those who found in it acceptance and meaning would be unlikely to accept the claims of a minority who invited them to become followers of a man whom the Jewish community had condemned. (Paul represents a very striking exception.) The 'outcasts of Israel' on the other hand would be far more likely to be drawn into a new community which offered to them what their society had persistently denied them. It was particularly this experience of a new justice that will have made the resurrection faith credible to its first hearers.

The absence of such a factor in the Christian community today, at any rate in Western countries, is undoubtedly relevant to our quest, for the community of the resurrection does not in our society experience much tension between its view of life and that which generally prevails; to this we shall return in the last chapter. But it is important at this point to notice that such a sociological factor in belief also brings with it great dangers. We have already referred to the use of resurrection symbolism in the rise of Nazism, and the plausibility of that imagery to a people for whom the democratic liberalism which prevailed previously appeared to offer no hope at all. It is here that the notion of appropriation differs from that of blind allegiance to a community come what may. Appropriation presupposes an object as well as a subject, something that is available to be made one's own. This external factor, which is the historical content of the resurrection faith, continues to have a life of its own in some degree independent of the community which holds it. It offers an authority to which to appeal and a standard against which to judge the particular life-style and aims of the believing community in the present. The story cannot be appropriated without the community; yet the story once appropriated becomes the community's judge. The events which lie behind the Easter faith continue to have a life of their own, subject at any time to the historian's investigation. To refuse to allow such an investigation of the event, however limited its chances of success, would mean to forfeit its credibility. Likewise a community which claimed the story while rejecting the values implicit in its own origins would have lost the essential congruity which is a vital factor if the story is to be appropriated by anyone else. It is the need for this congruity between fact and value that makes all stories which communities claim as their story at one and the same time totally demanding in the commitment they require and entirely provisional in terms of their vulnerability to historical criticism.

Yet in what way is the resurrection faith open to historical testing? The fact that converts were invited to appropriate the resurrection faith on other than strictly historical grounds, on the basis, that is, of the life-style of the community which proclaimed Christ as raised from the dead, was not merely due to the difficulty of obtaining verification or the time which would need to be spent in doing so. The resurrection of Jesus was something which could in principle not be verified in this way. The original accounts preserve this reticence in failing to give a description of the resurrection itself, and however far it might be possible to go in describing what the first disciples thought happened on the first Easter morning — and it seems hard to get very far at all — there is certainly no chance whatever of arriving at a definitive historical account of the raising of Jesus. This is because of the peculiarly eschatological nature of the resurrection; its subject is God and it stands in a unique relationship to other events in that it is the first of the last events. Appropriation is the only possible rational basis for belief about the resurrection, not because the historical investigation is difficult and the time short, nor because evidence is missing and must be sought for, but as a matter of principle, because the resurrection accounts as we have them are all framed within the context of an eschatological view of history which is not amenable to the procedures of modern historical criticism.

It must therefore be decided whether, in view of this, the provisionality and vulnerability which were stated above to be involved in decisions by appropriation are sincerely meant. Is the resurrection faith offered for acceptance in the genuine belief that subsequent research and discovery could cause a person to change his mind or not? Are the criteria for appropriation really met, and in particular, is there something which can be described and which can stand in some measure independently of the community which tells the Easter story? To put the matter another way, the appropriation of stories told by communities depends generally upon the trustworthiness of the community in question, and that trustworthiness is generally established by the discovery that there certain features of the story they tell which can be checked, and these features are true. The more amazing the story the community offers for belief, the greater the trustworthiness the community will need to establish for the story to be credible. If this is so, we have to ask how much we need to know to trust the church for the rest.

From the beginning, it can be observed that the answer to this question has varied considerably from person to person, and for that reason some have accepted the resurrection faith while others have not. Nevertheless something can be said in general terms. Doubt, it seems, was there from the beginning, and had to be met; allegations of dishonesty were also made and had to be answered. There was a concern, albeit a more limited one than we might wish for, to establish evidence. Some were convinced enough to respond, to act, and to wrestle for a congruity of their lives and that of their community with the substance of the story which they were telling. So far as it is possible to tell, the resurrection came to be believed by those who came to believe it without fraud or duress. When all this has been said, however, the answer given to the doubts, and the evidence produced, come out by modern historiographical standards as less than fully rigorous. There is a concern to insist that something had happened, but, from our point of view, a regrettably cavalier attitude to the modern virtues of precision and consistency. However much the Easter story is only half a story about human beings and the natural world and for the rest a story about God that words cannot adequately express, the fact is that the half that is about human beings has been considerably overshadowed in the telling, even though, despite that, it was never allowed to die. It remained for that community the happening of happenings which each individual had to display symbolically as he underwent death and resurrection at the waters of baptism and actually as the early Christians faced the hostility of the world around them. But the happening itself stood in the unrepeatable past as a sign of the real meaning of all events that were ever to follow it.

That being so, the vulnerability stands, for if it ever ceases to be the case that the resurrection of Jesus is subject to historical criticism the community of the present will come to have control over its own past and will thereby become sole judge and jury as to the values it professes. It is vulnerable to questions about the honesty of intention and the competence of execution of the original storytellers. We may judge their competence as reasonable by the standards of their time and their honesty by the standards of any time. Even if it be that a commitment to the truth of the resurrection faith will always depend on more than questions about the past, because the content of resurrection faith is related to more than the past, it is the indispensable role of the historian to attempt to ascertain what the New Testament writers were endeavouring to say and what their grounds were for saying it.

Yet, as has been pointed out, the resurrection storytellers get their own back because we are vulnerable to them. What they offer is a lofty complex of belief, community and commitment which, as the original resurrection faith, stands in judgment over those versions of resurrection faith which present themselves for acceptance or rejection in every generation.

> The presence of Christ will have to be determined not by a direct succession from a certain point in the past, but rather from such evidence as can be found in the empirical reality of communities whose action can be called redemptive. Wherever communities gather round acts of redeeming love, there we may look for the presence of Christ. The redemptive community of Christ in the world must be seen as ever coming into being again in the empirical history of man. It will be there implicitly wherever the redeeming gestures of love, hope and compassion are reiterated in human experience. It will become explicit wherever those gestures are seen in relation to the God who both created and redeems the world, who may well have been 'in Jesus', but who is ever again present in the human imitations of redemptive love. Every such community, whether implicitly in its action or explicitly in its worship, anticipates here and now the consummation of redemption toward which the world is moving.[4]

Such a theology of the presence of Christ, and therefore of the activity of God, like the theologies of Geering and Williams examined in chapter 2, is certainly to be applauded for what it implies about the present backing needed for the appropriation of the resurrection of Jesus. What it also implies about communities who, with the name church, have appropriated the story of Easter to propagate despair and perpetuate the reign of death is equally true. But such a theology can only be affirmed as true, as a fact of reality rather than a pious hope for what might be, by those who are prepared to engage in the quest implied by Peter Berger's words 'God . . . who may well have been in Jesus', for that quest requires, as well as certain aims for the community which declares Christ as risen, a continuing search for the truth about what happened in and to Jesus.

To summarize this section, it is now possible to say why resurrection faith has the character it has, and why it can only be believed by the process which has been designated appropriation. The resurrection is the name of something which is both historical and not historical; believing the resurrection involves believing something that concerns more than the past; it means being led to certain affirmations about both past and future by the experience of the believing community in the present. It has to be belief through others, because the resurrection itself cannot be traced by the processes of historical investigation.

Nevertheless, the resurrection stands for something which is at least historical. This means that what is appropriated is something which comes, once appropriated, to have a life independent of the community which appropriates it. It is more than what the community of those who believe it happen to accept at a particular time. It cannot be accounted for by, nor reduced to, the rise of faith in believers, because from the beginning believers have wished to say that in appropriating resurrection faith they had discovered something that was able to stand apart from, and if necessary over against, the judgments of any generation. If historical inquiry were able to show that there was nothing beyond the faith of the believers, and that the accounts could be explained entirely by the rise of that faith, then faith would be incredible, for it would ultimately be resting only on itself.

Believers in the resurrection have, then, been led through their membership and experience of the community of which they were a part to the discovery of that which stood beyond the community itself, and that which stood beyond it had reference not only to its own time, the time of the New Testament, but also to all times and places. It spoke not only about its own time but about man's present and future, but in order to do that the resurrection proclamation had at least to be understood as speaking about its own time, to be speaking the truth, that is, about what happened in and to Jesus Christ. Because of this, believers in this generation, with the methods of historical criticism to hand, will seek to do with them what believers of every generation have sought to do, namely to have some direct access to the risen Christ. The tools of historical criticism will lead to uncertainty and will fail, for reasons already stated, to produce agreed answers or a single picture. It is unlikely, as Downing concludes,[5] that there will be any speedy settlement of the historical questions; and yet that is no ground for allowing the questions to go unasked, even if it is recognized that the appropriation of the resurrection faith will depend now, as it always has done, upon the life of the believing community and upon the present experience of the believer. The indispensable role of historical questioning is as the source of renewal and judgment in relation to that experience.

> If a man accepts the prior commitment that here the saving love of God has come through to us most powerfully, there is no other course open than to continue the [historical] debate. To come

closer to the facts is to come closer to the gift. The conviction that here the love of God was most fully focussed will almost certainly be born in some experience of love among Christians today; but 'it is by this we know what love is: that Christ laid down his life for us'. The quest to come, as nearly objectively as possible, closer and always closer to the facts immediately and less immediately involved in this gift of love that we believe that we have received, must (for most if not for all types of Christian faith) be an urgent imperative, integral to that commitment of faith itself — difficult and inconclusive, but imperative.[6]

Belief is, then, both dependent upon and at the same time independent of the community of faith. What the community does is to bring a person closer to that which stands beyond the community as its support and its judge. This meets in some measure the earlier difficulty that resurrection faith understood as appropriation appeared to depend upon the authority of others in a way that jeopardized its being considered strictly rational. For the authority of 'the others' is always judged by that to which they testify. Not any story will do and not any community may tell the story. For authority can in the last resort only belong to the one who, it is claimed, raised Jesus from the dead. If the claim is true, all authority is limited to the extent to which it is able to lead back to the claim itself. The particular rationality of resurrection faith lies in the fact that, as we have shown, it consists of both a claim about the past and experience in the present, and these two elements interlock and support each other.

The Problem of Eschatology

Even if appropriation is a reasonable account of resurrection faith, there is a major problem still about appropriating that faith now. When it was originally proclaimed, the resurrection was part of the Jewish expectation of the last things. It was one thing to seek to persuade those who were awaiting the restoration of God's righteous rule that in a particular man this rule had been re-established; it is quite another to seek to persuade in this way those who have no such expectation. The authority of the New Testament community and the credibility of its preaching depended upon the correlation between the life-style which it displayed and the message which it proclaimed, but only within the specific context of an eschatology which it was possible to presuppose in their hearers. The message of the resurrection of Jesus had therefore a specifically eschatological rationality; the reasonableness, that is, of the decision which people were asked to make was a reasonableness which only arose because of the expectation of the end of all things. The rationality of the resurrection faith therefore is specific to the time and place in which it was first proclaimed, and is as dependent as its content and its implications on the culture in which it arose. The reasonableness of the proclamation of the raising of Jesus from the dead was then tied to the truthfulness of the claim that the end of all things was at hand.

The end of all things did not however take place and has not taken place. The rationality as well as the content of resurrection faith had therefore to change. It is not surprising that this change was in the direction of the individualistic and other-worldly understanding of the resurrection. From the point where eschatology determined the rationality and the content of the central proclamation of Christian faith it was a long but inevitable journey to the point where *scientia eschatologica* became the last item in a theological system and hope beyond the grave became its major content. Expounded often with great brilliance, as in Dante's *Divine Comedy*, resurrection became nevertheless the hope of the individual and no longer the last end of all things. Abelard's language is very clearly that of the eschatological resurrection faith, but its meaning was unmistakably different, as it undoubtedly had to be if the church of the twelfth century was to appropriate the language of the first:

> Now, in the meanwhile, with hearts raised on high,
> We for that country must yearn and must sigh,
> Seeking Jerusalem, dear native land,
> Through our long exile on Babylon's strand.[7]

The problem presses hard in contemporary theology, in that some of the most convincing expositions of the Christian faith in general and of the resurrection in particular, such as those of Pannenberg and Moltmann, depend on the conviction that the eschatological perspective of the first century must be recovered.

Only in connection with the end of the world that still remains to come can what has happened in Jesus through his resurrection from the dead possess and retain the character of revelation for us also. . . . . The delay of the end events, which now amounts to almost two thousand years, is not a refutation of the Christian hope and of the Christian perception of revelation as long as the unity between what happened in Jesus and the eschatological future is maintained. However, the Christian perception of what happened in Jesus will always retain an openness to the future. The ultimate divine confirmation of Jesus will take place only in the occurrence of his return.[8]

Inasmuch as the eschatological world-view of Judaism was presupposed in the proclamation of the resurrection of Jesus, the assumption of that world-view forms an essential element in the attempt to understand the meaning that proclamation had for the earliest disciples. In that sense what is appropriated is not resurrection proclamation on its own, but resurrection proclamation in context. The past can only be understood as the transmission of understanding through the media of the traditions available to the people passing them on. To this extent, Pannenberg's account of the way transmission occurs is entirely reasonable, and, indeed, is confirmed by the account we have given of the New Testament evidence.

> In the individual event something of general import is experienced, something relevant for other individuals. Therefore it is passed on in tradition and received by others. But because these others experience the general differently in new events, tradition is continually modified, even when, as is usually the case in archaic cultures, these alterations are repressed from consciousness.[9]

Yet, if this is the case, what does it mean to appropriate the resurrection faith? Are we concerned to appropriate the eschatological resurrection faith of the New Testament period — and then do we opt for the eschatology of Paul or John? Or do we opt for the resurrection faith of the medieval period, where the concern is still eschatological but has shifted in the direction of assuring the fate of the dead? This problem is raised most acutely for the understanding of the resurrection of Jesus, because of the claim that it is central to the Christian faith, but it can arise in connection with most of the doctrines of the Christian faith. As time passed, they were interpreted in ways which responded to questions implied in the culture to which the church was speaking. This alteration of meaning was, as Pannenberg points out in the last quotation, not always noticed, but with the rise of a historical consciousness such 'repression' becomes no longer possible.

Furthermore Pannenberg seems not to take seriously enough the difference between Jewish eschatology and man's current concern with the future (inasmuch as he has any). The rhetoric of his kerygmatic theology suggests that the second advent of Jesus can do duty as the Christian response to Marx's classless society or Hitler's thousand-year Reich. There is a frequent suggestion that the resurrection of Jesus, and the eschatological perspective in which alone it can be understood, represent a Christian understanding of human destiny. Yet it has already been observed (in chapter 3 above) that views of human destiny do not have much common currency among secular historians. It may well have been the case that it was belief in the existence of a human destiny being unfolded, and available to scientific discovery, which first gave the impetus to modern historical research; but outside Marxist circles that objective hardly remains the inspiration of historians in their work.

Moreover even if history could be expressed in terms of progress towards a human destiny, that would still not take account of the great difference of assumption between Jewish eschatology and modern views of historical advance. In particular, Jewish eschatology rested upon a belief in a God who was pictured as 'dealing with and in history', and in so doing contending with enemies of his purposes who are, in the words of M. J. Buss, 'not primarily mythical powers but are human forces, both within and outside of the elect people'.[10] Even if Buss, in his criticism of Pannenberg, places too much emphasis on the negative elements in Israel's estimate of history, when he says that 'human history is emphasised, not because it is good, but rather because God has to struggle against it'[11], the Jewish understanding of their own history was that it was the sphere of God's activity, not that it was intrinsically good. Even those views of history which continue at the present time to speak of human destiny do so on the basis of the assumption that it is something within the power of man to achieve. This can hardly be represented as a Jewish or a Christian view of the resurrection of the dead.

This change in the way history is thought about is also related to the matter of the centrality of the resurrection of Jesus to Christian faith. Both conservative and radical critics of the New Testament material agree that Paul's dictum 'If Christ has not been raised, then our preaching is in vain and your faith is in vain' (I Cor. 15.14) constitutes not only a true reflection of the views of all the first generation of Christians but the necessary starting-point for any discussion of the content of a contemporary expression of the resurrection faith. This commitment to a single text is, however, odd, since it clearly belongs within the context of the eschatology which Paul presupposes and the mission of which he was speaking. It was in that context that Paul could say that unless Christ was raised his preaching and their faith would be empty. Unless it is possible to take over the Pauline eschatological perspective, there would seem little ground for accepting this particular assertion as having eternal validity.

The relationship between the centrality of the resurrection to Christian faith and the understanding of the resurrection which was made available by the surrounding culture is confirmed by a fact clearly emerging from church history, that what doctrine turned out to be central at a particular time depended on the specific issue of the period. The Trinity, the Incarnation, the sacraments, justification by faith and other doctrines have at various times been central to the faith, and the belief that Jesus had been raised from the dead has, after the first century, very seldom been central in anything more than name.

If it is accepted that the resurrection faith was central to the Christian proclamation in the New Testament period, and that that centrality had to do with the presuppositions of Jewish eschatology by which the resurrection faith was apprehended, then it seems difficult not to relate the loss by the resurrection of its central place in the Christian proclamation to the decline in importance, and the eventual disappearance, of Jewish eschatology as a viable way of understanding the world, even if it remained as an appendage to a theological system. It is therefore necessary to consider further the precise relationship of the resurrection faith to Jewish eschatology, and also what is involved in something being 'central' to the Christian faith at any one time.

The use by the church of the idiom supplied by Jewish eschatology was of course by no means straightforward. That view of life spoke of an end of all things which was entirely in the future, and which, when it had taken place, would be the conclusion of all things, after which there would be no further future. It could not be spoken of in the past tense, and indeed it would never be the case that it could. The proclamation that Jesus had entered upon the end, which was implicit in the declaration that he had been raised from the dead, and that therefore Christians could also expect, at some future time, however imminent, to do the same, represented in itself a radical transformation of the eschatological frame of reference. To this must be added the fact that in the proclamation that it was Jesus who had been raised a new understanding had been given to the idea of God's intervention at the end of all things, as the vindication of those who had been faithful to the law. The resurrection of Jesus put the law in the wrong and justified the ungodly; it proclaimed the redemption not only of the outcasts of Israel but of the Gentile world as well. The idiom of Jewish eschatology was therefore not a mere vehicle of resur-

rection faith; it was that idiom which, as one of the basic presuppositions of a whole culture, allowed the church to be, and to be seen as,
the agency whose gospel would transform and ultimately break the
bounds of that idiom altogether. To regard belief in the resurrection
as involving the assumption of the categories of Jewish eschatology
in the modern world would be to ignore the fact that it was precisely
the proclamation of the resurrection of Jesus which meant that the
days of that world-view were numbered. In this way the enunciation
of the radical transformation occasioned by the gospel of Jesus in
the terms of the resurrection of the dead contributed, paradoxically, to
the inability of resurrection to be used for that purpose at a later time.

Centrality was then assumed by other forms of Christian proclamation. This is not the place to embark on even a short history of Christian doctrine, but it may be suggested that what became the issue in
each age, what appeared in that age to be the central tenet of the faith,
was that which was felt to challenge the framework of thinking of the
culture of that age at the point where that framework placed a con-
straint on the capacity of human beings to perceive and share in the
work of the one who breaks such constraints, and who is known to
Christians as the God who raised Jesus from the dead. The point at
which what a culture allows to be thought also limits what is able to
happen becomes the point of the Christian gospel's central impact, as
it was when it was first said that God had raised Jesus to life.

The rise of historical consciousness has brought about a situation
where these changes in what is central in Christian faith, and the idiom
in which it is expressed, cannot any longer pass unnoticed. It is not
possible to attach new ideas to inherited ways of speaking without
the seams showing, nor is it possible to offer translations of articles
of the faith which do not take account of the cultural impact made
when they were first proclaimed. The centrality is part of the meaning;
to believe Jesus had been raised was essential to being saved, and to
offer an interpretation of the resurrection which lacks that kind of
life-or-death centrality, that urgent statement about what was happening to the world in Jesus, is to offer the words of resurrection without
their meaning.[12] Nothing so eccentric as the issue of man's survival
of death nor so private as a man's personal choice of a new life-style
can begin to be central and therefore to be a valid translation of the
resurrection of Jesus.

Thus the task of translating the resurrection faith, that is, of provid-
ing ways of speaking of it which are exactly equivalent for us to the

words used in the original New Testament witness, is in principle beyond us. In so far as our words refer to resurrection at all or mention
the events which happened to Jesus they plunge us into a world that is
either private or other-worldly or simply past, whereas the words of the
New Testament proclamation plunged their hearers into a new way of
looking at the central purpose of living. We may say that we believe
what the New Testament writers say, but our belief may all too easily
lack the conviction which lies behind all they say, namely that the
limitations of their culture had been transcended by what had happened
to Jesus and that in him they had discovered the new possibility of
living. Our task is therefore to find a way of interpreting resurrection
that is different from what we normally mean by 'believing' or 'translating'.

It was for that reason that it was necessary to speak of appropriating
rather than of believing the story of the resurrection. The resurrection
story can be made their own by those who faithfully live in its wake,
who, that is to say, are engaged in the transcending of the limits of
what our culture allows to be thought in the way that the early Christians did when they proclaimed that Jesus was raised. But that original
proclamation, with all its original force displayed through historical
criticism of the evidence, is there not for belief with more or fewer
reservations, but as it stands to be made their own by those who
would wish in their generation also to believe what their culture calls
impossible. Once appropriated, the resurrection proclamation of the
earliest Christians will not allow a subsequent generation to believe any
impossibility it chooses, for the impossibilities to be believed in each
age are those which bear the marks of continuity with the things which
happened to Jesus. They will concern man's history and his society,
public truth and an expectancy towards the future, and will bear the
marks of the 'mind which was in Christ Jesus' and of the fruits of that
transformed living and thinking which we have noted in the earliest
Christian community.

The contemporary interpreter of the resurrection will do his utmost
to clarify the significance of the raising of Jesus from the dead as it
emerged in the words of the earliest Christians, so that those who
claim the resurrection of Jesus as their story may know what it is they
are appropriating, and so that those who are considering appropriating
it may see what the issues contained in that story are. He will not
obscure, but will rather seek to reveal, the extent to which the language
and impact of the resurrection faith depend upon a context of thought

and circumstance which are not ours and cannot be, and he will not seek to adjust the sense of the New Testament documents in order to make them more congenial or believable in the eyes of a contemporary audience. Such a procedure is not based merely upon an anticipation that the task of harmonizing the evidence will defeat the interpreter and accurate translation into the terms of the present day will elude him, but much more profoundly on the conviction to which the evidence inescapably leads that the proclamation of the raising of Jesus and its acceptance by the Christian community were supremely that which settled the question of the end of all things. In declaring that the end of all things had been set in train by Jesus of Nazareth, the church so transformed belief about the end of all things that very soon the central challenge of the gospel had to impinge on the world in different terms. Yet the stories of the appearances and the discovery of the empty tomb, together with the exposition by Paul and others of the centrality of the raising of Jesus, were preserved in the community which emerged from them not (we may say with hindsight) because the resurrection proclamation remained always the central one, but because the encounter between the resurrection of Jesus and the prevailing idea of resurrection was the encounter by which the community had taken its beginning and by which all subsequent encounters between the gospel and the world were to be recognized.

Nor was this the only reason for their preservation. It was found also that the resurrection of Jesus responded to other needs and answered other questions than those of the world in which it was first proclaimed. The history with which we have been concerned, as Pannenberg rightly points out, is the history of the transmission of traditions, and it has been clear at many points that the meaning of the resurrection has been changed radically as the tradition about it has been handed on. The desire to achieve a single and clear interpretation of the resurrection is invariably a desire to discover which of these subsequent meanings were 'misunderstandings' which no longer have any claim to attention; it can also conceal the fact that anything that is now said about the resurrection of Jesus is no less relative to this time and no less different from the meaning which it originally had than were those intervening misunderstandings.[13] This is a futile pursuit, and for a number of reasons. First, it has been shown already that differences of understanding about the resurrection began very early; the pluriformity of the resurrection proclamation within the New Testament itself is evidence of this. If the only meaning of resurrection which is to be called authentic is the one it had when it was itself the vehicle of the gospel's encounter with the world, then the fourth gospel might have to be regarded as a very early example of a 'misunderstanding'.[14] Secondly, if intervening understandings of the meaning of resurrection are to be regarded merely as misunderstandings, so might those which prevailed in late Judaism and which were the essential prerequisite for the capacity of the resurrection of Jesus to be the point at which the gospel encountered the world. Thirdly, the intervening understandings of the resurrection of Jesus were at least in part ways in which those who were confronting the world with the gospel could continue to speak of the resurrection at all. In doing so they not only responded to the living needs of their hearers, but also kept open a line of continuity between themselves and their beginnings in the New Testament, thus preventing any particular generation's presentation of the gospel from acquiring finality, and keeping themselves open to the one who alone possesses that finality. In theory they held that the period of the church's first beginnings were the unique canon by which its subsequent life was to be judged; in practice, as historical criticism allows us to perceive, the relationship between the New Testament period and subsequent periods was always and inevitably a mutual one.

The history of the transmission of traditions is the history of the preservation of the ways in which the gospel confronted the world at different times. Whatever the role played by the transmission of the tradition of the resurrection of Jesus at different times, it has enabled the questions asked of the world by the gospel to be in continuity with those asked by the raising of Jesus from the dead. Had the language of resurrection faith not been such as to be able to address other issues than those posed by Jewish eschatology (such as man's concern with his fate beyond death) it might not have been preserved at all; we should not then be able to elucidate the nature of the original confrontation of the gospel with the world, let alone to consider what the nature of that confrontation might be in the present age. So the meanings which resurrection has acquired in the centuries which have intervened between Paul and ourselves cannot be simply disowned, nor can the distinctive understanding of history which has emerged in the modern era, an understanding which while different from Jewish eschatology is nevertheless the one which has contributed so much to the elucidation of the complexity of the New Testament resurrection faith. Without a modern view of history there would have been no modern historical research and the eschatological significance of the original resurrection proclamation would not be known to us. To require therefore that the gospel should confront the world now in the language used by Paul, of resurrection and eschatology, is to ignore the many roles which have been played by resurrection language since Paul and to require of modern man that he should sacrifice his own distinctive historical awareness in favour of one which is not only certain to be uncongenial to him but has also been shown by all the evidence to have been unable to contain and survive that which happened in Jesus Christ.

It may even be that the language in which the gospel asks questions of the present world cannot be that of any cosmology yet known. Certainly those which have so far appeared in the history of the world have not seemed able to deal with the radical particularity of historical events, and modern secular history-writing appears singularly impatient of quests for some ongoing purpose which embraces all things. The infinite variety that scientific inquiry into nature and into history has disclosed has made cosmological thinking, of which eschatology may be said to have been one variety, far more difficult than it was in those ages when less was known and therefore more could be said. But cosmological thinking is not the only way in which it is possible to maintain a concern for man as a historical being, and as a person in solidarity with others who have been, are and will be. Those who appropriate the proclamation of the resurrection will continue to expect that in what happens to mankind there will be disclosed not merely meaning, but more specifically those discoveries which will overcome the barriers which are placed in the way of human development by inherited patterns of thought.

The capacity of resurrection faith to release untold power and love in a new community, the church, arose from the fact that in proclaiming that Jesus was risen the church also proclaimed that all the constraints of thought which had been part of Jewish eschatology — its insistence that the re-establishment of God's rule could only come at the end of all things, and that the judgment associated with that rule was to be bound by the values of the law — were at an end. This is the aspect of resurrection faith in the New Testament period which is there to be discovered by any who examine that faith as it was originally proclaimed, but in undertaking that investigation they will not be able to become first-century Jewish Christians, and indeed are likely to become more than ever aware of their inability to do so. Their own speaking of the resurrection, like that of their contemporaries who appropriate it without an understanding of its historical background, is likely to be based on the echoes which it strikes in their own quest for significant living, for hope for the future, for transcendence of death and for a greater capacity to mediate life to others. If, as has been suggested, the continued speaking of the resurrection proclamation has itself carried out a vital role not only in the transmission of the tradition but also in the confrontation of the world with the gospel, there would seem to be no ground for placing a ban on its being spoken and understood in any other than, say, a Pauline form, for that would only mean that it could not be spoken or understood at all. On the contrary, inasmuch as those quests, for significant living, for hope, for life beyond death, can be pursued by means of the language of resurrection faith, it leaves those quests open to the possibility of transformation and enrichment by some of the dimensions which historical inquiry into the resurrection proclamation of the New Testament period has brought to light.

The interpretation of the resurrection of Jesus Christ is something, then, which happens at a number of levels. Historical inquiry can discern more and more of the significance of the particular New Testament documents, and can shed some light on the understanding and experience which lay behind them. This is interpretation of the resurrection. The continued liturgical observance of Easter makes available, in the communal setting in which it was originally so made, the language of resurrection, in which the community retells the account of that crucial confrontation of the world by the gospel which gave it its beginning. It hears read in their original written form the language of that proclamation and the stories which root it in a particular period of the past. That also is interpretation of the resurrection. Poets and theologians discover ways in which the language of Jesus' being raised from death has echoes in the personal lives of believers and their quest for meaning in living, and this will save that language from dying on those who use it. That further interprets the resurrection. By those means the words which describe the crucial encounter between the gospel and the world can continue to be heard. Meanwhile, some will be challenging the points at which the inherited patterns of the world's thinking limit or destroy man's life, and they will claim to see in this event or that something which requires the thinking of new thoughts or the abandonment of old ones. There is no easy way in which such prophetic utterances can be assessed as true or false (and that is not a new problem); certainly it cannot be related simply to whether the language of resurrection is used in them; but if they carry forward the truth that was understood when Jesus was known to be raised from the dead into a new time and a new situation they are gospel, and as such also interpret the resurrection.

We have observed that many contemporary interpretations of the resurrection failed, at various points, to do justice to the proclamation as contained in the New Testament documents. The reason for this is now clear. The New Testament documents themselves, and certainly the subsequent history of the church, reveal the essential pluriformity of its expression and the reason for that pluriformity. The belief that it was Jesus who had been raised scattered meanings of resurrection, as it were, in all directions. As Evans has commented, 'Whatever the Easter event was, it must be supposed to be of such a kind as to be responsible for the production of these traditions as its deposit at whatever remove.'[15] It may be added that in the process the resurrection must have turned out to be of such a kind as to make the offering of a single interpretation of it out of the question. For even in its day it revealed the only language in which it could be apprehended, the language of eschatology, to be inadequate to its expression.

Theological interpretations are therefore unable to perform their task if they limit the pluriformity under which the resurrection can be apprehended, and this they do to the extent that they claim to make a particular world-view or certain presuppositions essential to resurrection faith. The language of resurrection has been able to function as a call to personal decision (Bultmann) or as an idiom of hope (Geering) or as a claim that something had taken place (Anderson and D. P. Fuller) or as the authentication of an eschatological view of history (Pannenberg and Moltmann) or as a pattern to be discerned in personal experience (Williams), but only because at a particular time and place it was gospel. It produced and continues to produce the variety of interpretation which it is possible to observe precisely because it was that which in its time served to break the natural succession of events and to break also the categories by which human beings had previously spoken of, and therefore limited, what was possible. The New Testament is not concerned with the writing of systematic history, or with describing what man's future will be like, or with stating the urgency of the decision facing human beings, or with presenting evidence to a court, though from time to time it is possible to see in it all these things. What it is *concerned* with is the only thing with which it could be concerned if that which it declares is the case. It is concerned, that is, with God.

The difficulties which have been encountered in speaking of the resurrection have been there from the beginning, and turn out not to have arisen simply from the difficulty of the research, let alone from the lack of ability of those who have tried to do it. In the last resort they are difficulties involved in speaking about God. These are more easily seen in the sphere of systematic theology than in the exposition of the New Testament tradition, which appears on the face of it more manageable, since its statements seem to be limited in scope and its size relatively small. This, together with the fact that it speaks of a particular time and place, makes it all the more likely that interpreters will imagine that further effort or refinement of skill will lead to the discovery of a single statement which would faithfully present the resurrection faith. In fact they achieve no more than the discovery of the limitations of the efforts of others.

The difficulties would also be less severe if God were being spoken of in a way which allowed the New Testament to be bypassed. Timeless proclamations are, by definition, without need of anything more than communication. The exposition of the New Testament, like the remainder of Christian theology, remains difficult precisely because it insists that at certain times and places, and specifically for the purpose of this discussion at the point called the resurrection of Jesus, God was to be discerned in the world of time. To say this is to imply that the work of the historian, uncovering as nearly as may be the evidence surrounding the early church, evaluating what different documents say and describing their significance, is essential, but also that its eventual failure is inevitable.

This situation is not avoided by forswearing the attempt to discover 'what happened' at the resurrection and asking only 'What did the church believe?' as Downing has shown, the quest for the historical primitive church is no easier than the quest for the historical Jesus,[16] and inasmuch as the resurrection functions as the link between these two it can hardly be any easier to discover what it was believed to have been. The intersection of the world of God with the world of time is not more amenable to detection and description as a belief than it is as a fact, because it appears to belong to the nature of the case that as a fact, if it is such, it has a unique capacity to defy expression, and therefore to generate a variety of belief. This is not to say that it generates only confusion, for it also produces power and renewed life, but that it both demands and defies the rational enterprise.

What historical inquiry succeeds in discovering is not a single event or a single belief, but a tradition which has been handed on. 'Christ is risen' is not a proposition offering itself for belief but a tradition which can be appropriated. The tradition has been handed on because at a certain time it represented the church's offering to the world of an experience which had transformed life for its members and promised transformation for the world because of what had happened to Jesus; more than that, it has been handed on because 'Christ is risen' has been able to mediate assurance and meaning for subsequent generations of Christians who, while not constrained as their forbears had been by a rigid eschatology, nevertheless found that only the God who raised Jesus was able to give significance to their life and hope beyond death. Those who have appropriated the resurrection tradition have done so, and can only do so, not on the strength of a belief about what happened to Jesus two days after he was crucified or will happen to them when they die, though either or both may be involved, but on the strength of a primary belief in the God to whom the resurrection tradition, at every phase of its transmission, has always pointed. On the strength of that belief the church has been able to confess that almost every aspect of its corporate experience, and of the personal experience of its members, can be seen as part of the Easter faith and as included in its meaning.

> This is the night, when you brought our fathers, the children of Israel, out of bondage in Egypt, and led them through the Red Sea on dry land.
>
> This is the night, when all who believe in Christ are delivered from the shade of sin, and are restored to grace and holiness of life.
>
> This is the night, when Christ broke the bonds of death and hell, and rose victorious from the grave . . .
>
> How holy is this night, when wickedness is put to flight, and sin is washed away. It restores innocence to the fallen and joy to those who mourn. It casts out pride and hatred, and brings peace and concord.
>
> How blessed is this night, when earth and heaven are joined, and man is reconciled to God.[17]

The God who is acclaimed in the Easter vigil hymn *Exsultet* has been known in each generation to meet the deepest needs and aspirations of the believing community; but he is acclaimed also as the one who was known at history's crucial moment by the raising of Jesus from the dead. Truly to interpret the resurrection is to lay bare the issue of belief in such a God.

Resurrection Rationality

If the handing on of the resurrection tradition and its appropriation by subsequent generations has been based upon belief in God who raised Jesus from the dead, this tradition must have major implications for the nature of rationality. It cannot be sufficient to ask, as has been our purpose hitherto, what account can be given of resurrection faith and its rational basis. The question which also arises is, what would be a structure of rationality which could be accepted if it is true that there is a God who raised Jesus from the dead? What is the role of reason in a world where God raises the dead?

Attempts have been made to demonstrate that the Christian's stake in history is no different from that of anyone else, so that the methods applied by any historian will be adequate to reach the conclusions required by the Christian believer. This is done in the cause of making history a sure ground of Christian apologetic. Such a position, with its implication that there is no distinction between fact and interpretation or between faith and knowledge, is highly tempting for those wishing to investigate the resurrection of Jesus. It could suggest that the death of Jesus and the redemption of the world are alike historical facts accessible to the historian, and on the other hand that the death of Jesus and the redemption of the world are both interpretations offered by the historian on the basis of his own perspective.

It is evident, however, that such a position can only be maintained if the canons of rationality which are currently applied in historical research are radically revised. Thus, for example, Richardson argues for miracle as a valid concept which the modern historian ought to reinstate, while Pannenberg argues that the assumption of an eschatological perspective is not only the essential prerequisite for understanding the original resurrection proclamation, but also a perspective which is available to modern man, and which would enable him to accept the resurrection of Jesus as something to be called, within that eschatological perspective, a historical event. With the first of Pannenberg's statements there is no reason to disagree; even if within the New Testament period radical changes in the significance of resurrection language begin to appear, there seems no doubt that the original proclamation acquired its significance from the perspective of late Jewish eschatology, though in so doing it also made that perspective obsolete. His second statement, on the other hand, that the assumption of an eschatological perspective on history would allow modern man to believe the resurrection as a historical event, is questionable. For an attempt to assume such a perspective, like the rehabilitation of miracle within history suggested by Richardson, could only be at the price of jettisoning one of the major achievements of modern secular history, which has been the careful consideration of the logic of historical explanation and the distinction between fact and interpretation.[18] Not only would the abolition of such a distinction make historical research as we know it impossible, but it would deprive theologians of what has been shown to be one of the major tools available to them for the clarification of the resurrection faith.

The search for the facts, whether the facts of the primitive church and its proclamation or the facts about Jesus, is precisely what has clarified the history of the transmission of traditions, and therefore the impact which the resurrection proclamation made at any particular time. It has in the process brought to light the gulf which is fixed between modern man's understanding of himself and the self-under-standing which could be assumed by the Jewish Christians of the first century. It has furthermore shown that even among early Christians there were such variations in world-view as to make the reinterpreta-tion of the language of the resurrection necessary from a very early date. If the history of the transmission of traditions is a desirable fruit of historical inquiry and of the distinction between fact and interpreta-tion, it is a fruit of the same tree as has produced modern man's aware-ness of his distance from the thought-patterns of a previous age. It hardly seems likely that the tree can be so doctored as to produce the first of these fruits without also producing the second.

There is however truth in the view that the appropriation of the resurrection faith must involve a willingness to contemplate some change in the pattern of our rationality, if only because the original proclamation involved that for those who first heard it, and the com-munity which has continued to speak of the resurrection has also continued to confront the world with a gospel which has required the world to transform its pattern of thinking. That which was previously unthinkable became under the impact of the Christian gospel an actual-ity, and in that way the pattern originally exhibited by the encounter of the resurrection of Jesus with the current idea of resurrection was exhibited again and again in the meeting of the gospel with the world. The continued proclamation of the gospel inevitably depends, therefore, upon the possibility of such transformations occurring in the limita-tions imposed by the canons of rationality. In that sense Pannenberg

rightly construes the current agenda of theology as that of so exhibiting
the past encounters of the gospel with human reason that the material
exists by which to evaluate and understand those points where events
come to transform what reason says is possible. The rise of Nazism
was a movement which challenged man's understanding of what was
possible; so is the rise of those movements of liberation which threaten
the existing social order in places where people are oppressed. Christian
theology has the capacity to provide the material for the making of at
least provisional judgments about which of such movements accord
with the gospel, through its access to the history of the encounter of
the resurrection of Jesus with the world of his day. In the history of
that encounter, and in that which followed from it, lies a summons to
expectancy in the face of the probability that the canons of rationality,
and that which the world calls possible in any age, must undergo
radical revision.

The particular revisions proposed by Pannenberg and Richardson,
however, are at once too great and too small. It is too great to require
that modern man should assume again that world-view in terms of
which the resurrection faith was originally expressed, but which the
resurrection itself made obsolete (even if that was not at first apparent);
to do so would require the sacrifice of that which, in making possible
historical inquiry as we know it, has given this generation the capacity
to understand the significance of that original proclamation, even if it
has also made it aware of the distance between its own world-view and
that of those who first proclaimed the resurrection of Jesus. Yet it is
too small in suggesting that the successors of those who proclaimed the
resurrection will only be required to return to some pattern of thought
which they already know and which their community has already
experienced. If that is indeed all that is required, it would be a much
lighter demand than that which confronted those who originally declared that it was Jesus who had been raised from the dead. The God
who was known as the one who raised Jesus from the dead and brought
into being the things which are not is unlikely to be known as the one
who reinstates the things that have passed away.

Niebuhr's solution, which takes its stand on the radical uniqueness
of all historical events, is also inadequate. The researches of the historian may no longer be dependent on the quest for an ongoing purpose
in history, but neither are they based on the need to produce radically
new explanations for every single thing. An understanding of the gospel
as that which, in some continuity with the things that happened to

Jesus, confounds the patterns of rationality of any generation, does not lead to the view that everything is new and unpredictable. Surprising events may happen every day, but that does not mean that surprising events are not surprising events. Nor is everything that is unpredictable surprising in the radical way that makes it gospel. For what has been shown is that it is only the diligent exercise of modern methods of rational historical criticism that has had the capacity to demonstrate in this age the radical newness of the original resurrection proclamation. The abandonment of those methods of inquiry would be the sacrifice of those patterns of thought which have proved themselves able to probe the limits of human reason in a way which can exhibit the radically new for what it is.

This issue of the relation of the old to the new in historical thinking received a treatment which can only be called prophetic in a work which came to be written during the period of the rise of totalitarian movements in the West, and which attempts to understand their significance for religious belief. This is V. A. Demant's *The Religious Prospect*. He observed that Christians in the West were seeing in the rise of communism and fascism a fundamental attack on the liberal doctrine of the status of persons, and he argued that this attack acquired most of its power from the failure of the liberal *dogma* to provide adequate support for that doctrine. He used the word 'dogma' for the deep-seated conviction out of which men act, in contrast to 'doctrine' which is their expressed belief. By the liberal dogma he meant the view that man was to be understood only in terms of his past and future, his 'becoming', and that he had no existence apart from the course of events. His contention was that this dogma, so far from supporting the liberal *doctrine* that persons had rights over and above the demands of their particular society, actually eroded it, and that it would be supported only by the recovery of man's being as well as his becoming.

> If there is nothing in man which is not derived from his temporal existence, then he has no claim against the collective life. The collective life on earth is of the temporal order. If the human person is likewise only of the temporal order he is but a fragmentary part of the collective whole; he is something less than the community, and therefore has no end other than its enhancement and power to survive. Because modern Liberalism has accepted a dogma of becoming only, the doctrine for which it wished to stand has been defeated by more deliberate and thorough embodiments of its dogma.[19]

If man is to be defined only in terms of the purpose revealed in his history, his becoming, then man's history is caught between those

totalitarian philosophies which take that argument to the logical conclusion of requiring that man the individual shall exist only for the
achievement of the collective destiny and reactions from them which
are inadequately based. The *dogma* of Liberalism, which assumes that
reality is only the flux of becoming, postulates no reality greater than
man's becoming and therefore possesses no understanding of man
which is more inclusive than the corporate destinies offered by totalitarian systems.

Demant does not envisage that the reassertion of the traditional
Catholic form of the dogma that man has his roots in an eternal realm
of being will enable him to resist the claims of totalitarianism and to
pursue again the liberal doctrine of the status of persons, but he does
suggest that only a philosophy of this kind will enable him to understand the conflict between totalitarianism and liberalism in a way which
will allow him not to give absolute loyalty to either. It will also give
him a ground upon which to stand in asserting the liberal doctrine of
the status of persons other than the liberal dogma that man is only
becoming, a dogma which can only lead logically to the totalitarian
attack on the rights of the individual.

> I am not arguing that the recovery of the two-world outlook will
> deliver mankind from the dialectical movements from one pole to
> another in the quest for abiding satisfaction. That process has been
> with man always, and has made its impression on Christian theology
> too. And it will be part of human existence to the end. But I am
> contending that only by recognition of the dependence and contin-
> gence of the process of becoming in relation to the Eternal Being
> will mankind be able to face the contrasts which emerge upon the
> historic stage and take an active part in history without giving abso-
> lute loyalty to one side of the contrast. . . . For he will see each
> movement as a tug of true being and be ready to learn from it; he
> will also know that it will be under judgment if it assumes that it
> fulfils the whole of man's being, and that it will provoke a new
> opposition.[20]

Demant judges that the theological movements of his time failed to
come to grips with the need to provide an understanding of the world
of man's becoming as rooted in his eternal being. At the one extreme
are those theological movements which tie man's apprehension of God
within the natural and cosmic process, either because they locate the
roots of religion in man's moral endeavour or because they identify
God with the process of becoming itself. At the other are those anti-
liberal protests, such as Barth made in his early writings, which speak of

the total otherness of God, and magnify the fallenness of man to such an extent that there is no relationship between man's belief and his understanding of the natural order, or of the workings of human history. Traditional Christian theology, on the other hand, spoke of a God who, while outside the cosmic order of becoming, and transcending it, was none the less active within it. God was not to be identified with the process of becoming, but neither, on the other hand, was his relationship to it to be severed. This traditional incarnational theology, which allowed man to discern the activity of the eternal God within the process of history was what emerged from the biblical understanding of 'saving events' when it encountered the Hellenistic concern with the eternal realm.

> The whole vitality of the formative Christian controversies which built up Christian doctrine came of the tension between belief in God, who in the Redeemer enters the cosmic process from the Eternal Places, and God who acts in the world process as Creator.[21]

The recovery of this tension is what Demant sees as the only future for religious belief. It was a tension which existed in the medieval synthesis and in its understanding of the relationship between natural and revealed theology.

> The religion which will preside over any renewed Christendom must find a dogmatic outlook which will hold in fruitful relation these two aspects of the full Christian faith which have fallen apart since the break-up of Medieval Catholicism. There can be no return to the synthesis attempted by the theology of the Middle Ages, which proved so fragile owing to its envisaging too narrow a universe. . . . What is clearly required is not a repetition of the medieval solution, but what Maritain calls 'an analogue' for our own day of the reality of God's relation to the world, of which the medieval dogmas was the 'analogue' in terms of that period.[22]

Demant's programme for theology has a remarkable resemblance to the seminal proposals of Bonhoeffer for a religion for a world come of age in which nevertheless God is known as the one who is edged out of the world on to a cross.[23] The need to retain a theology of redemptive action by a God who freely intervenes in a fallen natural and historic process remains, despite the need also to assert his lordship over the process itself. It is significant that in the categories of traditional Lutheranism the same fruitful tension can make its appearance as Demant sees in medieval Catholicism. It is significant also, and less encouraging, to note that for both the nature and style of such a theology remain as questions. What they are alike searching for is a way of speaking about that which is at the root of the being of man, who at times stands over against the particular movements in his becoming but not in such a way as to be absent from those movements.

This tension has been shown in this book to have been there in the proclamation of the gospel of the resurrection from the beginning. The statement that God had raised Jesus from the dead confirmed eschatological expectations to the extent that it spoke of God's radically new act in the life of the world. But in that it spoke of a resurrection of Jesus, which pointed to a future in which the continuing life of the church had a role and a significance, it continued to speak of a God who was active in the historical process. The ambiguity inherent in the antithesis between flesh and spirit in the New Testament is but one example of the expression of this tension. The flesh is there both as the locus of God's revelation of himself and also that which stands between the world and its apprehension of God's decisive action in Christ.

Demant's demand for a theology which expresses that tension is still relevant, for the words of the theologians who have been examined show them grappling with the fact that the resurrection contrives to be both that which is within history and that which, as something beyond history, breaks the bounds of historical development. Those who attempt to give to the raising of Jesus from the dead a purely historical content not only fail in the effort, but also lose its essential connection with the world which is beyond history and which impinged upon the world of history at the resurrection. Those who make its content entirely theological fail to retain its connection with the world of history. Those who attempt a theological statement which is also historical manage to do so only at the cost of injuring the integrity of the one or the other. It is not surprising that the major statements of the Christian faith, which have constituted Christian orthodoxy down the ages, have contained an element of contradiction.

Demant's criticism of the failure of theology as a rational discipline to provide a statement of the kind he desires is however somewhat wistful, and itself involves a failure to take seriously enough the absence of a world-view which made such statements in former theologies possible, or to see that those statements which emerged in the Christian tradition as statements of the gospel were not, in the modern sense of the word, statements of theology. Thus Paul's statements about the raising of Jesus were in fact the proclamation of the end of the only theology which he knew, and are only called theological statements with some degree of hindsight and anachronism. At the point at which they became theology, integrated, that is, within a structure of thought about God, they also ceased to be themselves statements of the gospel, and became instead statements about what the gospel might look like, and would, indeed, have to look like, if it were to be the gospel of the God who raised Jesus from the dead.

Demant offers an illuminating account of the way in which the medieval world-view of a world of becoming dependent on an eternal world of being provides a delineation of the shape of the gospel as that which alone breaks the self-sufficiency of the world of becoming, and deposes those idolatries which arise when men fail to take seriously the world of being upon which all becoming depends. It should be clear that the New Testament proclamation of the raising of Jesus from the dead can fulfil the same function. It has, however, also to be clear that a theology of the resurrection which now offers itself for appropriation cannot be, and must not be allowed to do duty for, a statement of the gospel which offers itself for belief. To expect that an interpretation of the resurrection might do this is to mistake the task of theology in particular and rationality in general. To the extent that the resurrection proclamation is an event within the history of the transmission of traditions it is material for theology; as such it has the potential for revealing in our time what occurs when the world which is describable in rational terms is shown not to be the only world there is, but to have to take account of the ever-present possibility of the radically new, and the name for that possibility is God. To the extent that theology deals with the natural processes of a part of the cosmos — as history or science does — it deals with that aspect of the divine activity which is discernible in the natural order of things. But theology also records occasions when the natural progression of nature and history has been interrupted by the impact of the radically new, by the bringing into being of that which is not, the gospel. Theology cannot itself bring about such interruptions of the natural and historical progression, for its function is the testing and recording of such interruptions in order that men may know the likely shape of the gospel, and know also that the world with which they are familiar and the structure of rationality which they understand may be broken by the God who makes all things new. It follows that theology by recalling and interpreting the New Testament resurrection proclamation maintains man's openness to the possibility that the God who raised Jesus from the dead will perform the radically new in our time.

If what the resurrection proclamation said about a God who in Jesus breaks through the limiting categories of human schemes of thought is true, then it could only be received in a context which allowed both rational exposition and decisive newness. Such a context was the Christian church. It was the community within which some could recount their experience and its results and others would themselves undergo the radical change which membership of the Christian church, with its new righteousness, mission and life, could bring. Within the church could be experienced the blessedness of those who had not seen and yet had believed, because they had undergone experiences which accorded with the shape of what they had not experienced but had heard about, and which therefore made what they heard believable.

The resurrection faith therefore manifests in itself what Christians hold to be the structure of the world's being. For the resurrection to have been apprehended required the existence of Judaism, which was the product of a long history. Not only the eschatological frame of reference but the whole life of the Jewish people formed the essential background to the apprehension of the raising of Jesus. On the other hand the raising of Jesus also represented a decisive break in that history; the bounds of Jewish thought and Jewish nationhood were burst under the impact of the raising of Jesus. That decisive break could only be accepted because it was proclaimed within the life of a community which the raising of Jesus brought into being. The historical development, the break in that development and the community in which that break can be accepted – these were the constituents of that rationality of appropriation by which the resurrection of Jesus was proclaimed and understood. And that rationality is discernible in the life of the world.

Christians, in common with others, have understood life as a creative process. It is amenable to rational inquiry, and can be affected by man's own creative ability and gifts. He builds on what he has inherited from the past with all the effort and ability he is able to muster in the present, and thereby participates in the building of his future. In such orderly creativity Christians have discerned the work of God the Father.

They have, however, also found that the creative process is not all there is to life. The disorder of the world is not in the end such as can be rectified merely by the forward movement of a process. They have from time to time discerned the radically new in history, a decisive act of rescue and deliverance. Such acts are as radically new as the first act of creation itself; they are new creation. As such they threaten even what have appeared to be the best results of man's own creativity, his systems of thought and structures of good government, things which they have believed to be the work of God. Yet these new creations, these decisive acts which appear to threaten what mankind under God has brought into being, are themselves perceived as the work of God, the Son, the Redeemer.

For that which is decisively new to be received as the work of God requires the coming into being of a new community by the life of which the new creation of God is experienced and can be tested. Thus the redemptive act carries with it the formation of a new community, apparently over against the old, but nevertheless perceived as God's creation because its life measures up to what the new redemptive act it proclaims seems to require. The new community is thus seen as the work of God, the Spirit, the Advocate.

The way in which the resurrection was and is believed thus reflects the character of the God who is claimed to have accomplished it. The resurrection proclamation built upon and shattered inherited patterns of understanding at one and the same time. It used the treasures of the old Israel but built up a new one. It was appropriated in community because it was creative of one. The unity of idea and life-style which we have noticed in resurrection faith reflects the trinitarian unity of God himself by building on and yet replacing the inherited treasures of the past.[24] Within new community it is possible to see the relation between what is old and what is new, and thus to have access to the God who raised Jesus from the dead.

6

WHAT THERE IS TO BE FOUND

To believe that God had raised Jesus from the dead was to believe he had accomplished his last act. It was also to believe that his last act was radically different from all that you had been led to expect: far from meaning the end of all futures it opened a new one; far from setting God's seal on the observance of the law it gave his approval to one whom the law had condemned. To believe God had raised Jesus from the dead was to enter upon a community experience which matched the story the community told; the radical nature of the raising of the dead was confirmed by the radically new understanding of justice, of mission, of life which the new community expressed. You entered upon that belief in the company of others and those others were part of that belief.

Easter faith has become something different from this; not focused upon the shared experience of a new community, it has come to belong instead in the areas of private experience and personal survival. Academically it has been a matter for historical research and ecclesiastically for liturgical repetition. The resurrection faith has undergone that transformation because in its original form it so radically transformed the categories of thought in which it was expressed as to make those categories unusable in their original sense. In the history of the handing on of the resurrection faith this is what has happened, and there is no chance whatever of reversing the process. Nor is there any reason to wish to do so: the life of the liturgy and the researches of historians, the concern of human beings to make sense of their experience by seeing patterns within it and to penetrate the mystery of their own death are all ways which have enabled and continue to enable Easter to be spoken of in a world very different from the one where the story began. But they fail as ways of looking for the living because that quest began and must begin in a new community whose life and experience matches the story which it tells. To tell the story of Easter, to research its probable origins, to enjoy and find meaning in the reverberations of its language is to occupy yourself with a moment of total transformation which broke the bounds of the available language and the existing society. To occupy yourself with that moment is not necessarily to experience in any way the power that moment brought to the world. To interpret the resurrection requires more than private or liturgical or historical interest; it requires also the interpretation of discipleship, the way by which corporate life reflects the power of which the Easter story speaks. This kind of interpretation will surely shed light on the questions which historians are asking and which trouble those who contemplate their own death; but first and foremost it will give access to the living as none of these other means can. This is the only possible conclusion from our detailed examination of attempts to find the resurrection by the route of individual questions about life or scholarly questions about history. We look for a resurrection faith which holds together, as the New Testament witness clearly does, searches that in our day have fallen apart. This means shedding new light on each of those searches by taking as a starting-point the corporate nature of the original Easter faith and seeing what kind of corporate discipleship would lend credibility to the story we tell.

This is not a question of starting with the community which at the moment tells the resurrection story and asking what modifications could be made to its life so as to make its witness more credible; that would be to handle the resurrection as the Pharisees handled the Torah, as a possession to be altered or disposed of in the most acceptable way. The New Testament community was not one which dealt in acceptable modifications of what they already knew, but one which found itself in coming to terms with events in the life of the world which gave it its agenda and to which it felt it had no choice but to respond.

Indeed its possession of the resurrection story is one of the major obstacles which stand in the way of the Christian community's ever going in search of the living one; confident that it is the rightful successor of the community which was, once for all, given new life, new hope, a new master and a new mission, it devotes its energies to maintaining its hold on its heritage, inviting others to share it, preserving it entire or checking whether this or that modification of it is acceptable. It was not so in the New Testament church: that was a community possessed by its experience, driven on by a mission which allowed no delay. To tell the resurrection story as the early church told it is to tell about that which empowers you and governs your community's life; it is to be convinced that what is driving you is nothing less than the meaning and destiny of the whole world, revealed in what has happened to a particular person at a particular point in time. The issue about what kind of community experience would provide a medium for looking for the living is not therefore a question about modification to the church but of response to the world, to the specific situations in which the meaning of human existence is revealed, and so of the formation of a community which expresses that response.

In the light of what we have seen about the nature and origins of the resurrection faith, what are the experiences within the life of the world which appear to contain the meaning and destiny of humanity and to which corporate response is required? And if we respond to the experiences that we find, how will this affect our looking for the resurrection of Christ? In what follows we shall take as a starting-point those theological motifs which appeared in conjunction with the resurrection in the New Testament and ask what are the equivalent motifs and corporate expressions of life which might be available to us today.

The New Justice

The earliest Christians in using the category of resurrection were speaking of something which, in so far as it was understood at all in contemporary Judaism, was understood to refer to the vindication of those who had suffered in obedience to the law. The righteous martyrs would receive from God the reward which in their life in the world they had been denied. Conversely, the unjust who had demanded that they apostatize from the law of God would also receive their due reward.

Such a justice is a static concept, which speaks to the one who is presently oppressed, and encourages him with the thought of eventual vengeance. It encourages him to aim for the recovery of power, and invites him to behave towards the oppressor in the manner that he himself has experienced. It states that the present unjust situation will be reversed, once and for all, by an act of God on behalf of those who have been loyal to him and against those who have defied him. The typical product of such thinking about justice was the zealot, a person who loved the law, was strongly nationalistic, fiercely opposed to Roman domination, and was ardently awaiting the arrival of the kingdom which was to change this situation.[1] The judgment of God is the direct reversal of the injustice of men.

There is no doubt that Jesus was understood as reflecting, in part, this view of the divine judgment, and there is a certain amount of evidence to suggest that those in authority at the time of his ministry associated him with that view, and with the aim of the overthrow of Roman occupation. Yet the proclamation of Jesus parted company with this view of judgment chiefly because in his view judgment was something which went deeper than the finding of superficial remedies to immediate situations. As Gustavo Gutierrez has written:

> For Jesus, oppression and injustice were not limited to a specific historical situation: their causes go deeper and cannot be truly eliminated without going to the very roots of the problem: the disintegration of brotherhood and communion among men. Besides, and this will have enormous consequences, Jesus is opposed to all politico-religious messianism which does not respect either the depth of the religious realm or the autonomy of political action.[2]

What is being noted here is the essential openness of the justice proclaimed by Jesus. It respects neither the boundaries of space nor those of time, because the issues with which it deals are such as pass beyond those of traditional eschatology. The depth of the religious realm and the autonomy of political action prevent the former being used to bless, and so give permanence to, the temporary achievements of the latter. Some, in observing this, have wished thereby to deny in the teaching of Jesus any implications for what we now call the political realm, and to range him on the side of the 'spiritual' values which are to be discovered in the personal rather than in the social or political realms.

Yet this would be no less an oversimplification than if Jesus were simply harnessed in the cause of this or that political movement. For the dialogue of Jesus with the powerful of his day can only be seen as political action inasmuch as it spoke of a new and transcendent justice which must transform the order through which, in his day, some were oppressed and others retained their authority. Such confrontations as took place were never simply a matter of taking the other side. They used the categories of God's kingdom in a way that liberated them from being the possession of this or that group and allowed them to stand over against any group who claimed to have laid hold upon them for themselves. That was why those who had hoped, in zealot terms, that Jesus was the one to redeem Israel were doomed to disappointment.

The zealots were not mistaken in feeling that Jesus was simultaneously near and far away. Neither were the leaders of the Jewish people mistaken in thinking that their position was imperilled by the preaching of Jesus, nor the oppressive political authorities when they sentenced him to die as a traitor. They were mistaken (and their followers have continued to be mistaken) only in thinking that it was all accidental and transitory, in thinking that with the death of Jesus the matter was closed, in supposing that no one would remember it.[3]

Gutierrez's theology of liberation is an attempt by a Latin American theologian to discover within the teaching of Jesus the roots of action for change in the direction of liberation and justice particularly within the South American situation. This is what lies behind his comment that the significance of the concern of Jesus with justice is not a transitory matter which terminated with his death. Yet the reason for the permanent significance of Jesus' preaching lies elsewhere, and in something which both as an event and as an idea lifts the notion of justice above what either a first-century Jew or a twentieth-century Latin American can portray, and that is his resurrection from the dead.

The discovery that Jesus was alive after his death, and the affirmation now that those who claimed to have made that discovery were speaking the truth, are not merely equivalent to saying that death was not the end of Jesus, or that Jesus' death was not the end of his teaching. The content of the teaching, and the nature of the life as it is portrayed to us, are both matched by the reinterpreted, Christian understanding of that which made death not the end for Jesus, namely his resurrection. The God who raised Jesus from the dead and brings into being things which are not can only be the God of a justice which is not static and of a demand for social righteousness which has continually to be reiterated. The permanence of the issue of justice is not inherent in the idea of justice itself, nor is it secured by the fact that the one who spoke of it was raised to life again after his death; it is the meaning of his being raised to life. For this reason, justice as the church proclaimed it could not be merely the vindication of the godly; it had also to be the justification which was not a single act but the perpetual demeanour of God towards his world. The resurrection of Jesus involved the discovery that the judgment of God is not the turning of the tables on those in power, but the radical and permanent demand for an ending of that way of looking at the world. The resurrection proclamation itself, and the teaching of the one who was raised, both declared the same thing, and it was this that had to be lived out in the life of the early church. The justification of the ungodly, which meant an end to the Jewish understanding of privilege in favour of the creation of an

Israel based solely on the faithfulness of God, was implied by the resurrection; the radical reversal of thinking and action from that which had sustained the Jews in their devotion could only be justified on the terms of the raising of the dead, for that is in fact what it was.

The teaching of Jesus, his resurrection and the community of the first Christian believers are the historical realities to which it is necessary to gain access. The New Testament pattern suggests that access can only be gained through the continued portrayal within the life of the believing community of that continuous exercise of the judgment of God which is the way the resurrection of the dead comes to be known. The position of Gutierrez is in that sense nearer to that which will enable the contemporary believer to gain access to belief than is that of Williams. The personal may be more accessible to experience and the intimate areas of living more likely to yield the experience of meaning, but if it is resurrection that is being sought, the communal must be the place of discovery, for the resurrection is about the bringing into being of that which is not, an Israel founded upon a divine demand which is continually heard. For it is concerned with a justice that remains discontented unless it includes all, and this is at once so radical and so impossible a demand as rightly to be called the resurrection of the dead. Inasmuch as the believer is offered the opportunity to engage in the quest for a community of that degree of newness, it is likely that he will encounter the question whether the dead are raised and the kind of evidence that will enable him to reach a decision about it. He will also be able to discover whether it is after all Jesus who was raised, whether, that is to say, the limited and exclusive justice which is actually national vengeance is all that can be hoped for, or whether there is something to be said about, and offered to, all mankind. At that point the uncertainty of the historical judgment about the resurrection of Jesus from the dead becomes more than a historical uncertainty; the doubt about the past becomes a question about the future and therefore about the appropriate style of living in the present. We may observe how rapidly the location of the cause of justice shifts, so that those who claim to be on the side of justice at one moment find themselves against it at the next; at one time it is with this nation, at another with a certain racial group, at another with women and at another with a natural order which no longer is willing to be taken for granted. To be committed to the justice of God is to join oneself to something that always moves, but which always raises the question what happens when the cause appears defeated, whether at that point it will all appear 'accidental and transitory', whether the matter is closed so that no one will remember it. To fail to be committed to the justice of God is to absent yourself from where the issue of the raising of the dead can be known about, and to deny yourself the possibility of discovering that the Easter proclamation is true.

Mission

Within the context in which the resurrection was expected in Judaism, the mission of God's people was clear. They had been entrusted with the Torah and were committed to the faithful keeping of it. Only by so doing could they be sure that at the coming of the Lord they would be worthy to be re-established as his kingdom. The heroism which this view frequently inspired was as clear as the desperation which must have lain behind it. For the great vision of the Second Isaiah, who was able to see the purpose of God being worked out in a pagan king (Isa. 41), had been lost under the pressure of two centuries of occupation, and the foreigner became synonymous with the enemy. His only use was to be rooted out when God came in triumph to vindicate his cause. Thus everything outside the small remnant of the faithful who were keeping the law was to be despaired of.

From the transformation which Jesus and his resurrection made in the understanding of the nature of the divine judgment, there followed a transformation in the understanding of mission. Indeed, mission was the name of that activity in the present which corresponded to the knowledge of what had been accomplished in Jesus and was to be accomplished for all mankind, the resurrection of the dead. The apostolate or mission of Paul and of the other apostles, and the commission to the church to proclaim the gospel to the ends of the earth, were both said to follow upon appearances of the risen Lord. So, if the new judgment was to be universal and inclusive, and was to take the form of something God had in store for the whole world, and if moreover it was to involve the justification of the ungodly, then there had to be an end to an understanding of mission that centred on a faithful remnant retaining its identity over against the world.

> Then what becomes of our boasting? It is excluded. On what principle? The principle of works? No, but on the principle of faith. For we hold that a man is justified by faith apart from the works of the law. Or is God the God of the Jews only? Is he not the God of Gentiles also? Yes, of Gentiles also, since God is one; and he will

justify the circumcised on the ground of their faith, and the uncircumcised because of their faith (Rom. 3.27 – 30).

Paul writes here of a transformation in the understanding of the context of mission, which was directly consequent upon the resurrection of Jesus, and was indeed part of its significance. For the resurrection was the putting of the righteous by the law, and indeed of the law itself, in the wrong, and Jesus, whom the law had declared accursed, in the right. Thus God had been shown to have justified the one who had been declared unrighteous by the law. It was therefore not an additional fact to be learned about Jesus that he was going before his disciples into Galilee (of the Gentiles) but was part of what was involved in his having been raised from the dead.

Thus the battle within the early church arising from the demand that Gentile Christians become Jews was in essence a battle for the resurrection. The issue was whether the community of believers was to bear witness in its own life to the universality which would appear in God's disclosed intention of judging the world.

Now God commands all men everywhere to repent, because he has fixed a day on which he will judge the world in righteousness by a man whom he has appointed, and of this he has given assurance to all men by raising him from the dead (Acts. 17.30f.).

Mission continued to mean faithfulness, not now to the needs of a small chosen remnant to retain its identity, but to that which was disclosed by the raising of Jesus from the dead; as Jesus had anticipated the end which was to come upon the world, so the church was to be in advance the community of the new justice. The active pursuit of mission in the declaration to all nations of what had been accomplished in Jesus arose out of the church's understanding of his resurrection, and this declaration was credible to those who heard it because the justification of all mankind was already in being in the church, the community of those who were proclaiming the news about Jesus.

In this sense, the church pursued in its own life the struggle necessary to bring into being the new order based on the justice of God. It cannot therefore stand apart from those conflicts under the pretext that mission can only take place if the church is united. As Gutierrez observes, the church is a 'Sacrament of History' precisely in so far as within it the struggle for a new social order in Latin America creates in microcosm the struggle for, as well as the achievement of, the justice of God. The battle in the early church about the Gentile mission, no less than the battle in the Latin American church about the nature of and remedy for social division, cannot be avoided if the church is to carry out its mission of being in advance that which is to come to all mankind.[4]

It is the experience of that struggle for the justification of the ungodly which in every age has offered the supreme opportunity of access for the believer to the historical reality proclaimed as the raising of Jesus from the dead. The rite of initiation into the church represents a 'death to sin', not primarily in the sense of the individual's own forsaking of personal sin, but in the sense of his identification with the only act which will bring about righteousness, namely resurrection. This reality is known within the Christian community as it struggles to become in advance what mankind is intended to become, and as, in so struggling, it retains its hold upon that which brought it into being, Jesus' own experiencing in advance of what is offered to all men.

It is thus characteristic of the resurrection of Jesus that access to it is gained not because a person happened to be a member of this or that family or community by descent, but by his taking into himself, and his being taken into, that community whose life and witness provide access to what has happened to Jesus and is the hope for all men; the metaphor characteristic of it in Paul's thinking, therefore, is not birth but adoption (cf. Rom. 8.12 - 17). To be a son of God is not a natural state, but one which men come to through the leading of the Spirit of God, that is to say, inasmuch as they are part of that community which the raising of Jesus called into being. The means by which they become children of Abraham is no longer birth but a participation in the mission of Christ, and it is that participation which allows the discovery of the resurrection faith. As the Baptist proclaims:

> Do not presume to say to yourselves, 'We have Abraham as our father': for I tell you, God is able from these stones to raise up children to Abraham (Matt. 3.9).

It is almost always an understanding of mission which presupposes that the resurrection story is something the church possesses and will share that prevents the kind of mission taking place which would bring us in touch with the truth of the Easter story. For the raising of Jesus poses the question about every struggle in which we involve ourselves: is this which the world finds despicable, unconvincing or even blasphemous (as they found Jesus) only that, or is it that which it is the purpose of God to exalt? To insist that mission is the taking of a story we possess to those who do not is to deny ourselves the involvement in the world's hidden and unidentified struggles that can raise the resurrection issue and put us in the way of finding an answer to it. For mission is not the preservation or aggrandizing of the sheltered identity of a faithful remnant but the active pursuit of what is known by faith born of the knowledge of the story of Jesus to be the meaning and destiny of human life. It is only such involvement that can really raise the issue of the raising of the dead.

The New Life

Life, as the fourth gospel offers it, is very different from the life which a Hellenistic audience would have been looking for. No longer is life that which is attained by the progressive abstraction of the self from the material world; it is instead that which God offers to the world in order to raise it from death. Not only is life offered to the world, but the sharing of life is part of the ministry of the Son in the world. Thus Jesus' words continue with what is clearly intended to be understood as a prophecy to be taken up in the later raising of Lazarus:

> Truly, truly, I say to you, the hour is coming, and now is, when the dead will hear the voice of the Son of God, and those who hear will live. For as the Father has life in himself, so he has granted the Son also to have life in himself, and has given him authority to execute judgment, because he is the Son of man. Do not marvel at this; for the hour is coming when all who are in the tombs will hear his voice and come forth, those who have done good to the resurrection of life, and those who have done evil, to the resurrection of judgment (John 5.2511–29).

Thus it is that the experience of life becomes a part of history. It is made available first through the history of the Son and then in the history of the church. By that means history itself, the story of man and of the world, is given life and made the source of life. This is the significance of the resurrection, and it is resurrection, and specifically the resurrection of Jesus, which causes life to become available in the history of the Son and of the Christian church.

> The hour has come for the Son of man to be glorified. Truly, truly, I say to you, unless a grain of wheat falls into the ground and dies, it remains alone. But if it dies it bears much fruit. He who loves his life loses it, and he who hates his life in this world will keep it for eternal life (John 12.23 – 25).

These words clearly point in two directions, to Jesus and his resurrection in the reference to the grain of wheat, and the growth of the church in the reference to the fruit which the grain bears when it has undergone the dying which occurs when it is sown in the ground. In this manner the writer takes the a-historical idea of life and roots it in the historical ministry of Christ and of the church, and thereby gives to it the historical reference which in Jewish understanding is associated with the concept of the kingdom of God.

The mediation of life through the Son and then through the church is the fruit of God's love for the *kosmos*, the structures of the world, which God willed to save by the sending of his own Son (John 3.16f.). Thus the sending of the Son, and through him of the church, makes the structures of the world and the processes of human history not the source of death but of life. It was this experience of life within the Christian community which allowed the believer access to a new understanding of the role of the world and of history in the divine purpose. It was not sufficient to proclaim that the destiny of the world was life, and that this was shown to be so by the life and teaching of Jesus; the proclamation was experienced as true because that life was realized in advance in the life of the church. That life was experienced as an imperishable one in contrast to the life of the old Israel, which was only in the past.

> Your fathers ate the manna in the wilderness, and they died. This is the bread which comes down from heaven, that a man may eat of it and not die. I am the living bread which came down from heaven; if any one eats of this bread, he will live for ever; and the bread which I shall give for the life of the world is my flesh (John 6.49 – 51).

The eucharistic life of the church is here represented as the image of that life which has been lived in the ministry of Jesus, and is to be given for the life of the world.

Thus the New Testament points unmistakably in the direction of the historical for any proclamation of the resurrection, however contemporary. Experiences which enhance personal life are possible; for the painter, the influx of inspiration which had failed him suddenly and unexpectedly reappears; for the family, the rediscovery of the possibility of growth in intimate relationships which had appeared to be dead; for the person in psychotherapy, the uncovering of the source of the emotional paralysis he has endured may seem like life from the dead. Such experiences and many others may give those who have them illumination in their understanding of the resurrection, but they cannot provide access to the resurrection itself, nor may they form the content of a contemporary resurrection faith because they are not historical experiences. The burden of the Johannine expression of the gospel is that precisely the life which was being sought in the exercise of the philosophical reason, or in the detachment of the self from the flux of events, is to be found within the *events* of Jesus and the church, inasmuch as Jesus has been raised and has given to the church the gift of life to be shared within the world's history.

The contrast being made here between the personal and the historical is not a contrast between good and bad, but between what naturally is and what by the divine miracle can be. This is presented as the contrast between the flesh and the spirit. Thus Nicodemus is told that he must be born again‛ of the Spirit and the spirit does not share in the predictability of the world of the flesh. The second birth which is required of him is therefore unlike the first birth.

> That which is born of the flesh is flesh, and that which is born of the Spirit is spirit. Do not marvel that I said to you, 'You must be born anew'. The wind blows where it wills, and you hear the sound of it, but you do not know where it comes from or where it goes; so is everyone who is born of the Spirit (John 3.6 – 8).

When Nicodemus asks how this can happen, he receives an answer which is so clearly the preaching of the early church that it has not even been put into the singular: 'Truly, truly, I say to you, we speak of what we know, and we testify to what we have seen; but you do not receive our testimony' (John 3.11). There follows the prophecy of the death-glorification, the 'lifting up' of the Son of man for those who believe in him to have eternal life. The story of what happened to Jesus, 'what we have seen', and the creation of the church, both of which are events within the world's history, are thus the facts to which the early church appeals in its proclamation that life has entered the world, and that it is not necessary to leave the world in order to find it.

The evidence for this argument is the resurrection of Jesus, which is also its conclusion. The creation of a life-giving community provides its members with access to, and understanding of, that which brought it into being. The life which the resurrection of Christ implies, and which will persuade the believer that his resurrection is true, is that which takes him beyond the individual and the private into the community which is committed to the offering of life to the world. To the extent that the church confines its energies within its own existence or within the private lives of its members, it may provide refreshment and renewal, and these may illuminate the idea of resurrection, but it will not provide access to the resurrection itself, for that is only available in those things which take human beings beyond their interior lives into the world of public fact.

> That which was from the beginning, which we have heard, which we have seen with our eyes, which we have looked upon and touched with our hands, concerning the word of life – the life was made manifest, and we saw it, and testify to it, and proclaim to you the eternal life which was with the Father and was made manifest to us – that which we have seen and heard we proclaim also to you, so that you may have fellowship with us; and our fellowship is with the Father and with his Son Jesus Christ (I John 1.1 – 3).

The discovery of the resurrection of Christ within the corporate life of humanity is not only the key to personal meaningfulness and significant living for the individual; it also relates to that most ultimately personal issues, our fate beyond death. For Paul as for John, what had to be said about this was related to their understanding of the cause of Christ; if he had been raised from the dead, if his mission and his life had been restored by the act of God, then so would be the mission and the life of his followers. There are no Christian answers to the issue of our fate beyond death apart from those issues of the purpose of man's common life which alone were the basis on which the raising of Christ came to be believed. When the question of life after death is raised apart from those issues, it is quite understandable that what emerge are bizarre speculations about how the life which has evidently come to an end can in fact continue. It is possible that the evidence of parapsychological research may have some bearing upon such an attenuated hope and even provide some comfort in distress; what that evidence cannot do is provide access to a belief in the resurrection, that is to say a belief that the life of the world will be raised from death in a reversal that will include any particular individual. Access to such a belief can only come through participation in the struggles of the world towards life, where the frequent failures and setbacks really do raise the question, 'Are the dead raised?' In a community committed to that struggle there might indeed occur the dawning of a faith that all, both alive and dead, will be included in the final triumphing of life, when the last enemy is overcome. The raising of the dead is faith's final and most daring utterance, born of shared commitment and struggle; offered as itself the way into faith, it never overcomes the desperation from which it springs, and the language of the final great reverse is tamed into the sad longing for mere continuation.

The Exaltation of Christ

There is no struggle for the common life of humanity without an issue about authority. The Christian tradition rings with this battle, and so do the agonies of present-day society. The accounts of the last days of Jesus' life raise this issue in almost every line, and so does nearly every story that can be told about the attempt to secure an inclusive justice for the world. The proclamation of the resurrection was, as we saw, among other things the bold answer of the New Testament community to those who would say that they had no authority for what they were saying and that Jesus, having been condemned by the law, had no authority either. The authority of Christ is the authority of the cause of God, and God declared this to be so, say the New Testament writers, by raising him from the dead.

The crisis of authority inherent in the cause of Christ is not precipitated for its own sake, out of a doctrinaire commitment to anarchism, let alone a childish demand to have it one's own way; it is precipitated only in relation to the struggle of society for justice and truth, and it is precipitated by those who hold authority in their refusal to recognize that their authority is subject to the ultimate authority of justice and truth. Those who oppose them and take their authority from the justice and truth of their claims come sooner or later face to face with the question whether authority really does reside in the cause they are pursuing or whether it resides with those who brand resistance as proud, or unlawful, or immoral or sick. There is no separating Christ's authority from his resurrection.

No community can credibly speak of the resurrection unless it has placed itself in the situations of the struggle for justice and truth in human affairs which raise the question of who has authority. The blind acceptance of inherited authority patterns without any testing of them to see whether they serve the cause of justice and truth is bound to lead to a sense of remoteness and inaccessibility when the story of the resurrection is told: in such circumstances to point to the benefits of the virtues of compliance and obedience is simply to avoid the intense risks and conflicts which arise in any engagement with the world's struggle. It is not only, of course, the church which speaks of the resurrection and at the same time calls for obedience and order; it is also educational institutions who put obedience above the truth for which they exist and which will be their judge, and political organizations who earn contempt for preferring the maintenance of order and tranquillity to the interests of those who need the justice they claim to serve.

The raising of the dead can only be found at the point where courage is taken for the breaking of that pattern and daring affirmations can be made about the meaning of the resulting pain and failure. That is the meaning of the discovery that it was, after all, Jesus to whom God declared that he had given his authority by raising him from the dead; he was known at that point as the one by whom the world was to be judged and who had faithfully pursued the divine cause among men. To go looking for resurrection faith is necessarily to expose oneself to all the ultimate doubts which we find in the story of the last days of Jesus about who has authority, who is in the right and where the truth lies. Resurrection faith is to have entered that arena and still to have hope.

The New Future

By contrast with the New Testament writers we do not find that our society is predicated on the belief that the days surely come when sudden divine intervention will set the world right. We find ourselves as a society committed to the view that the future is for planning. Resurrection faith is not pleading for a return to a *deus ex machina* kind of eschatology, nor is it a demand for the throwing away of all that human ingenuity has brought about. It is about the issue of where hope lies.

What is noticeable about much commitment to planning the future is its utter half-heartedness. We believe we can plan to overcome this difficulty or right that wrong, and we use our skill to attempt to predict for years rather than merely weeks or months. But hope is demanded only at the point where the responsible implementation of a vision is the goal. Only at the point of striving after the constantly recurring issue of the justice of God is there any real question whether the future of Christ is any more than a dream. Against all the planning which implicitly or explicitly asserts that the future most to be desired is the least modification of the present, the resurrection faith asserts that the future belongs to Christ, the one who for what awaited him despised the failure and the shame. Where the community that holds the resurrection story at the same time espouses by its living a view of the future as a minor modification of the present it is not surprising that the story it tells loses all purchase on the decisive factors in living, and its hearers find themselves required to form a conclusion in the absence of the evidence.

To look for the living in hope is to cease assuming that what we must plan for is sustaining the present, and to begin entertaining the vision of a society in which plunder is not the only possibility and the world does not groan under the depredations of a humanity that avoids facing its own disorder by taking ever more and more from the earth. At the point where that hope is confronted by the militant declaration that present reality is the only one to be reckoned with, it will be possible to raise the question whether the future belongs to Christ and his cause, and that is the question whether God even now before that future dawns raises the dead.

Resurrection and the World of Hard Fact

It is at that point that the historic question of the future of the world becomes the historical question of the raising of Jesus. For at the point of that striving and that confrontation the issue must arise whether the vision is mere rhetoric or has the capacity to be actualized in the world of hard fact. It is not difficult to accept the world as it is and plan for its continuance, and it is perfectly possible, even while that is going on, to entertain dreams of a different world and use the language of miracle to describe what is a pious hope totally unconnected with life in the present. At the point of the vision's apparent failure to be capable of realization there arises the question whether resurrection is factual, whether it belongs in this world, whether it represents a divine response to the rebuff administered by the world to those who remain faithful to the vision, and whether that response has any real meaning in the present.

The only real evidence for an affirmative answer to that question comes at the point where the story of the resurrection appearances and of the transformed life of the earliest Christian community is seen to match our experience – however unlike in externals – of the divine response to the world's rebuff. On the basis of that experience it is both legitimate and possible to accept the disciples' claim of an external source for their belief that Christ was alive. Although their descriptions of their experience are often confusing, those who seek a way of discipleship in the world are able to discover that the disciples' assertion that a divine act occurred in the world of hard fact and not merely in their dreams is true. That our experience may match their accounts of theirs is the best hope we have of finding both meaning for and confirmation of our resurrection faith.

It is the greatest travesty of resurrection faith that it is used to support a doctrine of divine activity and human passivity. It is used to suggest that relying on God in advance is a stance towards living that corresponds to the biblical witness; in fact the discovery of the power of God comes not instead of human action but when human hopes and vision have been pursued to the limit of our efforts. Resurrection is what is promised at the limit of our wholeheartedness and not as support in our detachment.

To work wholeheartedly at the resurrection traditions with the tools of the historian produces absolute clarity and absolute confusion: clarity, that people were collecting and handing on material that expressed the greatest shout of their conviction that their looking for a new justice and a new hope against all odds did not in the end go unvindicated; clarity, that the future for which they were preparing was God's future, that he had placed it in the hands of Jesus and the world's rebuff would not negate that; confusion, because it *is* confusing to speak of the last end of all things in the language of causes and effects which is the only language of human endeavour; and it is confusing to say that the vindication which belongs only to God and is from outside the chain of events was in fact decisively revealed in that chain of events, of actions and of sufferings, whose name is Jesus of Nazareth; it is doubly confusing to have to tell such a story when all you have are memories of some people finding a grave empty and being told that that was not where you looked for the living one, and of others having seen Jesus alive after his death and being told that the real blessedness was faith without such seeing.

Yet what other confusion and what other clarity could there be for those who would seek to pursue in any generation the hard and detailed engagement which is necessary if the recurrent issue of justice is to be raised? and what other vindication would be worth anything except one that offers itself within the detail of plans and cities and foodstuffs and minerals, cruelty, affection, enjoyment and hope that are human history? and what promise would be worth entertaining that was not the upholding of our most committed action at its point of failure?

To say this is not simply to wish that a resurrection of Jesus might be so but to describe what at the end of much looking seems there to be found; it is to describe what can be known by means of a search made up of inquiry and discipleship. It is not to answer the questions we still want to ask about what happened to a body or to graveclothes or who saw what, but neither is it to outlaw those questions on the basis of some paralysing and demeaning call to mere faith; on the contrary, those detailed and factual questions which have to be asked about the past have their counterparts in the detailed questioning and striving which have to be undertaken in the present in the service of a vision for the future. But what sets the seal of validity on all those questionings and strivings is not merely that which they are able to achieve in their own way and on their own terms. What really vindicates our inquiring and our discipleship alike is that from outside their own terms and their own time, but from the source of the vision itself, in guises that are as many as those who see it, at the point where the strivings fail, where life appears gone and the vision itself a fraud, a new beginning captures us, and the dying one and the living one are seen to be one.

Abbreviations

ET   English translation
JB   Jerusalem Bible -
NEB   New English Bible
NEPT A. G. N. Flew and A. MacIntyre (eds.), *New Essays in Philosophical Theology*, 1956
NFT   J. M. Robinson and J. B. Cobb Jr. (eds.), *Theology as History* (New Frontiers in Theology, Vol. 3), 1967
NTI   R. Batey (ed.), *New Testament Issues*, 1970
SBT   Studies in Biblical Theology
SMR   C. F. D. Moule (ed.), *The Significance of the Message of the Resurrection for Faith in Jesus Christ*, SBT 2.8, 1968
TH   P. Gardiner (ed.), *Theories of History*, 1959

Unless otherwise stated, biblical quotations are taken from the Revised Standard Version of the Bible.

Notes

1. What are we looking for?

1. For the views of some of the church fathers and subsequent writers, see J. McLeman, *Resurrection Then and Now*, 1965, pp. 197 - 208. The development of ideas about the resurrection during the patristic period is also described in L. Geering, *(Resurrection – a Symbol of Hope*, 1971, pp. 174 - 94.

2. See particularly F. G. Downing, *The Church and Jesus*, 1968; A. O. Dyson, *The Immortality of the Past*, 1974; V. A. Harvey, *The Historian and the Believer*, 1967; A. Richardson, *History Sacred and Profane*, 1964; T. A. Roberts, *History and Christian Apologetic*, 1960. As will become clear, this book owes much to Downing's analysis of the issues.

3. See for example A. M. Ramsey, *The Resurrection of Christ*, 1945, p. 36; G. O'Collins, *The Easter Jesus*, 1973, p. 72.

4. B. F. Westcott, *The Gospel of the Resurrection*, 1898, p. 116. This and Westcott's other work on the resurrection, *The Revelation of the Risen Lord*, 1881, remain classics, even if the challenging of some of his historical assumptions means that his understanding of the resurrection cannot be presented unchanged today.

5. C. Gore, *The Reconstruction of Belief*, 1926, p. 370

2. Where are people looking?

1. M. C. Perry, *The Easter Enigma*, 1959, p. 292. This book is commended by J. A. T. Robinson (*The Human Face of God*, p. 130, n. 110) as 'an important but neglected study', but as Robinson himself says (ibid.), the kind of evidence which Perry adduces would not establish resurrection in the New Testament sense.

2. M. C. Perry, op. cit., p. 191.

3. Ibid., p. 192.

4. Ibid., p. 195.

5. Ibid., pp. 229 - 38.

6. Ibid., pp. 240 - 3.

7. Ibid., p. 71. It is noticeable that in Perry's later book, *The Resurrection of Man*, 1975, which appeared after this book was completed, he makes much more use of New Testament criticism. On the other hand, it is still true that his main interest in the resurrection is in its relevance to the question of life beyond death, and to that extent the criticisms made in this section still apply.

8. H. H. Price, *Essays in the Philosophy of Religion*, 1972.

9. Op. cit., Preface

10. Ibid., pp. 82 - 90.

11. Ibid., p. 120.

12. Ibid., pp. 120f.

13. Athenagoras, *De Resurrectione* 3 - 11.

14. See particularly Tertullian, *Adversus Marcionem* V.10 and Irenaeus, *Adversus omnes haereses* V. iii. 3.

15. R. A. Norris, *God and World in Early Christian Thought*, 1965, p. 167 (1967, p. 137).

16. H. A. Williams, *True Resurrection*, 1972, p. 33. See below, pp. 20 - 25.

17. The New Testament appears to have very little interest in offering consolation for grief, as indeed it has little concern for the psychological reaction of the disciples to the death of Jesus or their subsequent transformation by the resurrection. The concern of Paul may be said to relate to 'eschatological grief', that is to say for the fact that a person appears, on the face of it, to have been excluded by death from God's coming victory – as Jesus was on the face of it by his crucifixion.

18. It is interesting to observe that the germination of a seed can only be used as an analogy of the resurrection by employing the picture of the seed *dying* before growth can take place. This is, of course, botanically false, but parallels the fact that birth is not used as an analogy for resurrection except in the case of birth from a *barren* womb in the case of Sarah (Rom. 4. 18 - 25). Resurrection refers to something beyond the ordinary natural progression.

19. W. Stringfellow, 'Harlem, Rebellion and Resurrection', *The Christian Century*, 11 November 1970, pp. 1345 - 8. A similarly all-embracing hope is more fully worked out in J. Baillie's classic book, *And the Life Everlasting*, 1933; he begins, however, with the contemporary quest for survival and not with the proclamation of the resurrection of Jesus, and thus no account is taken in his book of the difference between modern questions and those with which the New Testament was concerned.

20. H. A. Williams, *True Resurrection*, p. 4.

21. Ibid.

22. Ibid., p. 5.

23. Ibid., pp. 10f.

24. Ibid., p. 33.

25. Ibid., p. 54.

26. Ibid., p. 80.

27. Ibid., p. 131.

28. Ibid.
29. Ibid., p. 118.
30. Ibid., pp. 123f.
31. Ibid., pp. 147–51.
32. Ibid., p. 154.
33. Ibid., p. 171.
34. Ibid., p. 180.
35. But not sufficiently to do justice to a book filled with poetic expression and insight. Williams provides the necessary description of what G. O'Collins in *The Easter Jesus*, 1973, calls 'the experiential correlate' in resurrection and what S. H. Hooke in *The Resurrection of Christ as History and Experience*, 1967, means by experience. Both of these books pay more attention than Williams does to the historical data, but have very little to say about what are the kinds of experience which at the present time would count as 'resurrection'.
36. 'The Finkenwalde Seminary to the Council of Brethren of the Old Prussian Union', a letter written 10 November 1935. See D. Bonhoeffer, *The Way to Freedom*, 1972, pp. 36f.
37. H. A. Williams, op. cit., pp. 110f.
38. See for example G. E. Mendenhall, 'The Hebrew Conquest of Palestine', *Biblical Archaeologist* 25.3, September 1962, pp. 67–87, or M. Noth, 'The Homes of the Tribes in Palestine', in S. Sandmel (ed.), *Old Testament Issues*, 1969, pp. 121–56.

3. More looking than finding

1. G. W. F. Hegel, *Lectures on the Philosophy of History*, 1944; A. Comte, *The Positive Philosophy of Auguste Comte*, 1893; K. H. Marx, *Selected Writings in Sociology and Social Philosophy*, ed. T. Bottomore and M. Rubel, 1956.
2. K. R. Popper, *The Poverty of Historicism*, 1957.
3. See G. Vico, *The New Science*, 1948, quoted *TH*, pp. 12–21; J. G. Herder, *Reflections on the Philosophy of the History of Mankind*, 1969, quoted *TH*, p. 35.
4. See particularly Kant's 'eighth proposition' in his 'Idea of a Universal History from a Cosmopolitan Point of View', trans. W. Hastie, *TH*, pp. 30–32; also in *Eternal Peace and Other International Essays*, 1914.
5. A. N. de Condorcet, *Sketch for a Historical Picture of the Progress of Mankind*, 1955, quoted *TH*, p. 58; H. T. Buckle, *History of Civilization in England*, 1899, quoted *TH*, pp. 106–24.
6. A. Toynbee, *Civilization on Trial*, 1948, ch. 1. See *TH*, p. 210.
7. R. Aron, 'The Philosophy of History', *Chambers's Encyclopaedia*, Vol. 7, 1966, pp. 150–5.
8. W. B. Gallie, 'Explanations in History and the Genetic Sciences' *Mind* 64, May 1955, pp. 160–80 reprinted *TH*, pp. 386–402; also his *Philosophy and the Historical Understanding*, 1964; A. C. Danto, *The*

Analytical Philosophy of History, 1965. There is an important critique of the narrative models of Gallie and Danto in F. G. Downing, *The Church and Jesus*, 1968, pp. 164ff., p. 170 n. 66. On form criticism, see R. Bultmann, *The History of the Synoptic Tradition*, 1963.

9. H. A. Williams, *Jesus and the Resurrection*, 1951, p. 111.

10. M. Barth and V. H. Fletcher, *Acquittal by Resurrection*, 1964.

11. Op. cit., pp. 99 – 122.

12. A. M. Ramsey, *The Resurrection of Christ*, 1945, p. 56.

13. E.g. ibid., p. 71, 'Is it not reasonable to suppose that there may have been appearances in both localities [Galilee and Jerusalem]?' But if it is possible to account for the differences between the narratives on *theological* grounds, what are the *historical* grounds for accepting either place?

14. J. Moltmann, *Theology of Hope*, 1967, p. 226.

15. L. Geering, *Resurrection – a Symbol of Hope*, 1971, p. 232.

16. W. Marxsen, *The Resurrection of Jesus of Nazareth*, 1968, p. 148.

17. W. Künneth, *Theology of the Resurrection*, 1965, pp. 285ff.

18. W. Pannenberg, *Jesus – God and Man*, 1968, p. 107.

19. G. W. H. Lampe and D. M. MacKinnon, *The Resurrection*, 1966, p. 10.

20. C. F. Evans, *Resurrection and the New Testament*, 1970, pp. 170ff.

21. H. - G. Geyer, 'Survey of the Debate', *SMR*, p. 105.

22. Ibid.

23. D. P. Fuller, *Easter Faith and History*, 1968, p. 60. But his evaluation of the evidence is open to criticism; see below pp. 56f.

24. C. F. D. Moule, 'Introduction', *SMR*, pp. 1 – 11.

25. In practice, these subdivisions are somewhat rough. The fourth view, in particular, is sometimes combined with one or more of the others.

26. Barth expresses the same view in *The Epistle to the Romans*, 1933, p. 30.

27. R. Bultmann, 'New Testament and Mythology' in H. -W. Bartsch (ed.), *Kerygma and Myth* I, 1954, p. 42. Bultmann's view is also found in his *Theology of the New Testament* I, 1952, pp. 292 – 306; e.g., 'Christ's death and resurrection, accordingly, are cosmic occurrences, not incidents that took place once upon a time in the past' (p. 299). See also *Jesus Christ and Mythology*, 1958. For a critique of Bultmann's use of the New Testament evidence, see A. D. Churchill, *The Resurrection of Christ* (unpublished D.Phil. thesis, Oxford 1968), but this work does not take account of Bultmann's *theological* objections to a historical resurrection, being concerned only to establish what views were held by the New Testament writers. Bultmann's theological and philosophical presuppositions are critically examined in D. Cairns, *A Gospel without Myth?*, 1960, esp. pp. 159 – 63; R. W. Hepburn, 'Demythologizing and the Problem of Validity', *NEPT*, pp. 227 – 42; and E. W. Good, 'The Meaning of Demythologization', in C.W.

Kegley (ed.), *The Theology of Rudolf Bultmann*, 1966, esp. pp. 34 – 40.
28. See K. Barth, *Church Dogmatics* III. 2, 1960, pp. 437ff.
29. L. Geering, op. cit., pp. 218f.
30. Ibid., p. 67.
31. Ibid., p. 66.
32. W. Marxsen, op. cit., p. 141.
33. W. Marxsen, 'The Resurrection of Jesus as a Historical and Theological Problem', *SMR*, p. 30.
34. G. W. H. Lampe, 'Easter – a Statement', in G. W. H. Lampe and D. M. MacKinnon, *The Resurrection*, pp. 29 – 60.
35. *Interpreter's Dictionary of the Bible*, Vol. 4, 1962, pp. 43 – 53.
36. Op. cit., pp. 45 – 47. C. H. Dodd expresses the same view, though with different theological conclusions; see *The Founder of Christianity*, 1971, p. 167.
37. J. A. T. Robinson, *The Human Face of God*, 1973, pp. 127 – 41.
38. N. Clark, *Interpreting the Resurrection*, 1967, p. 95.
39. R. Gregor Smith, *Secular Christianity*, 1960, pp. 103ff.
40. *The Human Face of God*, p. 130.
41. Ibid., p. 131.
42. C. F. D. Moule and D. Cupitt, 'The Resurrection – a Disagreement', *Theology* 75, October 1972, pp. 507 – 19.
43. D. P. Fuller, op. cit., pp. 188ff.
44. F. Morison, *Who Moved the Stone?*, 1930.
45. H. J. Schonfield, *The Passover Plot*, 1965.
46. J. N. D. Anderson, *A Lawyer among the Theologians*, 1973.
47. The criticisms advanced here of approaches such as Morison's are not intended to rule out the use of imaginative techniques such as belong to novels or drama in the presentation of Easter. (See, for example, S. Jackman, *The Davidson Affair*, 1968.) Such approaches, however, are not to be confused with historical reconstruction.
48. J. N. D. Anderson, op. cit., p. 103. Anderson considers his viewpoint is supported by D. H. van Daalen's comment (*The Real Resurrection*, 1972, p. 41) that 'Traditions may serve a particular purpose in the community, but that does not necessarily mean that they were invented for the purpose.' But this is hardly the point. What the discovery of the theological function of the resurrection narratives within the primitive church has done is not to prove them false but to raise questions about their meaning and about the capacity of historical research to separate their historical from their theological content.
49. See J. A. Baker, *The Foolishness of God*, 1970, pp. 244 – 74.
50. Ibid., p. 274.
51. C. F. Evans, op. cit., p. 128.
52. Ibid., p. 130.
53. See particularly *The Epistle to the Romans*.
54. Op. cit., p. 195.
55. K. Barth, *Church Dogmatics* III.2, p. 448.
56. Ibid., p. 446. See V. A. Harvey, *The Historian and the Believer*, where Barth's later view is rightly criticized.

57. Op. cit., p. 441.
58. P. Tillich, *Systematic Theology* II, University of Chicago Press 1957, p. 153 (Nisbet 1957, p. 176).
59. Ibid., p. 153 (p. 177).
60. Ibid., p. 154 (p. 178).
61. See below, pp. 85ff., C. F. Evans, op. cit., pp. 11ff., and J. A. Baker, op. cit., pp. 253 - 5.
62. P. Tillich, op. cit., p. 154 (p. 178).
63. Ibid., p. 155 (p. 179).
64. Ibid.
65. Ibid.
66. Ibid., p. 154 (p. 178).
67. See, for example, A. Richardson, *Science, History and Faith*, 1950, p. 61. It is only in his later book, *History Sacred and Profane*, that Richardson takes the view that *all* history-writing involves interpretation and therefore faith; see below, pp. 73ff.
68. W. Künneth, *Theology of the Resurrection*, p. 103.
69. Ibid.
70. Ibid., pp. 104f.
71. Ibid., p. 107.
72. See ibid., pp. 180 - 9.
73. W. Pannenberg, 'Did Jesus Really Rise from the Dead?', *NTI*, pp. 102 - 17.
74. See also his essay, 'The Revelation of God in Jesus of Nazareth', *NFT*, pp. 101 - 33.
75. E.g., *Jesus - God and Man*, p. 104.
76. Ibid., p. 98.
77. Ibid., p. 81.
78. Ibid.
79. See below, pp. 85ff.
80. *Jesus - God and Man*, p. 85.
81. Ibid., p. 88.
82. J. Moltmann, *Theology of Hope*, p. 145.
83. Ibid., p. 174.
84. Moltmann devotes hardly any space to these questions.
85. Ibid., p. 191. This is quoted by Robinson (*The Human Face of God*, p. 136n.), but his dismissal of it as 'playing with words' may relate in some measure to his own failure to take seriously enough the effect of kerygmatic and eschatological motifs on the form of the resurrection accounts.
86. J. Moltmann, op. cit., p. 182.
87. C. F. Evans, op. cit., p. 131.
88. R. R. Niebuhr, *Resurrection and Historical Reason*, 1957.
89. Op. cit., p. 173.
90. Ibid.
91. Ibid., p. 177. As V. A. Harvey states (*The Historian and the Believer*, pp. 227f.), the difficulty with this argument is that death in fact occurs often enough for its defeat to be fairly surprising.

92. A. Richardson, *History Sacred and Profane*, 1964.

93. See I. T. Ramsey, *Religious Language: an Empirical Placing of Theological Phrases*, 1957.

94. A. Richardson, op. cit., p. 226.

95. Ibid., pp. 195ff. For a critique of Richardson's view about the resurrection, see F. G. Downing, *The Church and Jesus*, 1968, p. 145n.

96. V. A. Harvey, op. cit., p. 249.

97. Ibid., pp. 255ff.

98. Ibid., p. 274. But does the repeated 'in fact' stand for more than emphasis, and if so are we dealing with more than mere perspective?

99. F. G. Downing, op. cit., p. 74.

100. Ibid., pp. 26ff.

101. Ibid., p. 180.

102. Ibid., pp. 191f.; see below, pp. 141f.

103. This is not dissimilar to the conclusion vigorously expressed by J. McLeman, *Resurrection Then and Now*, though he is less disposed than Downing to be involved in the continuing historical debate. 'That Jesus is the only person of whom it could be believed that he rose from the dead in any sense which is not synonymous with magic is the fact that created the Christian faith' (op. cit., p. 243). But is it?

104. H. Price, 'Is the Resurrection of Christ to be Explained by Theologians?', *Theology* 70, March 1967, pp. 109f.

105. B. G. Mitchell, 'What Philosophical Problems Arise from Belief in the Resurrection?', *Theology* 70, March 1967, p. 112.

106. See A. Loades and J. Cumpsty, 'What is Belief in the Resurrection?', *Theology* 70, March 1967, pp. 99 - 104.

107. Op. cit., p. 101.

108. Ibid., p. 103.

109. N. Smart, 'What are the Dimensions of Belief in the Resurrection?', *Theology* 70, March 1967, p. 118.

110. For a very clear account of the way in which much Protestantism takes its stand on commitment alone, and the vulnerability of such a position, see W. W. Bartley III, *The Retreat to Commitment*, 1966.

4. Looking at the New Testament

1. It is impossible to use the New Testament evidence for even this limited purpose without presupposing the great amount of detailed work which has been done on the various texts which relate to the resurrection, even though the inclusion of much of it within the body of this chapter would have detracted from its main concern. While it is not possible to give a summary of agreed results of current research, for scholars' judgments differ at many points, the aim of this chapter in using the texts for the purpose of giving the best possible account of the convictions of the various New Testament writers is shared by many. The accounts that are emerging of the development of the resurrection traditions are of vital importance in this endeavour. A very full

account of the current state of research into the texts can be found in
B. Rigaux, *Dieu l'a ressuscité*, 1973. See also particularly C. F. Evans,
Resurrection and the New Testament, 1970; R. H. Fuller, *The Forma-
tion of the Resurrection Narratives*, 1972; A. D. Churchill, *The Resur-
rection of Christ*, 1968. On the narratives of the appearances, see C. H.
Dodd, 'The Appearances of the Risen Christ: an Essay in Form-Criticism
of the Gospel' in *More New Testament Studies*, 1968, pp. 102-33. On
the traditions concerning the empty tomb, see E. L. Bode, *The First
Easter Morning*, 1970, and on the Pauline tradition in I Corinthians see
J. C. Hurd Jr., *The Origin of I Corinthians*, 1965.

2. See G. W. E. Nickelsburg, *Resurrection, Immortality and Eternal Life in Intertestamental Judaism*, 1973.

3. M. E. Dahl, *The Resurrection of the Body*, 1962, p. 95. The
word 'sacramental' of course introduces a later thought-form. Dahl's
consideration of the doctrine of resurrection is very full, but omits to
give due weight to the motif of judgment.

4. J. Moltmann, *Theology of Hope*, p. 192.

5. Ibid., p. 193.

6. L. Geering surveys much of this material in *Resurrection – a
Symbol of Hope*, pp. 75 - 85, but fails to note the way in which the significance of the idea is changed in its use by the early church.

7. For an account of this transformation of cultural expectations,
see J. A. Baker, *The Foolishness of God*, pp. 253 - 5.

8. Cf. R. H. Fuller, op. cit., p. 170: Those appearances 'fall into
two groups, those concerned with the establishment of the eschatological community, and those concerned with the inauguration of the
community's mission'.

9. Cf. W. Marxsen, *The Resurrection of Jesus of Nazareth*, especially chs. 3 and 4.

10. W. Marxsen, op. cit., pp. 63ff.

11. This point is made by E. Schweizer, *Lordship and Discipleship*,
1960, p. 38. Cf. R. H. Fuller, op. cit., pp. 33f., 170.

12. Cf. C. F. Evans, op. cit., p. 142. This does not, of course,
exclude A. D. Churchill's conclusion (op. cit.) that the reason why the
resurrection narratives could not be replaced simply by the proclamation of Christ's exaltation was that the disciples had in fact experienced
Christ as having been raised bodily from the tomb. But the fact that the
resurrection narratives fulfilled the theological function of asserting the
continuity of the exalted Christ with the earthly Jesus cannot be ignored and may cause one to hesitate before accepting Churchill's account
as conclusive.

13. C. F. Evans, op. cit., p. 49.

14. See J. C. Hurd, op. cit., pp. 195f.

15. Ibid., pp. 282 - 7.

16. *Theology of Hope*, pp. 154 - 65.

17. Ibid., p. 155.

18. For the significance of *soma* as the totality of the person, see
M. E. Dahl, op. cit., pp. 59 - 73.

19. J. Moltmann, op. cit., p. 164.

20. R. H. Fuller, op. cit., pp. 36, 170.

21. At least this much can be said in opposition to Marxsen's claim (op. cit., p. 111) that Paul 'nowhere offers factual evidence'.

22. R. H. Fuller asserts (op. cit., p. 170) that on the basis of Paul's apocalyptic presuppositions he must have believed in the empty tomb. But E. L. Bode is surely right in saying (op. cit., pp. 90 - 100) that such 'doctrinal' thinking is not borne out by the text.

23. A later attempt was made, presumably in the light of Luke 24.24 to add v. 12 to the manuscript, describing an apostolic visit to the tomb.

24. Cf. W. Marxsen, op. cit., ch. 3.

25. The account in John 20.8 of the two disciples running, the beloved disciple arriving first but Peter actually entering the tomb first, and the beloved disciple 'seeing and believing' seems to be part of the preoccupation of the last two chapters of John with the relative status of John and Peter.

26. See J. A. Baker, op. cit., pp. 252ff.

27. It can also be observed that the idea of resurrection becomes linked with that of rebirth: 'Blessed be the God and Father of our Lord Jesus Christ, who in his great mercy has given us a new birth as his sons, by raising Jesus Christ from the dead' (I Peter 1.2, JB). The idea of a circle of belief containing a number of elements parallels Smart's idea of the 'dimensions' of belief in the resurrection. See above, pp. 80f.

5. *Many ways of looking*

1. See R. M. Hare, 'Theology and Falsification', *NEPT*, pp. 99 - 102.

2. D. Bonhoeffer to E. Bethge, 30 April 1944, *Letters and Papers from Prison*, 1971, p. 279.

3. See W. Marxsen, *The Resurrection of Jesus of Nazareth*, pp. 138f.

4. P. Berger, *A Rumour of Angels*, 1970, p. 116.

5. F. G. Downing, *The Church and Jesus*, pp. 132f.

6. Ibid., pp. 191f.

7. P. Abelard, *'O Quanta Qualia'* (*English Hymnal*, 1933, no. 465, v.6).

8. W. Pannenberg, *Jesus - God and Man*, pp. 107f.

9. W. Pannenberg, 'Response to the Discussion', *NFT*, p. 256.

10. M. J. Buss, 'The Meaning of History', *NFT*, p. 144.

11. Ibid., pp. 144f.

12. Cf. the suggestion in the proposed prayer book of 1928 that the Athanasian Creed be recited without the blessings and curses at the beginning and end. No doubt this might make that creed in some ways more congenial, though no more comprehensible; but to do so would also conceal the all-important key to understanding its meaning, which is that it was once thought to be a matter of life and death.

13. This is the important conclusion of Berger's chapter on 'Relativizing the Relativizers', op. cit., pp. 53–65.

14. Because, as has been pointed out, the resurrection is commended in the fourth gospel primarily as the answer to the (quite different) Hellenistic search for 'life'.

15. C. F. Evans, *Resurrection and the New Testament*, p. 130.

16. F. G. Downing, op. cit., pp. 1–44.

17. From *Exsultet*, the seventh-century hymn sung at the lighting of the paschal candle on the eve of Easter.

18. Downing's criticism of such attempts to revise history's agenda and presuppositions (op. cit., esp. pp. 132–70) is unanswerable, and what he says about Richardson would apply equally to Pannenberg (on whom cf. W. Hamilton: 'The Character of Pannenberg's Theology', *NFT*, p. 180: 'It is rather hard to understand, or take seriously, a theology that can by a definition dispose of the secularism which has been an important segment of Western history for the past four hundred years.' Cf. also A. O. Dyson, *The Immortality of the Past*, 1974, p. 112: 'Thus, against all theological enterprises which seek to repeat "earlier constellations of thought", which try to bring the past into the present, we must continually struggle for the elaboration of a theological method which is appropriate to both transcendence and historical existence.'

19. V. A. Demant, *The Religious Prospect*, 1939, pp. 56f.

20. Ibid., pp. 151f.

21. Ibid., p. 199.

22. Ibid., p. 200.

23. D. Bonhoeffer to E. Bethge, 16 July 1944, op. cit., p. 360. That particular letter shows Bonhoeffer attempting to reconcile (or at any rate to do justice to) the 'adulthood' of the world and its self-sufficiency and the demands of radical obedience to God. His language inevitably possesses the same quality as much of Demant's: 'And we cannot be honest unless we recognize that we have to live in the world *etsi deus non daretur*. And this is just what we do recognize – before God! God himself compels us to recognize it. So our coming of age leads us to a true recognition of our situation before God. God would have us know that we must live as men who manage our lives without him. The God who is with us is the God who forsakes us. . . . The God who lets us live in the world without the working hypothesis of God is the God before whom we stand continually. Before God and with God we live without God. God lets himself be pushed out of the world on to the cross.' Bonhoeffer goes on to speak of the powerlessness of God in the world as the only means by which he is able to help man. Thus on the one hand adulthood, maturity and responsibility are affirmed and in that sense creativity is celebrated; on the other hand the need for that which is not part of the world's self-sufficiency – in Bonhoeffer's terms, the suffering God (ibid., p. 361).

24. The introduction of the Trinity at this point is intended only to draw attention to the fact that the nature of resurrection faith as it has

been elucidated in this book is not different from the way in which Christians have very frequently discerned the meaning of their faith, and in particular that it shares in the mysterious way in which believers have understood the activity and nature of God. An exposition of the resurrection is in the last resort an exposition of what is believed to have been an action of God in the world and has therefore to do justice to two poles at once. The resurrection thus exhibits the dialectical relationship of which Dyson speaks (op. cit., pp. 100ff.) between God and the world, of which trinitarian theology also speaks. As Dyson points out, it is precisely because the divine-human relationship has this character that Christian theology will always find itself torn between a concern for the discovery of historical truth and the realization that the historical process is not in the last resort the only process, as the material world of becoming was not, in Demant's terms, the only world. The discernment of the nature of the relationship between God and the world at any moment is the work of prophecy (and it is doubtful whether theology should claim for itself the capacity for that kind of discernment, *pace* Dyson, op. cit., p. 111: 'The theologian is above all concerned with the historical actuality of the divine-human relationship at successive points in history, and especially in his own present age'). But theology does have the task of displaying that relationship as it was crucially displayed in what happened in and through Jesus, including his death and resurrection.

6.   *What there is to be found*

1. G. Gutierrez, *A Theology of Liberation*, p. 227.
2. Ibid., p. 227f.
3. Ibid., p. 231.
4. Gutierrez, op. cit., pp. 272-9.

List of Works Cited

Anderson, J. N. D., *A Lawyer among the Theologians*, Hodder & Stoughton 1973

Aron, R., 'The Philosophy of History', *Chambers's Encyclopaedia*, Vol. 7, Pergamon Press 1966, pp. 150 – 5.

Baillie, J., *And the Life Everlasting*, Scribner 1933, Oxford University Press 1934

Baker, J. A., *The Foolishness of God*, Darton, Longman & Todd 1970

Barth, K., *Church Dogmatics* III.2, ET T. & T. Clark and Scribner 1960

Barth, K., *The Epistle to the Romans*, ET Oxford University Press 1933

Barth, K., *The Resurrection of the Dead*, ET Hodder & Stoughton and Revell 1933

Barth, M., and Fletcher, V. H., *Acquittal by Resurrection*, Holt, Rinehart & Winston 1964

Bartley, W. W., III, *The Retreat to Commitment*, Knopf 1962, Chatto & Windus 1964

Batey, R., (ed.), *New Testament Issues*, SCM Press and Harper & Row 1970 (cited as *NTI*)

Berger, P., *A Rumour of Angels* (1969), Penguin 1971

Bode, E. L., *The First Easter Morning*, Biblical Institute Press, Rome, 1970

Bonhoeffer, D., *Letters and Papers from Prison*, ET, enlarged ed., SCM Press 1971, Macmillan (NY) 1972

Bonhoeffer, D., *The Way to Freedom*, ET (1966), Fontana 1972

Buckle, H. T., *History of Civilization in England*, London 1899; see *TH*, pp. 106 – 24

Bultmann, R., *The History of the Synoptic Tradition*, ET Blackwell and Harper & Row 1963

Bultmann, R., *Jesus Christ and Mythology*, ET Scribner 1958, SCM Press 1960

Bultmann, R., 'New Testament and Mythology' in H. W. Bartsch (ed.), *Kerygma and Myth*, SPCK 1953, Macmillan (NY) 1954

Bultmann, R., 'On the Problem of Demythologizing', *NTI*, pp. 35 – 44

Bultmann, R., *Theology of the New Testament* I, ET SCM Press and Scribner 1952

Buss, M. J., 'The Meaning of History', *NFT*, pp. 135 – 54

Cairns, D., *A Gospel without Myth?*, SCM Press 1960

Churchill, A. D., *The Resurrection of Christ*, unpublished D.Phil. thesis, Oxford University 1968

Clark, N., *Interpreting the Resurrection*, SCM Press and Allenson 1967

Collingwood, R. G., *The Idea of History*, Clarendon Press 1946

Comte, A., *The Positive Philosophy of Auguste Comte*, trans. H. Martineau, London 1893

Condorcet, A. N. de, *Sketch for a Historical Picture of the Progress of the Human Mind*, ET Weidenfeld & Nicholson and Noonday Press 1955

Dahl, M. E., *The Resurrection of the Body*, SBT 36, SCM Press and Allenson 1962

Danto, A. C., *The Analytical Philosophy of History*, Cambridge University Press 1965

Demant, V. A., *The Religious Prospect*, Frederick Muller 1939

Dodd, C. H., 'The Appearances of the Risen Christ' in D. E. Nineham (ed.), *Studies in the Gospels: Essays in memory of R. H. Lightfoot*, Blackwell 1955, pp. 9 – 35, reprinted in *More New Testament Studies*, Manchester University Press 1968, pp. 102 – 33

Dodd, C. H., *The Founder of Christianity*, Collins and Macmillan (NY) 1971

Downing, F. G., *The Church and Jesus*, SBT 2.10, SCM Press and Allenson 1968

Dyson, A. C., *The Immortality of the Past*, SCM Press 1974

Evans, C. F., *Resurrection and the New Testament*, SBT 2.12, SCM Press and Allenson 1970

Flew, A. G. N., and MacIntyre, A. (eds.), *New Essays in Philosophical Theology*, SCM Press and Macmillan (NY) 1956 (cited as *NEPT*)

Fuller, D. P., *Easter Faith and History*, Eerdmans 1965, Tyndale Press 1968

Fuller, R. H., *The Formation of the Resurrection Narratives*, SPCK and Macmillan (NY) 1972

Gallie, W. B., 'Explanations in History and the Genetic Sciences', *Mind* 64, May 1955, pp. 160 – 80, reprinted *TH*, pp. 386 – 402

Gallie, W. B., *Philosophy and the Historical Understanding*, Chatto & Windus and Schocken Books 1964

Gardiner, P. (ed.), *Theories of History*, The Free Press, New York, 1959 (cited as *TH*)

Geering, L., *Resurrection – a Symbol of Hope*, Hodder & Stoughton 1971

Geyer, H. -G., 'Survey of the Debate', *SMR*, pp. 105 – 35

Good, E. W., 'The Meaning of Demythologization' in C. W. Kegley (ed.), *The Theology of Rudolf Bultmann*, SCM Press and Harper & Row 1966, pp. 21 – 40

Gore, C., *The Reconstruction of Belief*, John Murray 1926

Gutierrez, G., *A Theology of Liberation*, ET Orbis Books 1973, SCM Press 1974

Hamilton, W., 'The Character of Pannenberg's Theology', *NFT*, pp. 176 – 96

Hare, R. M., 'Theology and Falsification', *NEPT*, pp. 99 – 103

Harvey, V. A., *The Historian and the Believer*, SCM Press and Macmillan (NY) 1967

Hegel, G. W. F., *Lectures on the Philosophy of History*, trans. J. Sibree, Dover Publications 1944, W. H. Allen 1947

Hepburn, R. W., 'Demythologizing and the Problem of Validity', *NEPT*, pp. 227 – 42

Herder, J. G., *Reflections on the Philosophy of the History of Mankind*, ET Chicago University Press 1969

Hooke, S. H., *The Resurrection of Christ as History and Experience*, Darton, Longman & Todd 1967

Hurd, J. C., Jr., *The Origin of I Corinthians*, Seabury Press and SPCK 1965

Jackman, S., *The Davidson Affair*, Eerdmans 1967, Faber & Faber 1968

Kant, I., *Eternal Peace and Other International Essays*, ET World Peace Foundation, Boston, 1914

Künneth, W., *The Theology of the Resurrection*, ET SCM Press and Westminster Press 1965

Lampe, G. W. H., and MacKinnon, D. M., *The Resurrection*, Mowbray 1966, Westminster Press 1967

Loades, A., and Cumpsty, J., 'What is Belief in the Resurrection?', *Theology* 70, March 1967, pp. 99 – 104

Marx, K. H., *Selected Writings in Sociology and Social Philosophy*, ed. T. B. Bottomore and M. Rubel (1956), Penguin 1970

Marxsen, W., *The Resurrection of Jesus of Nazareth*, SCM Press and Fortress Press 1968

Marxsen, W., 'The Resurrection of Jesus as a Historical and Theological Problem', *SMR*, pp. 15 – 50

McLeman, J., *Resurrection Then and Now*, Hodder & Stoughton 1965

Mendenhall, G. E., 'The Hebrew Conquest of Palestine', *Biblical Archaeologist* 25.3, September 1962, pp. 67 – 87

Mitchell, B. C., 'What Philosophical Problems Arise from Belief in the Resurrection?', *Theology* 70, March 1967, pp. 110 – 14

Moltmann, J., *Theology of Hope*, ET SCM Press and Harper & Row 1967

Morison, F., *Who Moved the Stone?*, Faber & Faber 1930

Moule, C. F. D., (ed.), *The Significance of the Message of the Resurrection for Faith in Jesus Christ*, SBT 2.8, SCM Press and Allenson 1968

Moule, C. F. D., and Cupitt, D., 'The Resurrection – a Disagreement', *Theology* 75, October 1972, pp. 507 – 19

Nickelsburg, G. W. E., *Resurrection, Immortality and Eternal Life in Intertestamental Judaism*, Oxford University Press 1973

Niebuhr, R. R., *Resurrection and Historical Reason*, Scribner 1957

Norris, R. A., *God and World in Early Christian Thought*, Seabury Press 1965, A. & C. Black 1967

Noth, M., 'The Homes of the Tribes in Palestine' in S. Sandmel (ed.), *Old Testament Issues*, SCM Press and Harper & Row 1969, pp. 121–56

O'Collins, G., *The Easter Jesus*, Darton, Longman & Todd 1973

Pannenberg, W., 'Did Jesus Really Rise from the Dead?', *NTI*, pp. 102–17

Pannenberg, W., *Jesus – God and Man*, ET SCM Press and Westminster Press 1970

Pannenberg, W., 'The Revelation of God in Jesus of Nazareth', *NFT*, pp. 101–33

Pannenberg, W., 'Response to the Discussion', *NFT*, pp. 221–76

Perry, M. C., *The Easter Enigma*, Faber & Faber 1959

Perry, M. C., *The Resurrection of Man*, Mowbray 1975

Popper, K. R., *The Poverty of Historicism*, Routledge & Kegan Paul and Beacon Press 1957

Price, H., 'Is the Resurrection of Christ to be Explained by Theologians?', *Theology* 70, March 1967, pp. 105–10

Price, H. H., *Essays in the Philosophy of Religion*, Oxford University Press 1972

Ramsey, A. M., *The Resurrection of Christ*, Geoffrey Bles and Westminster Press 1945

Ramsey, I. T., *Religious Language: an Empirical Placing of Theological Phrases*, SCM Press and Allenson 1964

Richardson, A., *History Sacred and Profane*, SCM Press and Westminster Press 1964

Richardson, A., *Science, History and Faith*, Oxford University Press 1950

Rigaux, B., *Dieu l'a ressuscité*, Duculot, Gembloux, 1973

Roberts, T. A., *History and Christian Apologetic*, SPCK 1960

Robinson, J. A. T., *The Human Face of God*, SCM Press and Westminster Press 1973

Robinson, J. A. T., 'Resurrection in the New Testament' in *The Interpreter's Dictionary of the Bible*, Vol. 4, Abingdon Press 1962, pp. 43–53

Robinson, J. M., and Cobb, J. B., Jr. (eds.), *Theology as History* (New Frontiers in Theology, Vol. 3), Harper & Row 1967 (cited as *NFT*)

Schonfield, H. J., *The Passover Plot*, Hutchinson and Bernard Geis 1965

Schweizer, E., *Lordship and Discipleship*, ET, SBT 28, SCM Press and Allenson 1960

Smart, N., 'What are the Dimensions of Belief in the Resurrection?', Theology 70, March 1967, pp. 114–18

Smith, R. Gregor, *Secular Christianity*, Collins 1960

Stringfellow, W., 'Harlem, Rebellion and Resurrection', *The Christian Century*, 11 November 1970, pp. 1345–8

Tillich, P., *Systematic Theology* II, ET University of Chicago Press and Nisbet 1957

Toynbee, A., *Civilization on Trial*, Oxford University Press 1948

Van Daalen, D. H., *The Real Resurrection*, Collins 1972

Vico, G., *The New Science of Giambattista Vico*, trans. T. E. Burgin and H. H. Finch, Cornell University Press and Oxford University Press 1948

Westcott, B. F., *The Gospel of the Resurrection*, Macmillan 1898

Westcott, B. F., *The Revelation of the Risen Lord*, Macmillan 1881

Williams, H. A., *Jesus and the Resurrection*, Longmans Green 1951

Williams, H. A., *True Resurrection*, Mitchell Beasley and Holt, Rinehart & Winston 1972

Index of Names and Subjects

Index of Modern Authors

Index of Biblical References